View from the Hill

by Mick Jones

www.1889books.co.uk

ISBN:978-1-9163622-0-8

Mick's work shines a light on a Sheffield that has been bulldozed from our history, honestly capturing the hard times and hardened people. His artistic eye enables him to bring out the warmth of those captured and tells the narrative of his mates, who are the subject of much of this work. A unique vision.
– Pete McKee

Living in Sheffield 'born and bred', I found the book full of powerful images that I can personally relate to, with extremely fond memories. I, and I expect many others, will recognise every single photo, together with similar stories for each and every one. It provides a visual expression of the grit, pride, resilience, joy and all the emotions that we remember whilst growing up and living through the best of times and the toughest of times. As the Leader of the city, and therefore a 'place shaper', seeing how our city looked, felt and the interactions between place and people, during a particular time, and the comparison with how it looks, feels and operates now, will help us understand what we want and need for our future. Do not underestimate the 'simple image' that conveys the essence of a place, a life lived and a real time story. This book is full of them. It has been a pleasure to read and return to time and time again.
– Councillor Julie Dore, Leader of the Council
& Member for Park & Arbourthorne Ward

The wonderful and talented photographer, Mick Jones – not *The Clash* or *Foreigner* fame – however better with a capture box than an axe, sent me his book today. I look through this and, yes, I'm back! I was 7/8 years old when these images were created, in 69/70. I can see three of my previous homes on these shots and that is so precious to me. Thank you Mick, I will see you at the Crucible Theatre, we will be Standing at the Sky's Edge, I will buy you a pint of Hendos, stay safe. Excellent work I'm honoured!!!
– Neil Kitson, Professional Photographer

Really enjoyed having all the pictures together in that format. Overwhelmingly nostalgic, not normally something I'm susceptible to. At some points it felt like I must have been following you around at that time. The great thing that comes across is the intimacy and that you were observing from the inside rather than coming from the outside with a ready formed agenda. We're conditioned into thinking that black and white photography imbues images with a certain grimness, but the main emotion I get from this is how optimistic it all felt, it was a time of renewal, anything was possible or so it seemed – five O levels and the world was yours. It's an achievement, Mick, and deserves every success.
– Michael Dolby, Artist/Illustrator

This is what happens when you hit the bullseye without aiming for it.
– Richard Hawley

Foreword

Sheffield in the 60's was a city experiencing significant change. Its steel industry was in terminal decline, smokeless zones cleared the air, and bold housing schemes were replacing nineteenth century, unsanitary back-to-back housing. The largest and most notable of these was the Park Hill Estate, built on the rising ground on the other side of the tracks above the railway station. Here, the utopian vision of high density community living, with streets and bridges in the sky, was carried out in a stark, minimalist style that subsequently became known as brutalism.

Shortly after the estate was opened in 1961 Mick Jones and his family moved into their apartment on Long Henry Row where their new home felt spacious even luxurious. As Mick subsequently noted "I thought we had won the pools." He was just 10 years old.

In 1968 Mick enrolled at the Sheffield College of Art to take the two years vocational course in graphic design. In addition to the usual skills with pen and paint brush, the curricula also included typography and photography as these were now regarded as key elements of 1960's design. I had just been appointed to look after the photography component, largely based on my experience as a commercial and industrial photographer. It was here that I taught Mick as a first year student. The course was largely structured around individual projects, one of which Mick reminds us, was based on the "slum Clearance" that was such a feature of Sheffield's urban landscape.

During this decade Photography had become more fully integrated into the social fabric of the nation as a key visual element in the iconography of the "swinging sixties". The appearance of the Sunday colour supplements during the same decade became a powerful influence through work of an emerging generation of photo-journalists, many of whom worked with 35mm cameras and grainy black & white film. They belonged to the new   avant-garde with photography regarded as an exciting means of self-expression. It had, in effect, escaped from its traditional role of wedding, birthday and holiday snapshot, to become the more democratic medium that we now enjoy on our mobile phones.

One senses that when Mick was first introduced to photography during his first term at college in 1968 it was something of a revelation. Here was a new technology, one that offered new experiences and gave him a status and street credibility that he quickly adopted. He came down "from the hill", ventured forth, and began to explore with the confidence of a streetwise lad with a camera to his eye. His photographs are those of an insider looking out, and not, as so often is the case, those of an outsider looking in.

The resulting images have the freshness and innocence that one expects of a seventeen-year-old let loose with a camera where everyone, everything, and everywhere was of equal importance. But instead of taking random, meaningless snapshots, Mick engaged with his subject matter, struggled with his exposure times, paid careful attention to his framing, and valued everything he had created.

Now, fifty years later these photographs have adopted the significance and meaning of historic documents, ones that offer a brief insight into a world that now seems strangely distant and unfamiliar. They are neither nostalgic, or glamorous, but are the highly personal statement of a young man at large in a city experiencing a social and economic transformation. We are fortunate to have them.

Roger Taylor, Professor Emeritus, De Montfort University

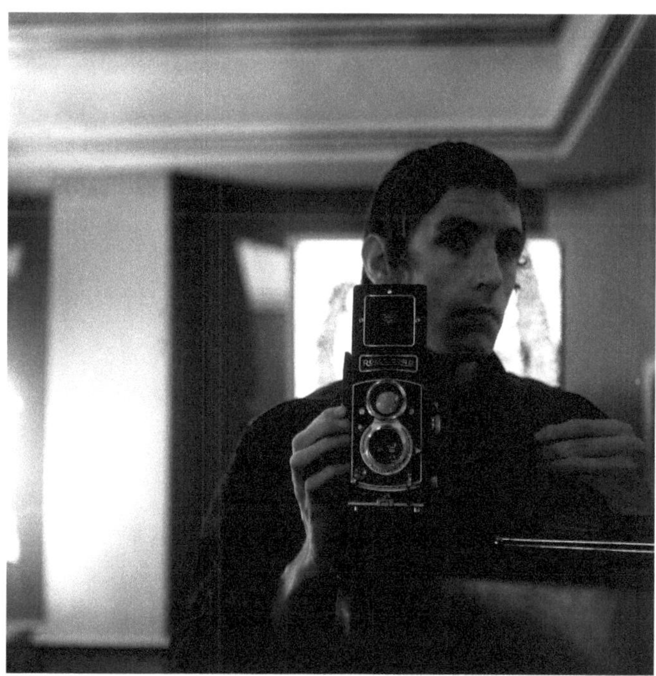

The photographs in this book were all taken from early 1969 to the summer of 1970 when I studied photography as part of a graphic design course at Sheffield College of Art. My tutor in the first year was Roger Taylor, now an Emeritus Professor — I can't thank him enough for all his advice and help. We did projects related to graphic design and the commercial world, one of them being to take photographs to a brief: capturing scenes of what was then referred to as "slum clearance" or of industrial Sheffield.

Roger Taylor left at the end of 1969. Then, during the summer holidays I saw one of my mates from college out and about with a college camera. "Where have you got that from?" I said. "It's Mr Grant (the new tutor) — he's lending them out." So I went and got hold of two cameras: a 2 ¼ inch film Rolleicord twin lens reflex camera, and a Pentax SLR 35mm film camera. I then started taking photographs as and when I liked.

I used to like to go out and have a drink, so one thing I did was to take a camera with me to experiment with some new fast film. Not many of them came out very well but this one did: a self-portrait taken in the foyer of the Heartbeat nightclub which was above the Silver Blades ice rink.

I took the cameras around Park Hill and around town. The results are a snapshot of a city and a community at a time of great change — of places and ordinary people going about their lives. Most of the negatives had remained undeveloped for 50 years and sadly a few have been lost.

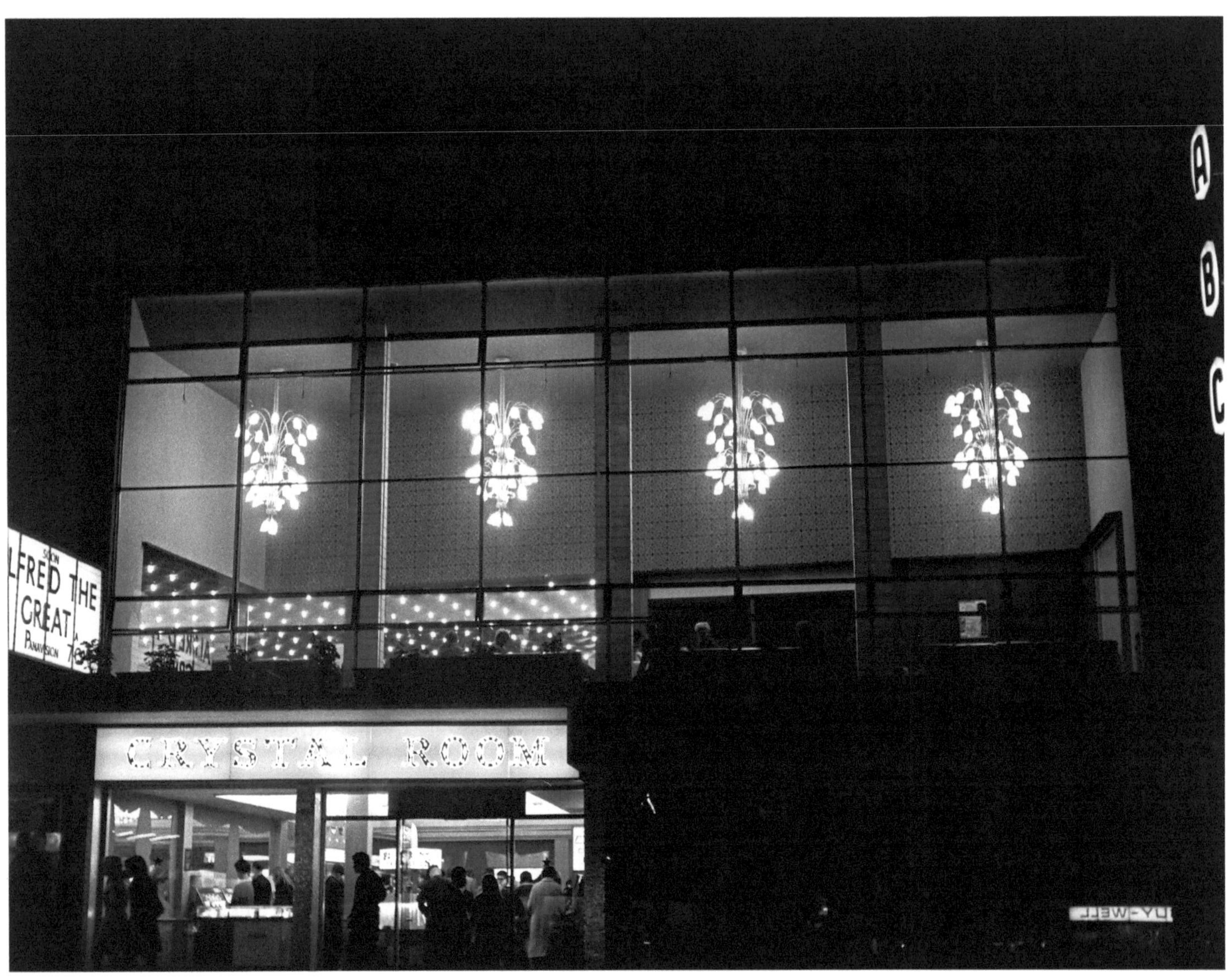

The Crystal Room at night — again experimenting with fast film. I never used to use a flash or a lightmeter for most of my photos: basically because I couldn't be bothered, so I just used estimated settings and mostly got away with it. The Crystal Room underneath the ABC cinema was a slot machine place where mods and skinheads used to meet.

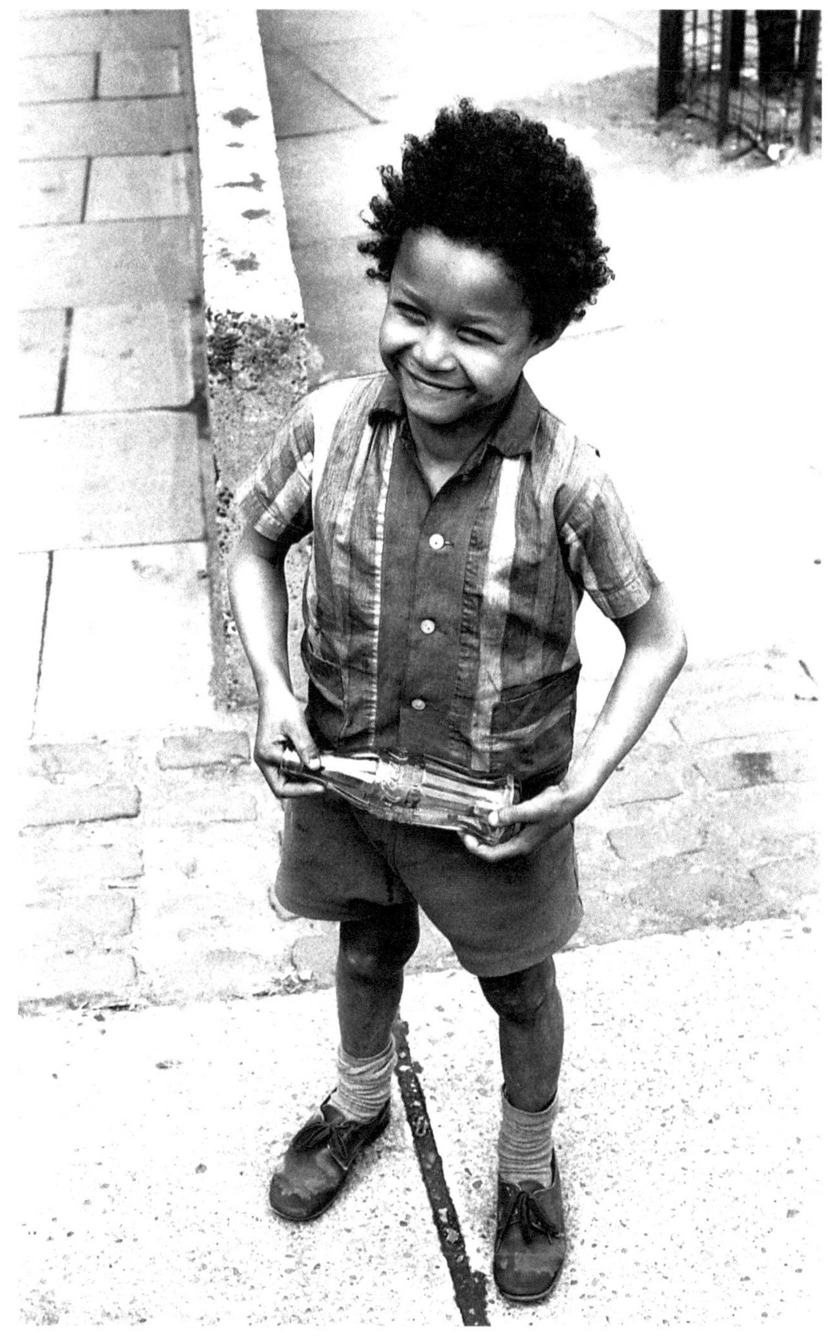

Alan Jones: such a happy lad! Looks like he's just finished his pop and ready to take his bottle back for his penny deposit. The Jones family lived near "The Pavement" on Park Hill and were lovely people. He's probably talking to my brother; I liked to take photographs where people were just going about their business and not posing.

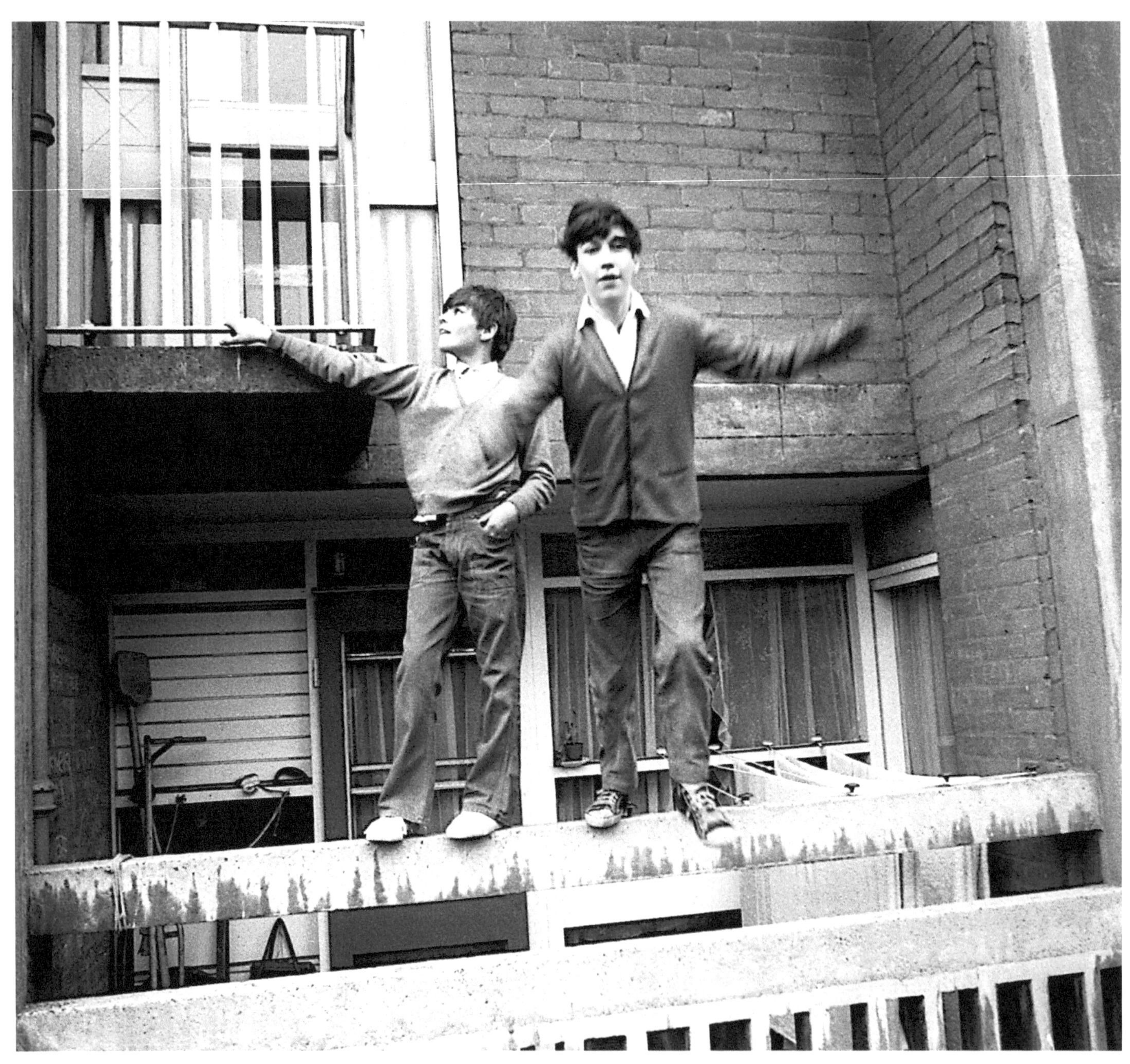

This was taken on Talbot Street: Ben Roe and Dave "Flo" Foster jumping off a balcony on Park Hill Flats. Don't worry though it was the ground floor.

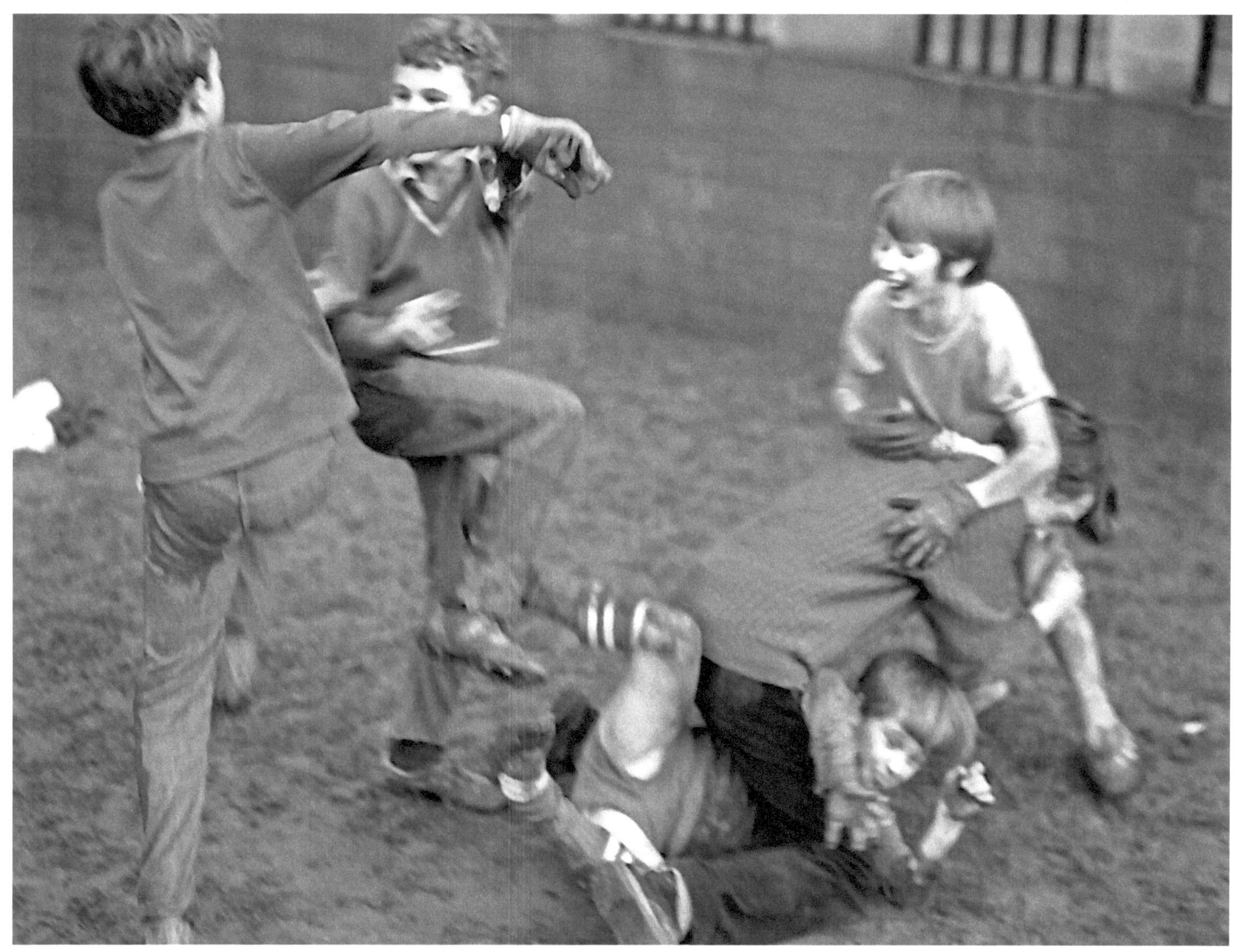

On the grass at Park Hill: we weren't supposed to play football there. The porters would chase us off — then when the coast was clear we'd be back again. This is David Crossland with William and Robert King and Ray Wright — this game has clearly descended into chaos, or it might have been a game of British bulldog. To coin a phrase they look a bit "loppy."

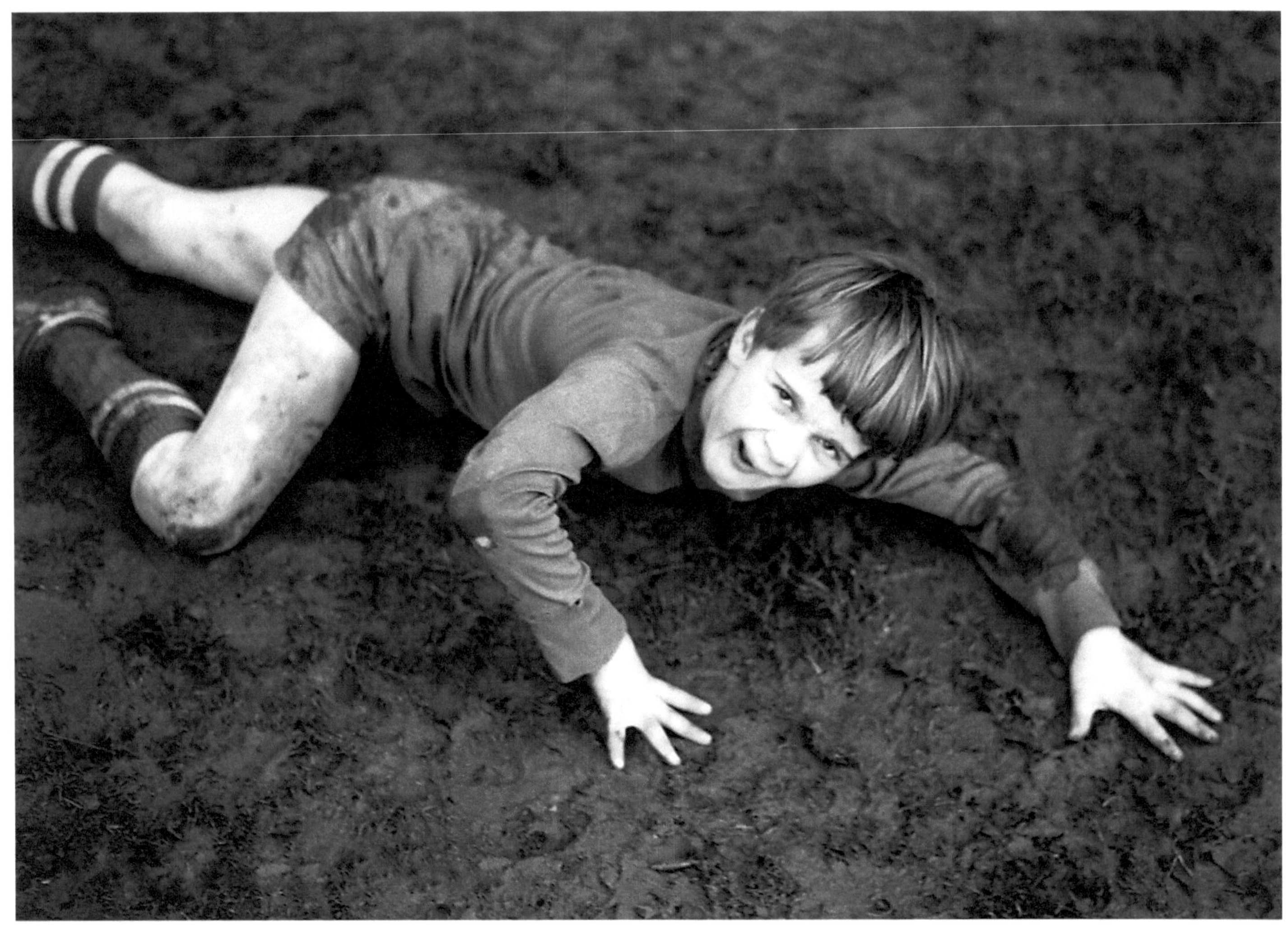

Robert King was a good goalkeeper — clearly not scared of a bit of mud. Bet his mum was none too pleased when he got home though. That said we were always scruffy — it was a sign of having had fun; when my brother Sean was little he was given the nickname "The Black Knight" in honour of his cleanliness.

Robert appeared in later life in Melvyn Bragg's *Reel History of Britain* series, in the episode *Streets in the Sky* — he is sadly no longer with us.

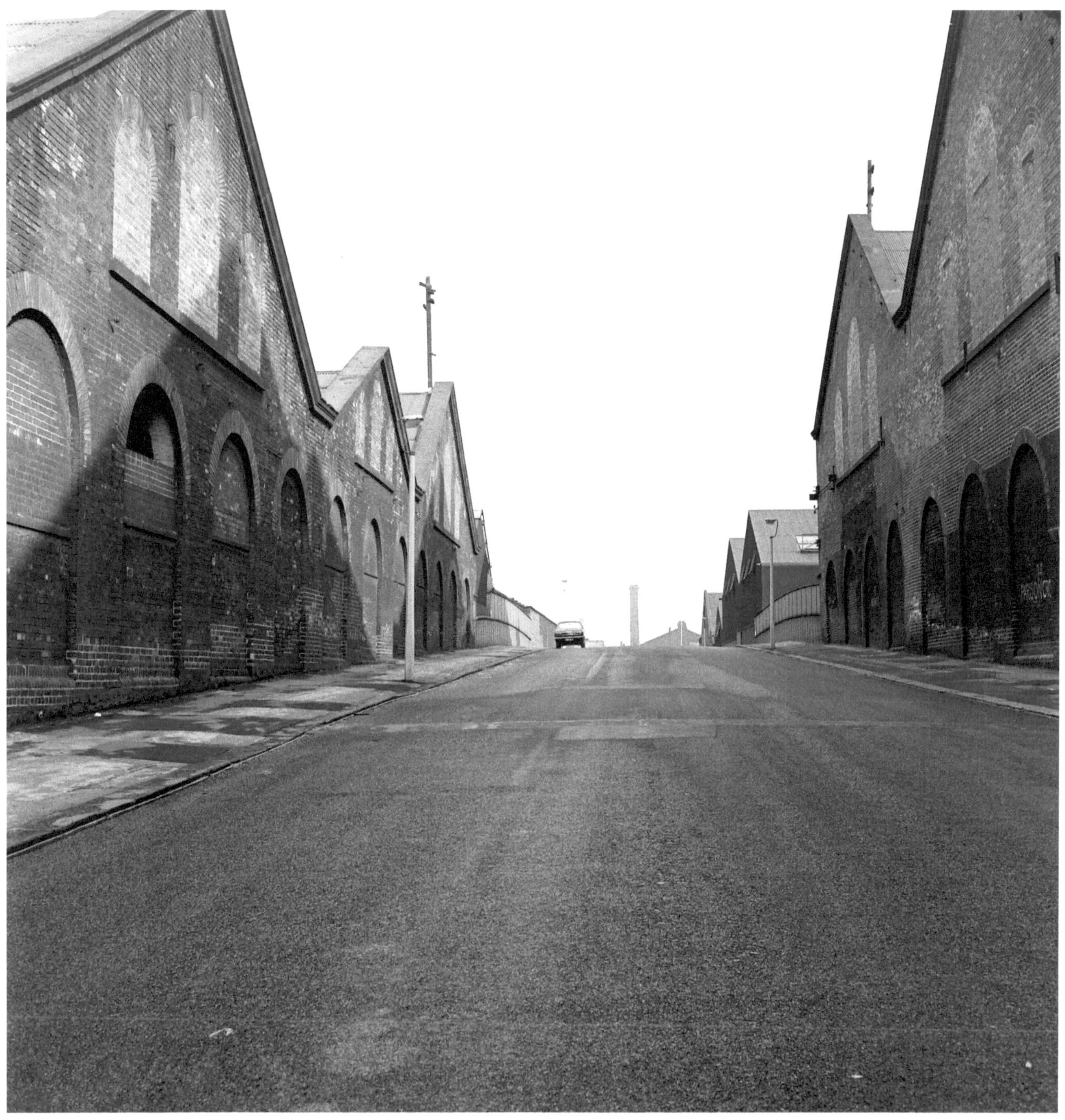

Carwood Road 1969. This was one of the pictures taken for the industrial areas brief at college. It meant we captured industrial areas that were starting to disappear. I often preferred shots without people in them; although it's amazing how often there were figures in my photos that I had not spotted.

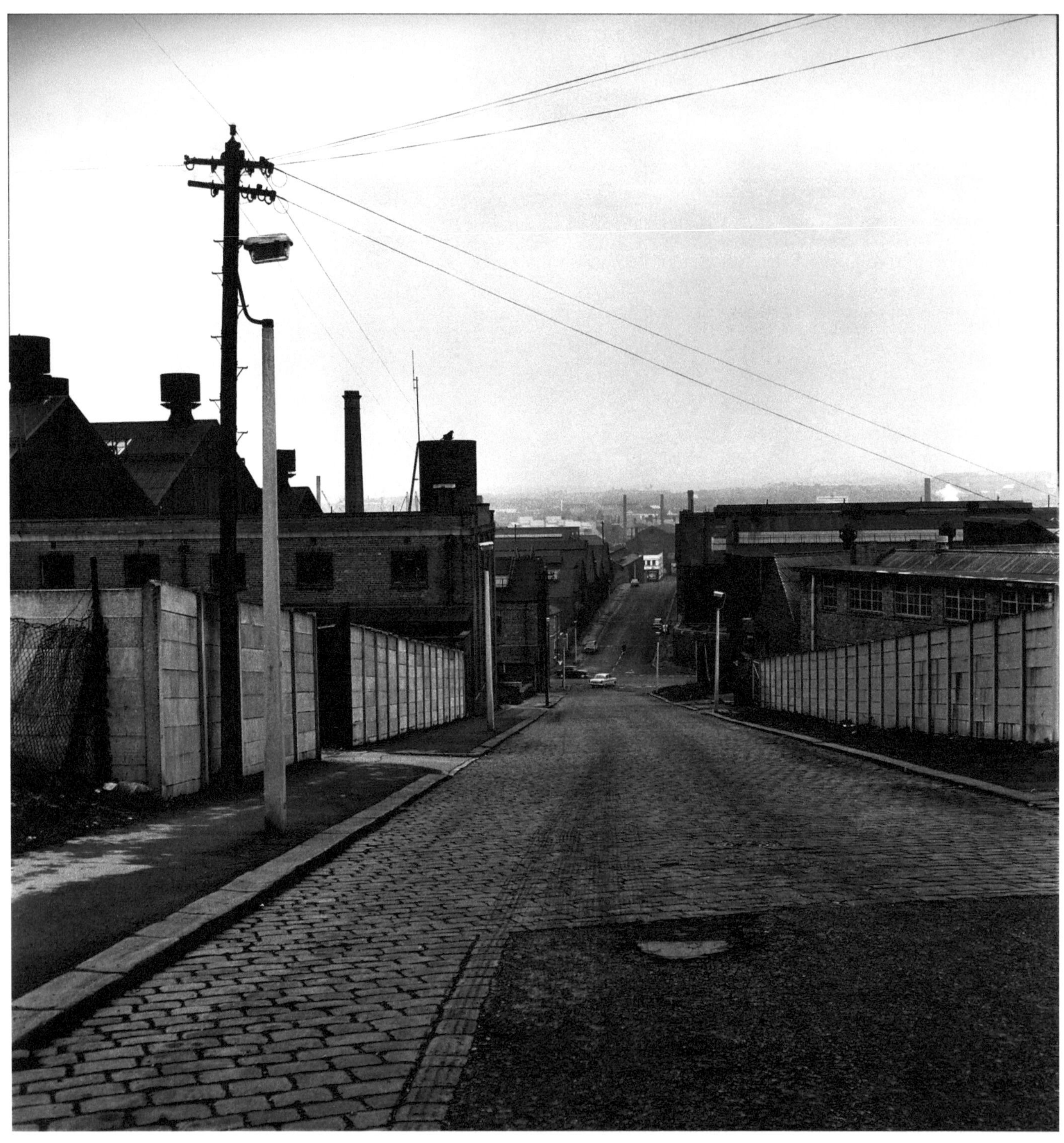

Carwood Road again: higher up, looking from Pitsmoor. I believe the turret on the left was an old anti-airgraft gun emplacement from the Second World War.

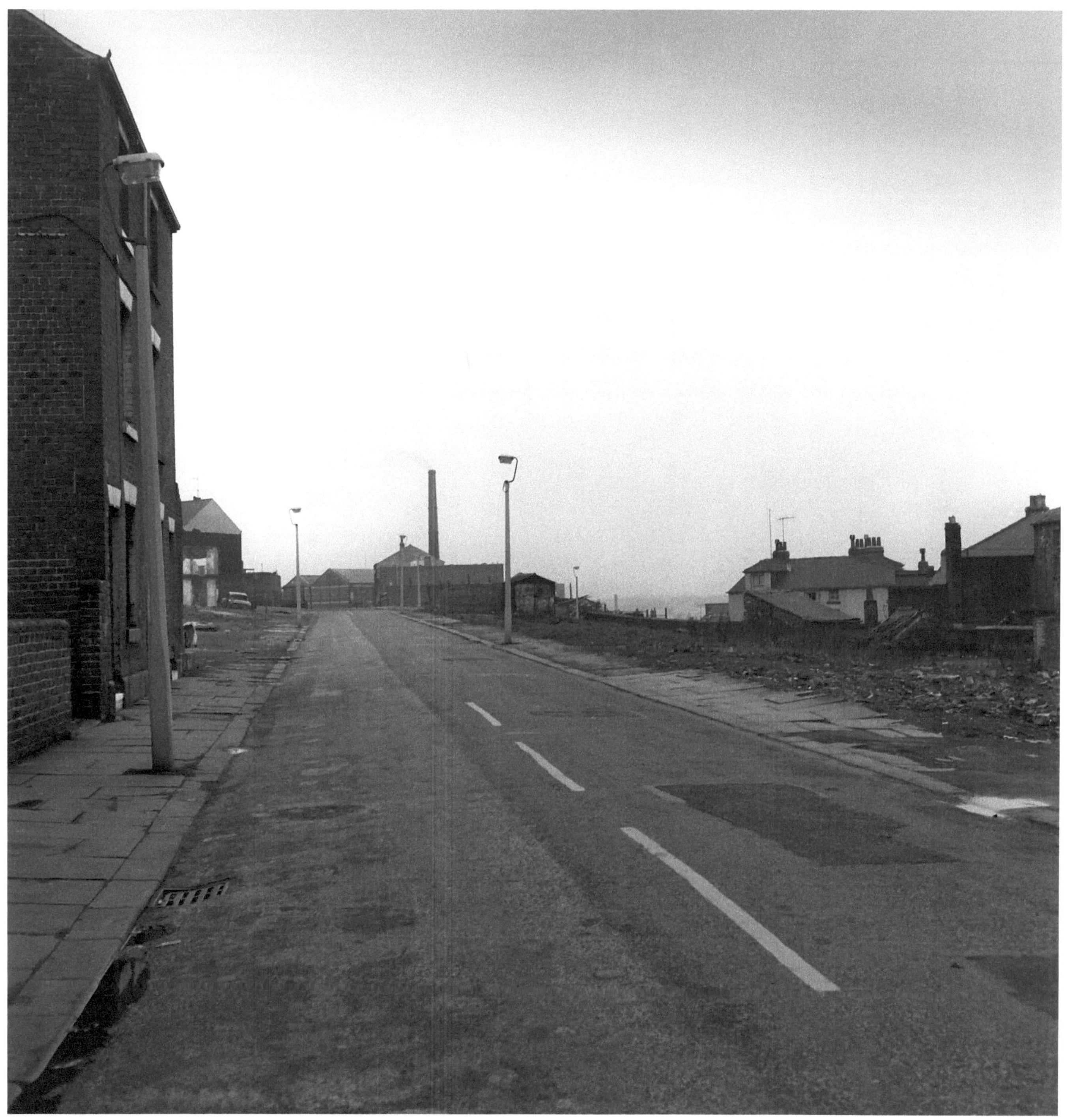

Clun Street, Burngreave. Note the abandoned, partly dismantled car in the distance. We often used old abandoned cars as dens on Park Hill, until one of our rival gangs set fire to ours. From then on all the kids were warned off.

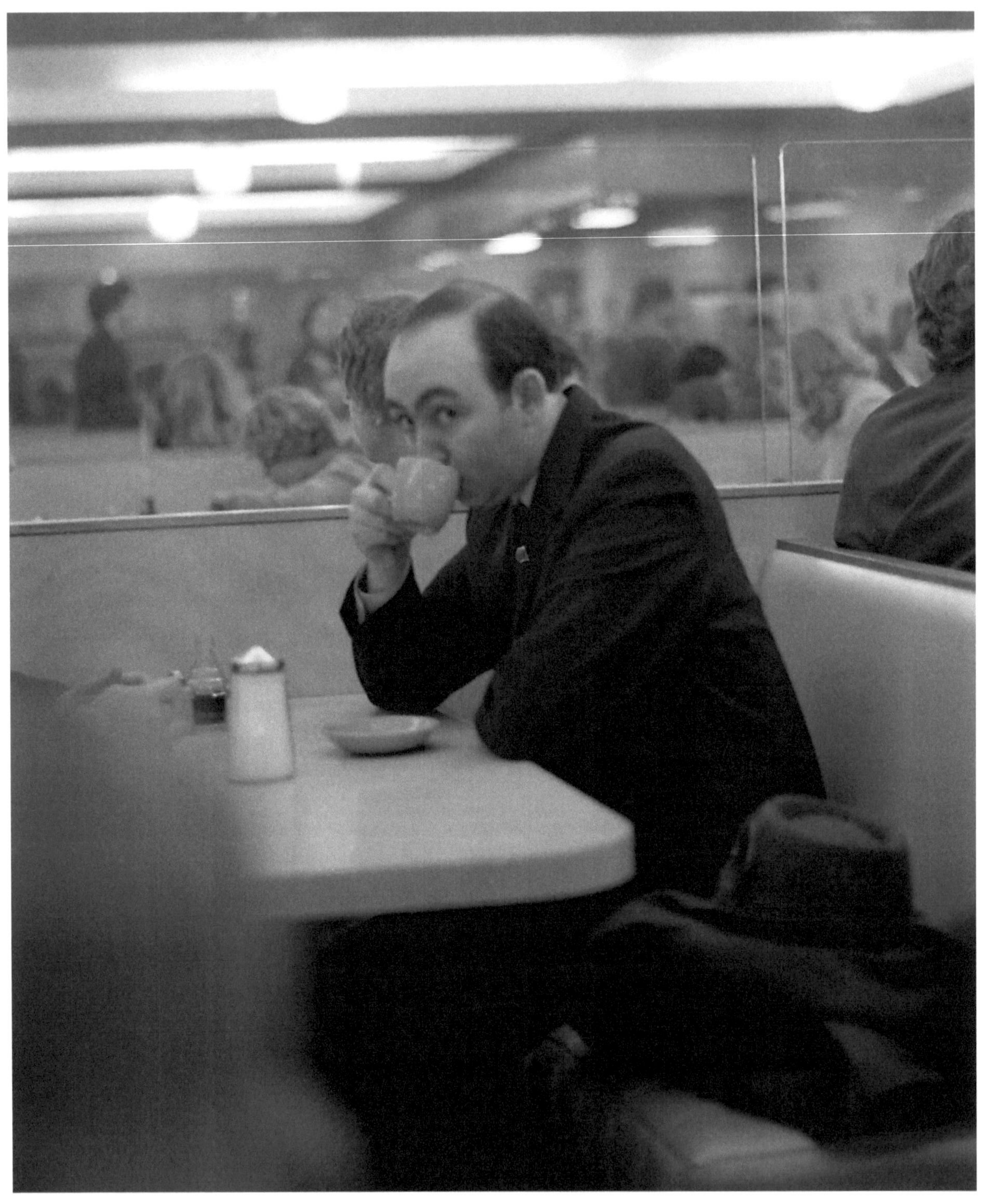

The cafe at Pauldens department store on the Moor (later became Debenhams).

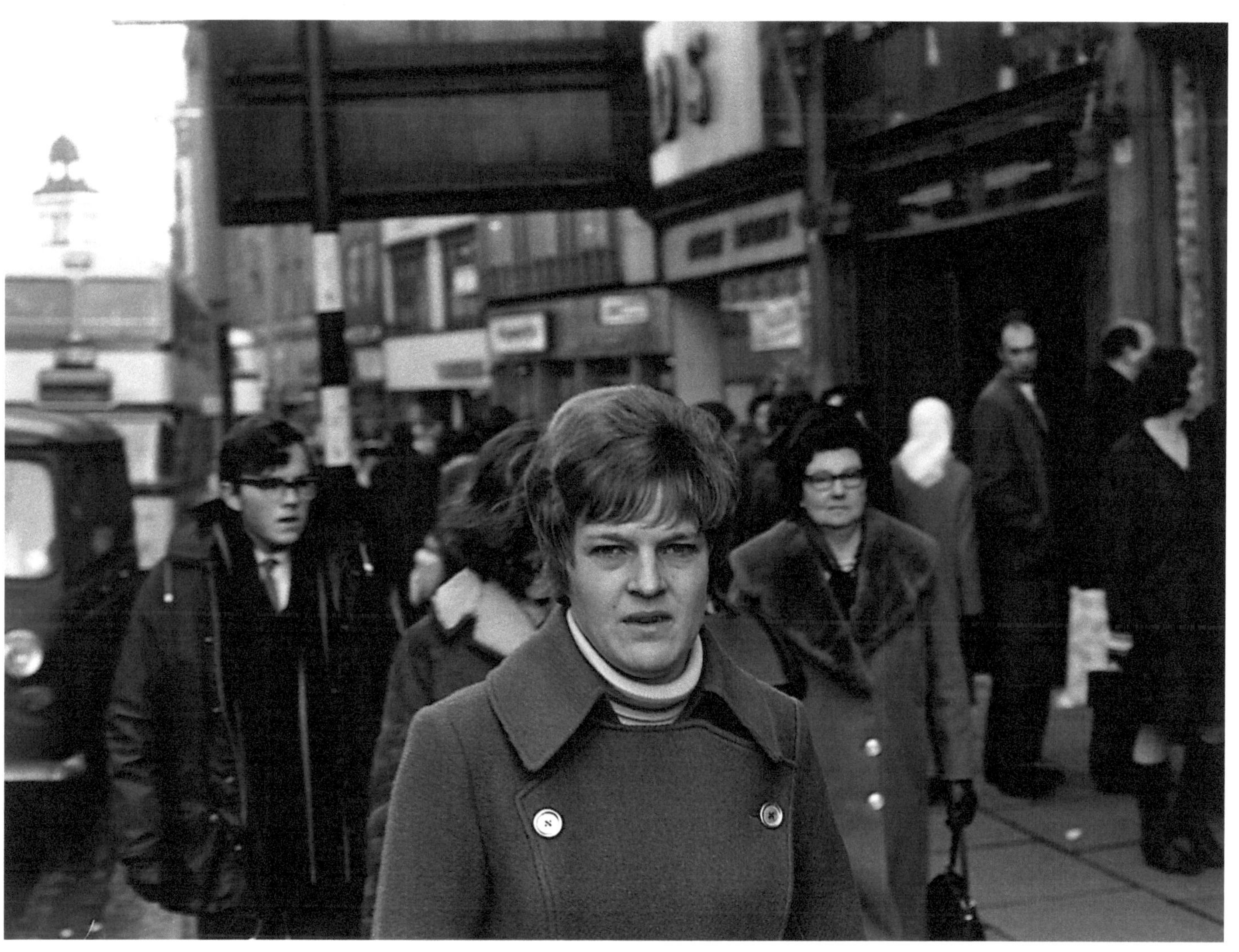

Shoppers on Fargate back in the days when town was really busy — totally different to what it is now: when there was a real heart in the town.

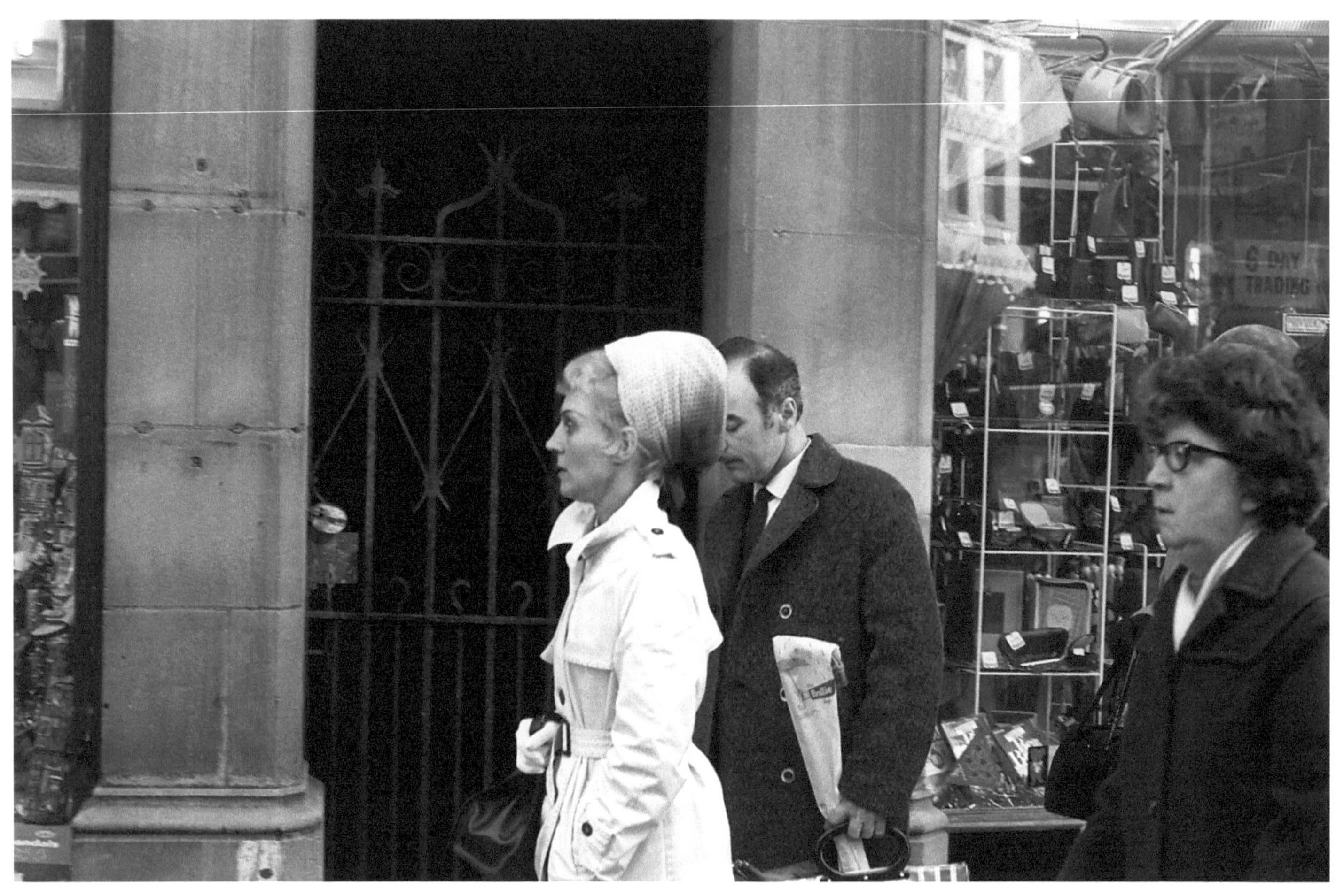

Christmas shoppers in town in 1969. Those raincoats were all the rage in the late 60s.

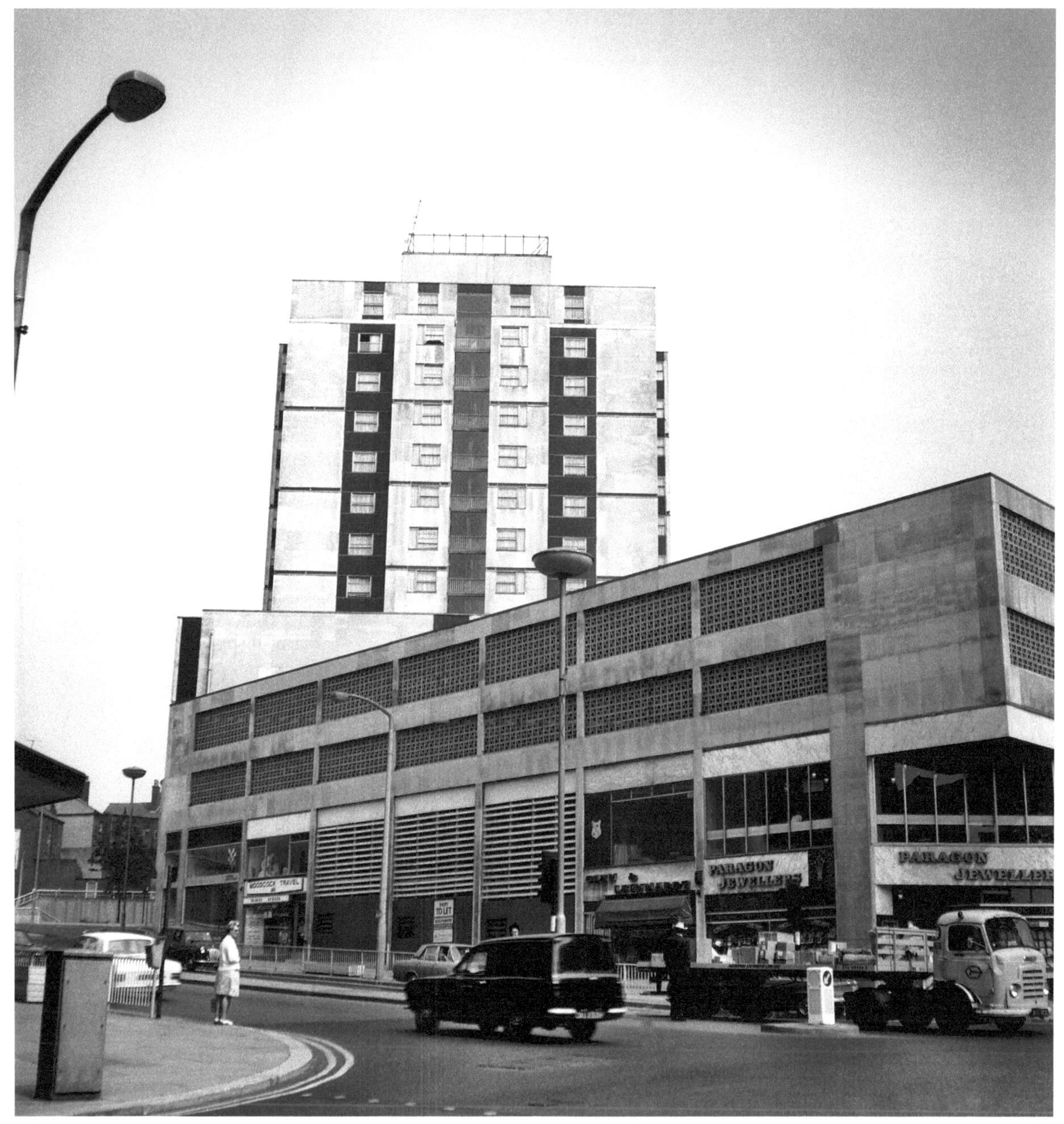

The Grosvenor: Sheffield's poshest hotel. Just before starting college I got an evening job here as a pot washer — loading the machine. It paid quite well and I got fed. Ted Rhodes my first year tutor said we finished at 7 p.m. on a Wednesday. When I said I couldn't he went mad — that was until I said I was working. "You mean you go to college and then to work after?" He then held me up as some sort of role model for hard work. I never had the heart to tell him when a few months later I'd had enough and packed the job in!

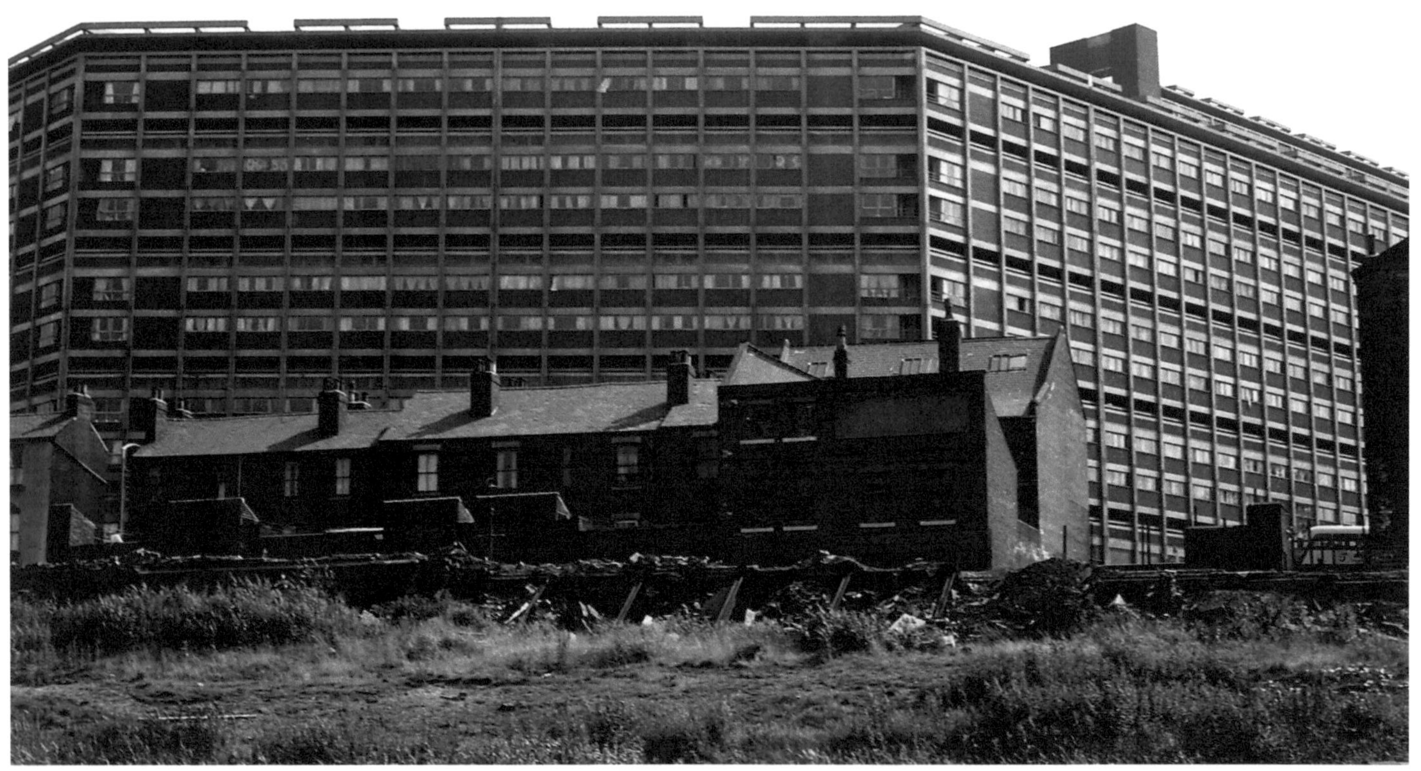

I took this because I loved the contrast between the old and the new. This is Hyde Park flats with the old back-to-back houses of Bernard Road in the foreground ready for demolition. Little did I know that not that many years later that part of Hyde Park would also be demolished.

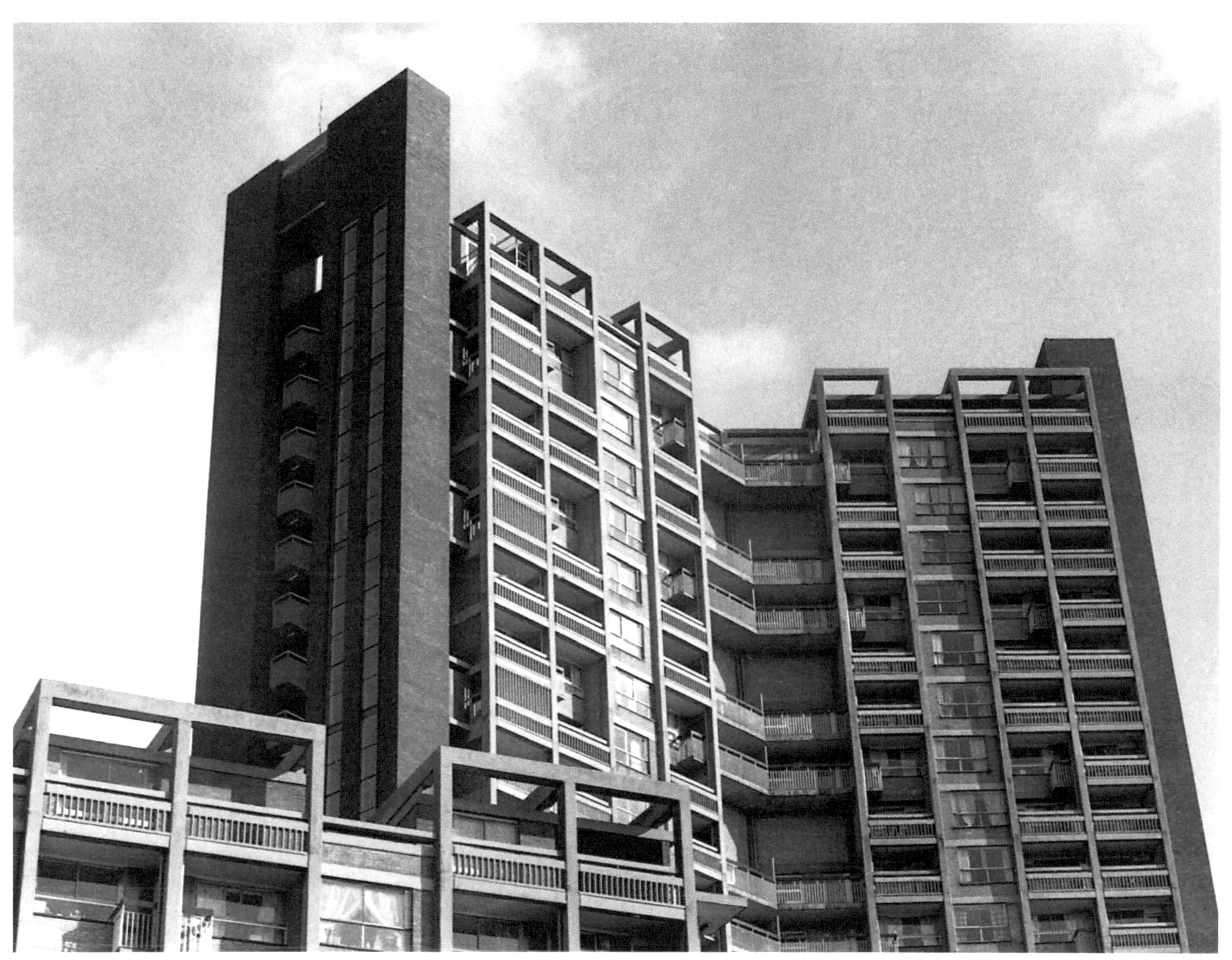

Looking up at one of the blocks on Hyde Park flats. I quite liked the brutalist architecture. Maybe I was biased because I lived on Park Hill.

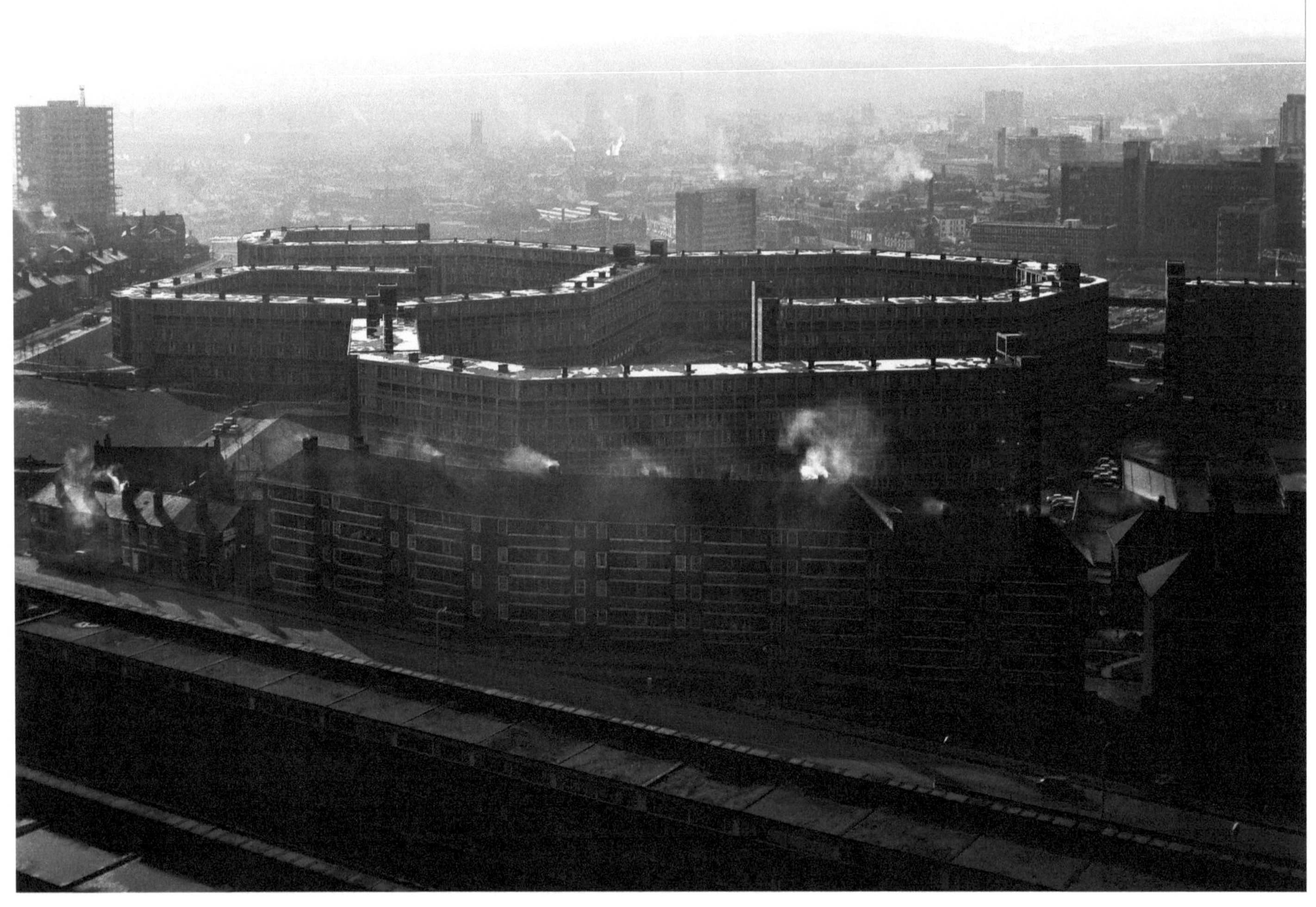

This was taken from Hyde Park flats with Claywood flats on the left still under construction. I liked the contrast between the Bard Street flats 1930s architecture and the newness of the Park Hill estate with town in the background. The Clean Air Act had been in force for some time but you wouldn't know it looking at this image.

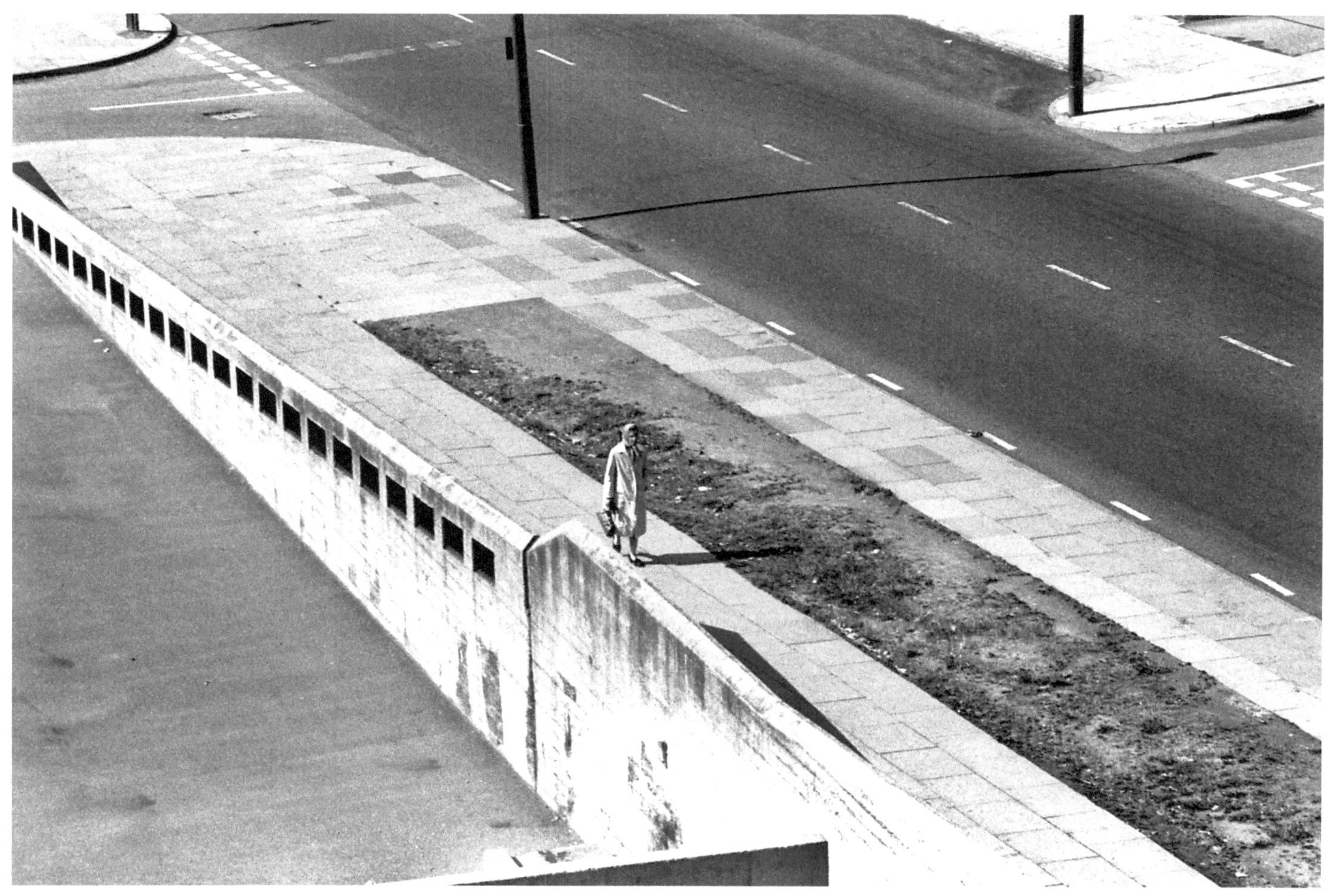

Walking up Duke Street. Taken from our landing on Long Henry Row near the lifts. The school yard is on the left. As kids we used to get a roller skate and put a book on it and race down that slope at a speed of knots — you had to make sure you stopped before the end otherwise you were in the road. Other dangers were the scraping of knuckles and getting a rollicking from pedestrians who had to jump out of the way and usually told our parents.

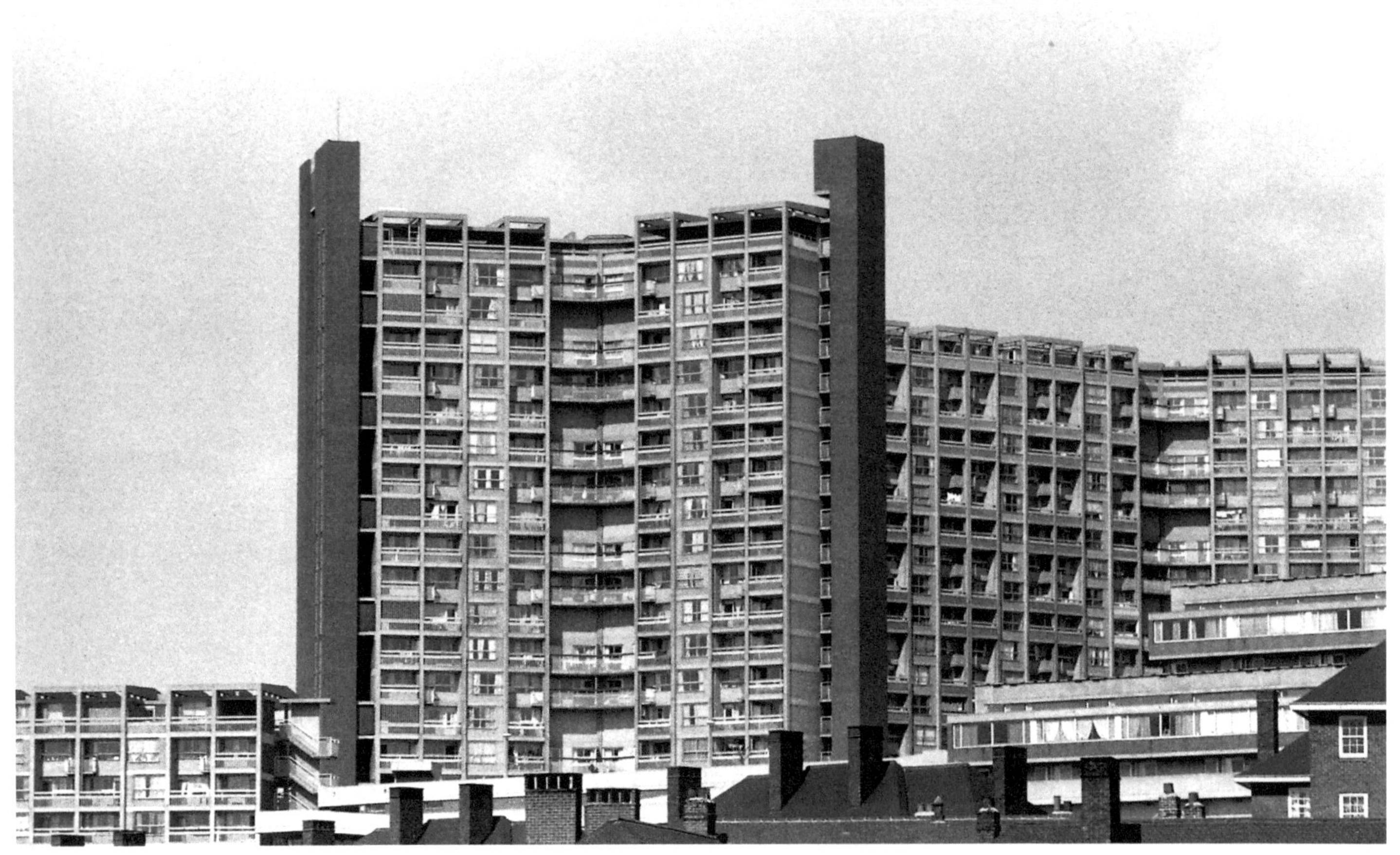

Hyde Park flats from Long Henry Row. Parts of Hyde Park Terrace and Hyde Park Walk are visible with a little bit of Bard Street in the foreground. We used to call the flats on Bard Street "Bardyland, " its residents being "Bardylanders."

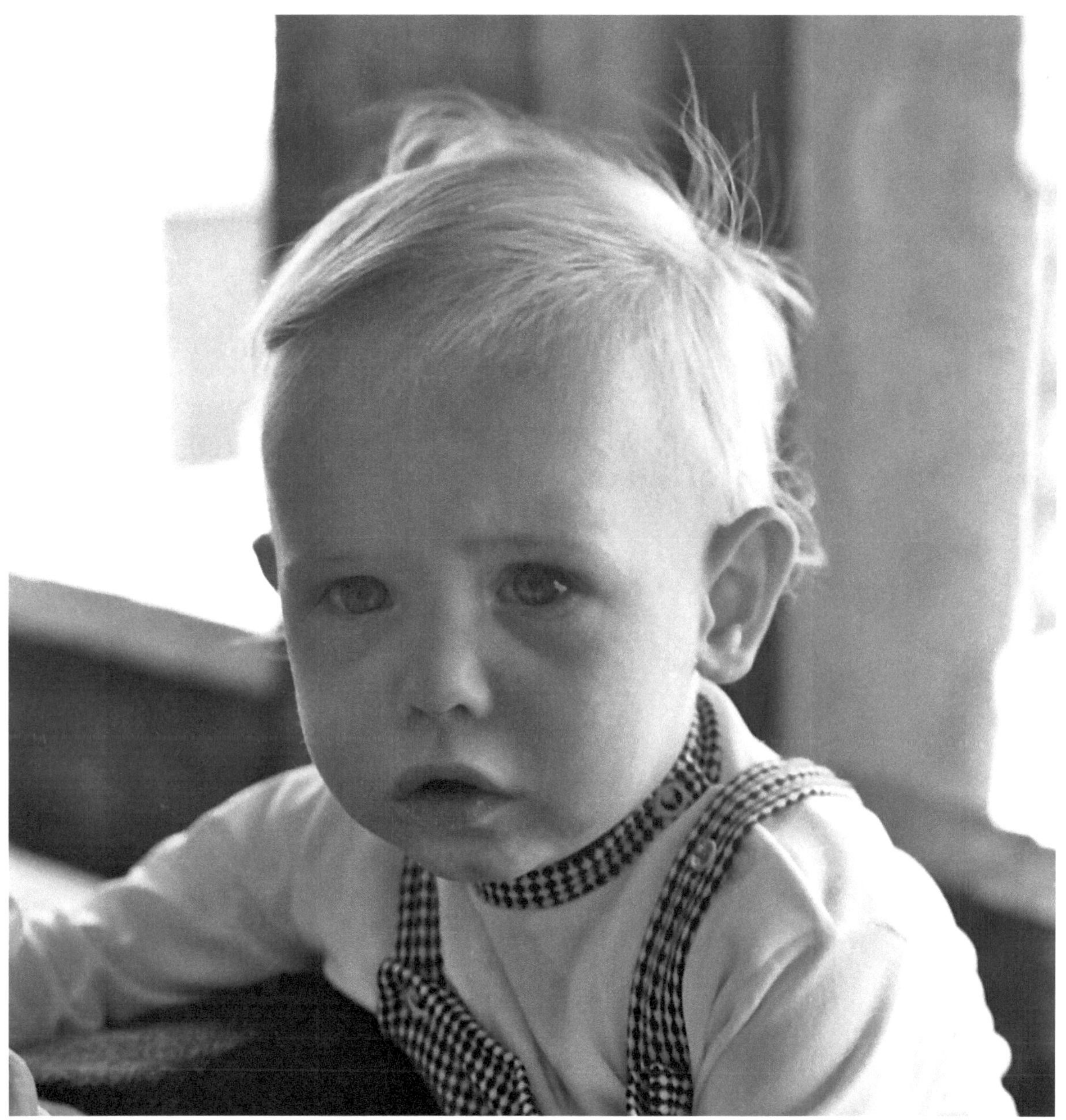

At Whitsuntide I made a bit of pocket money taking photos of people dressed in their best clothes for the day. Once I'd taken a few, word got round and everyone was asking me. Whit was a massive event in the calendar back then: one of the few times of the year when everyone had to look their best for church or parades. Our new clothes were funded through "Banners" cheques: a sort of loan in those days from Banners store down Attercliffe. This lad looks as if he's about to cry — looking at me he would do! Or maybe he's found out the interest rate Banners charged.

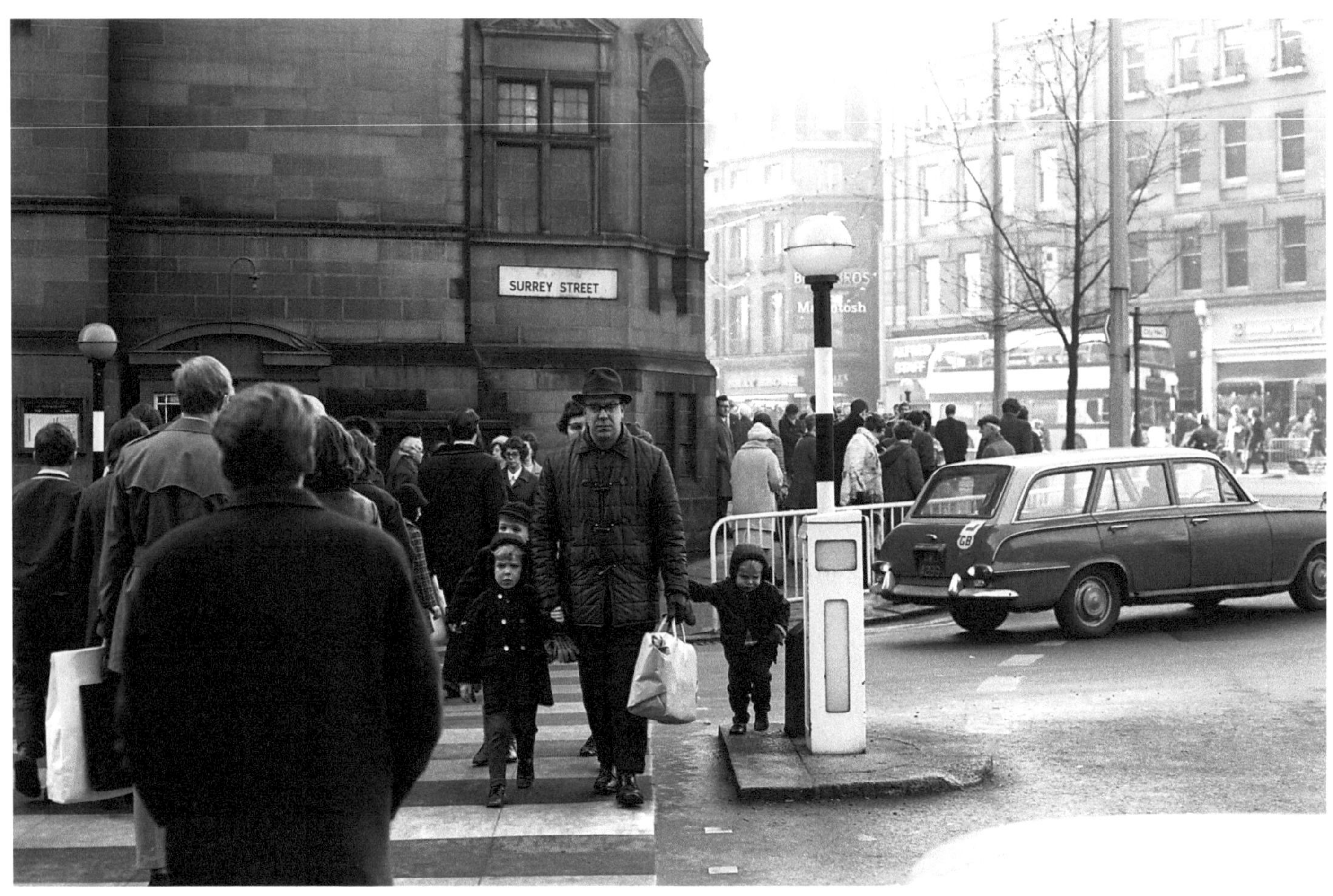

The zebra crossing on Surrey Street next to the Town Hall, Christmas 1969.

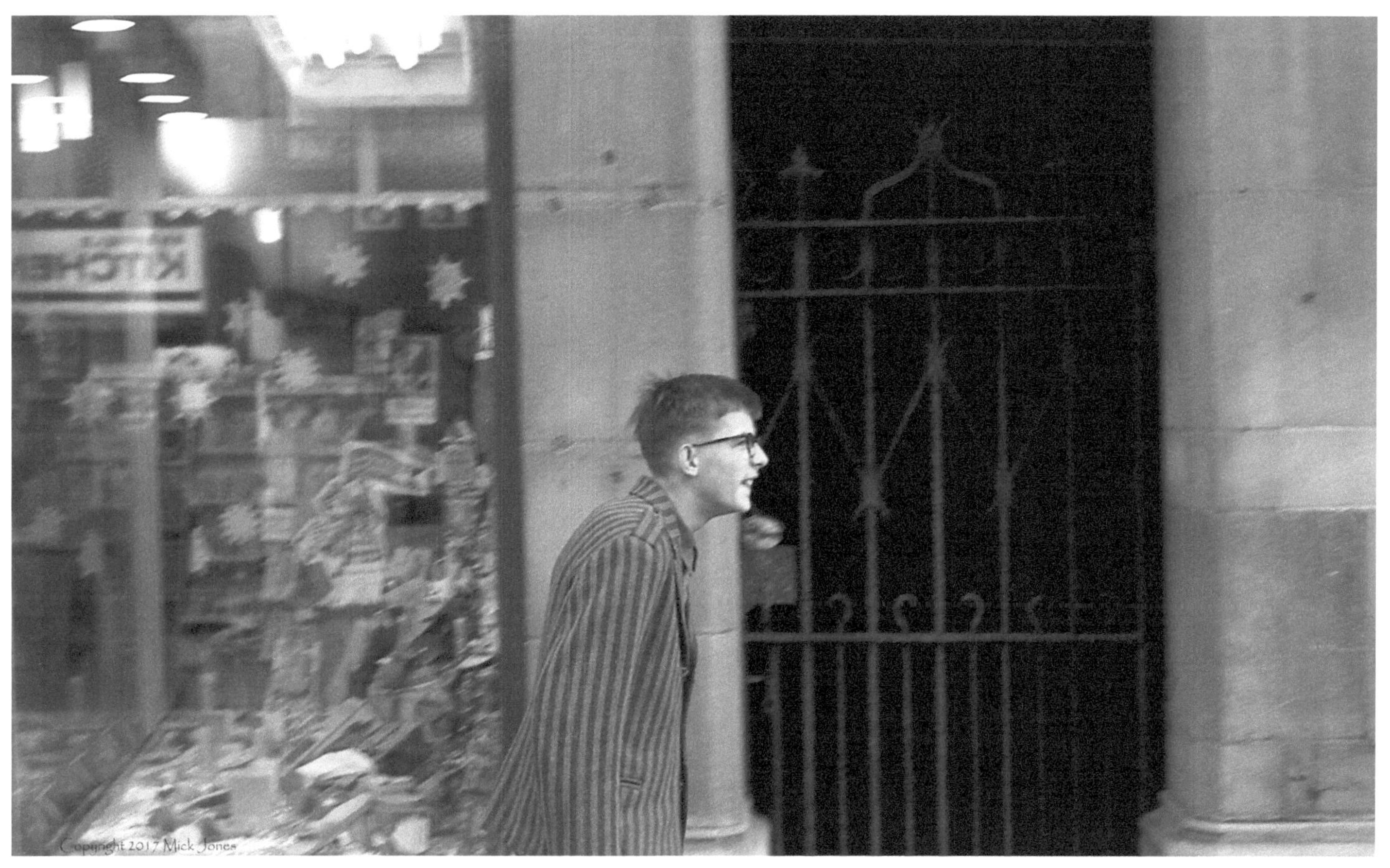

I reckon I took this one because I liked this lad's jacket: it was purple and orange, or something like that. He was probably a boy wizard.

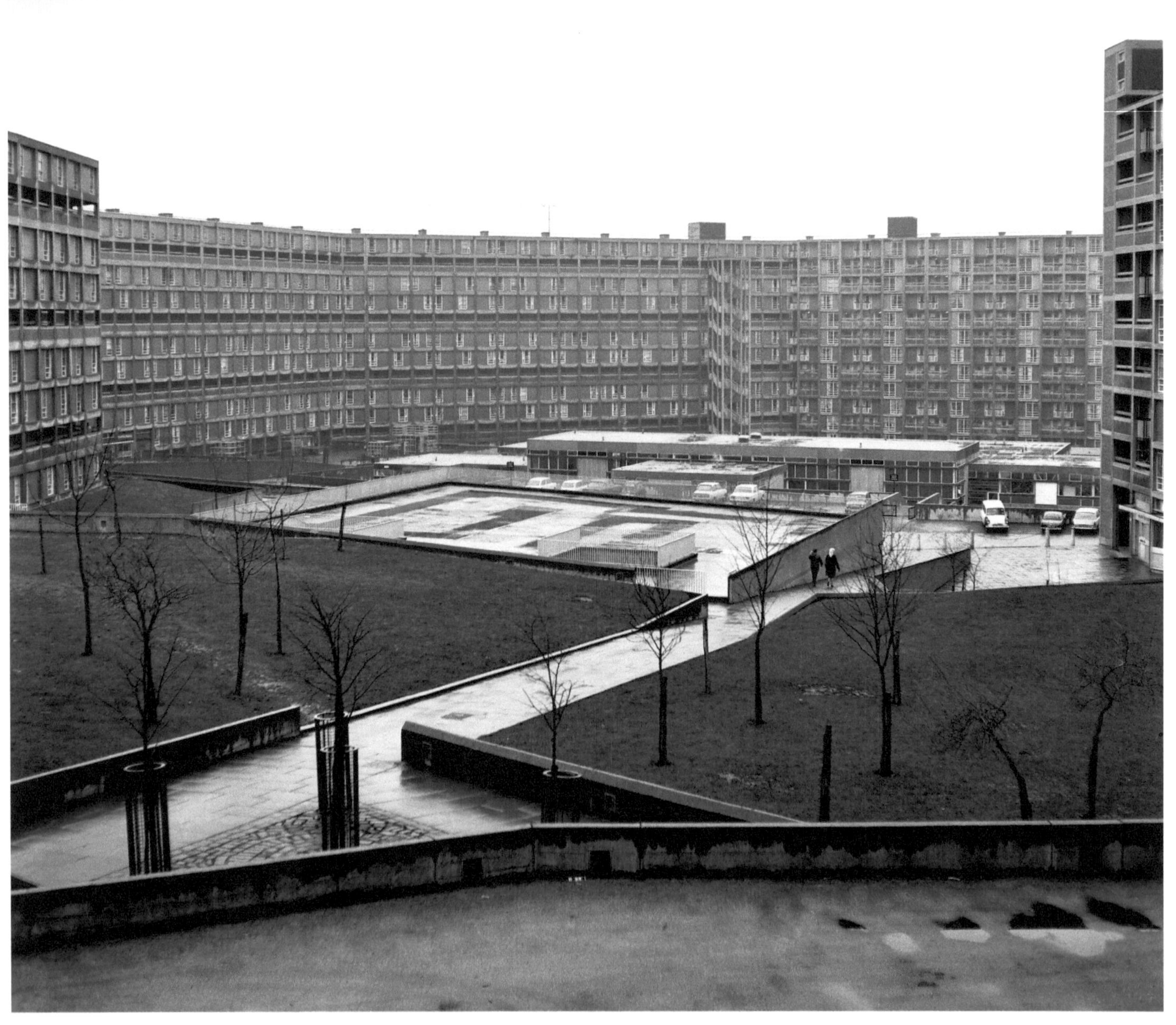

This was home from 1961; I thought we'd won the pools. We had a fitted kitchen, under-floor heating and an inside toilet and bath. You can see the Link pub, the school, the Scottish Queen and the launderette, or the washhouse as it was known.

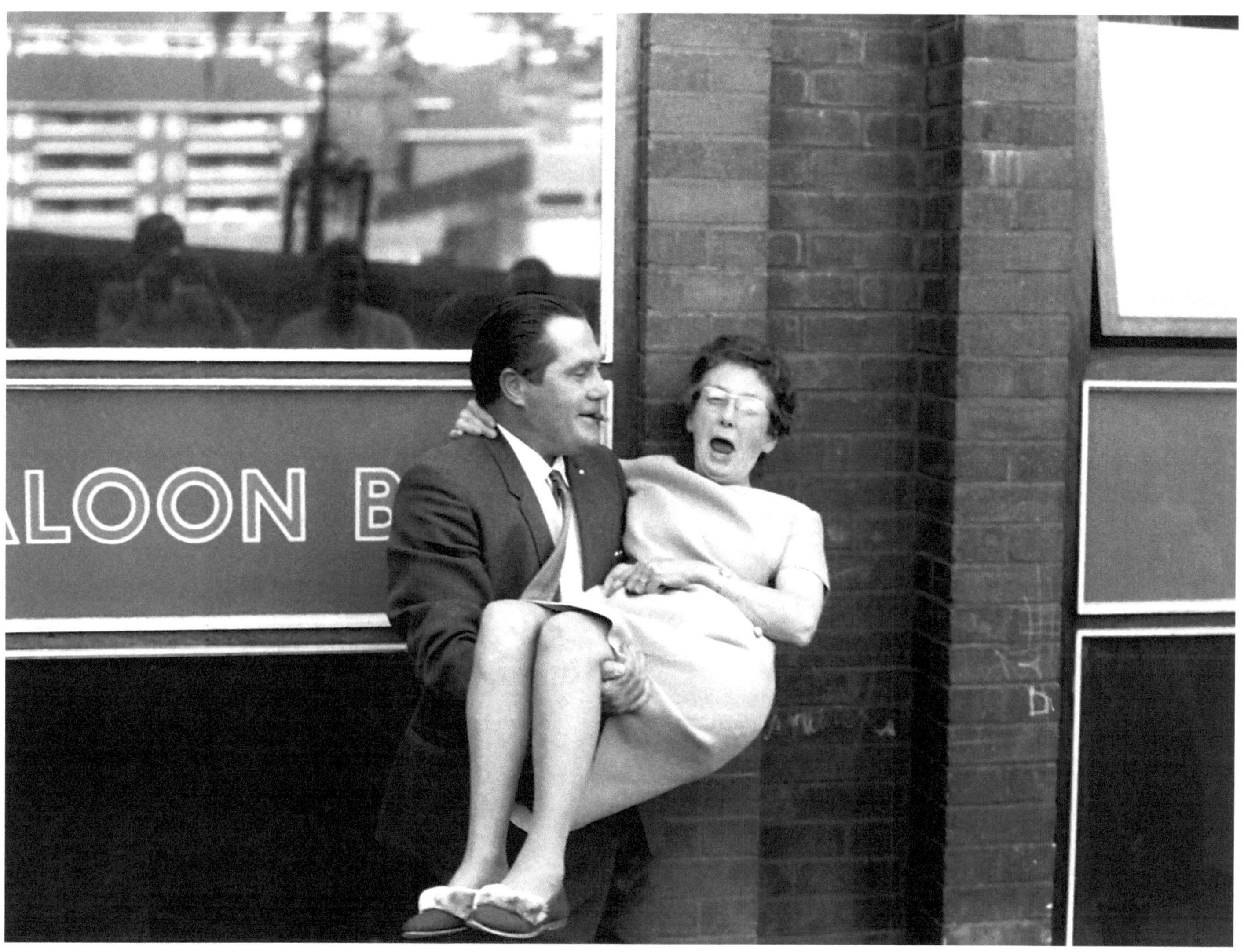

Taken outside the Scottish Queen pub, you can see me and Mick Marshall (and Bardyland) in the window's reflection. It was Mick asking me to take a picture of his new baby sister at Whit that led to lots of others asking for their pictures taking. This was of a friend of Mick's dad, a chap called Jack, who used to keep the Royal Standard. The woman is Ma Grain.

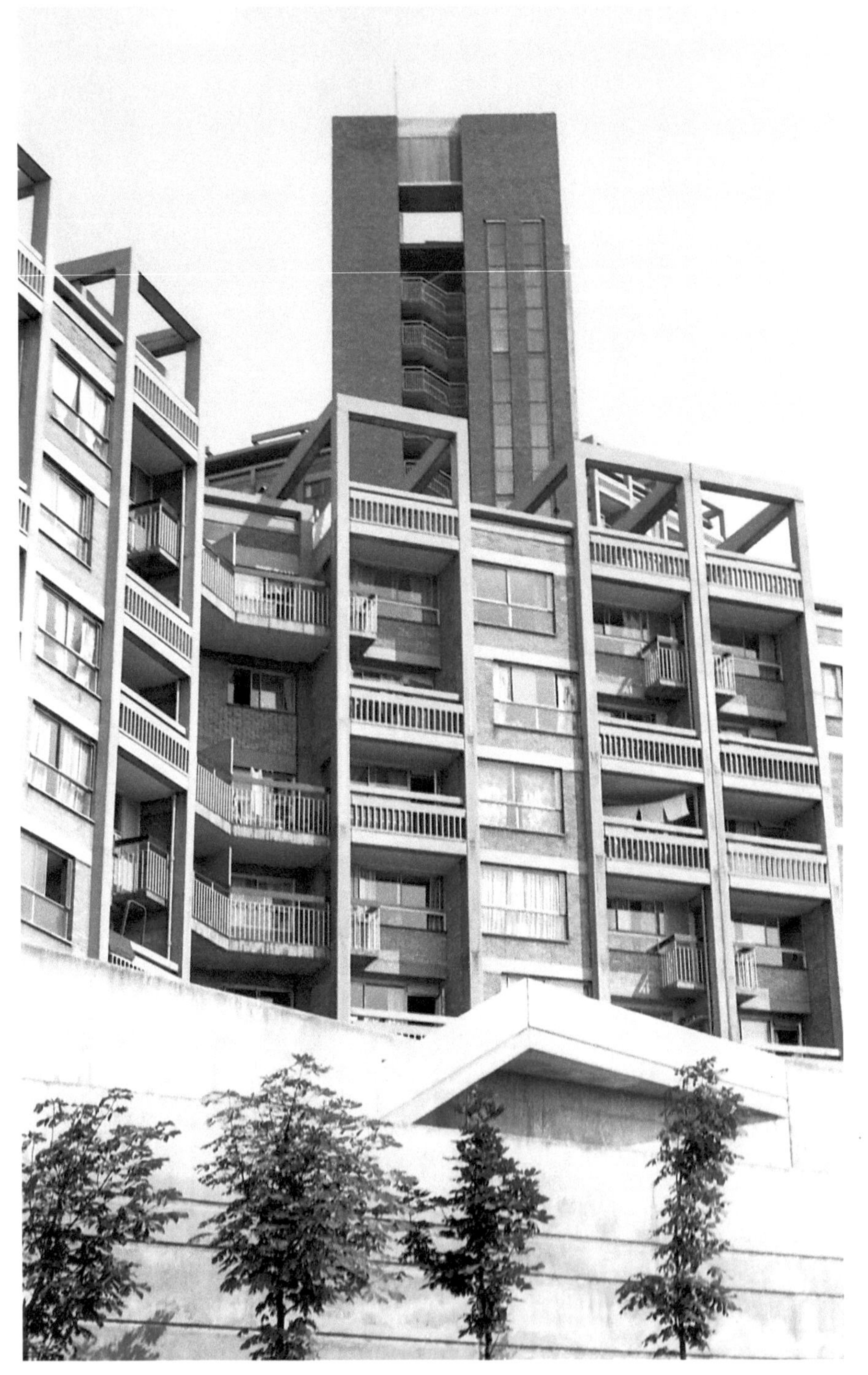

Hyde Park Flats looking good in the sunshine, the brutalism contrasting with the softness of the trees.

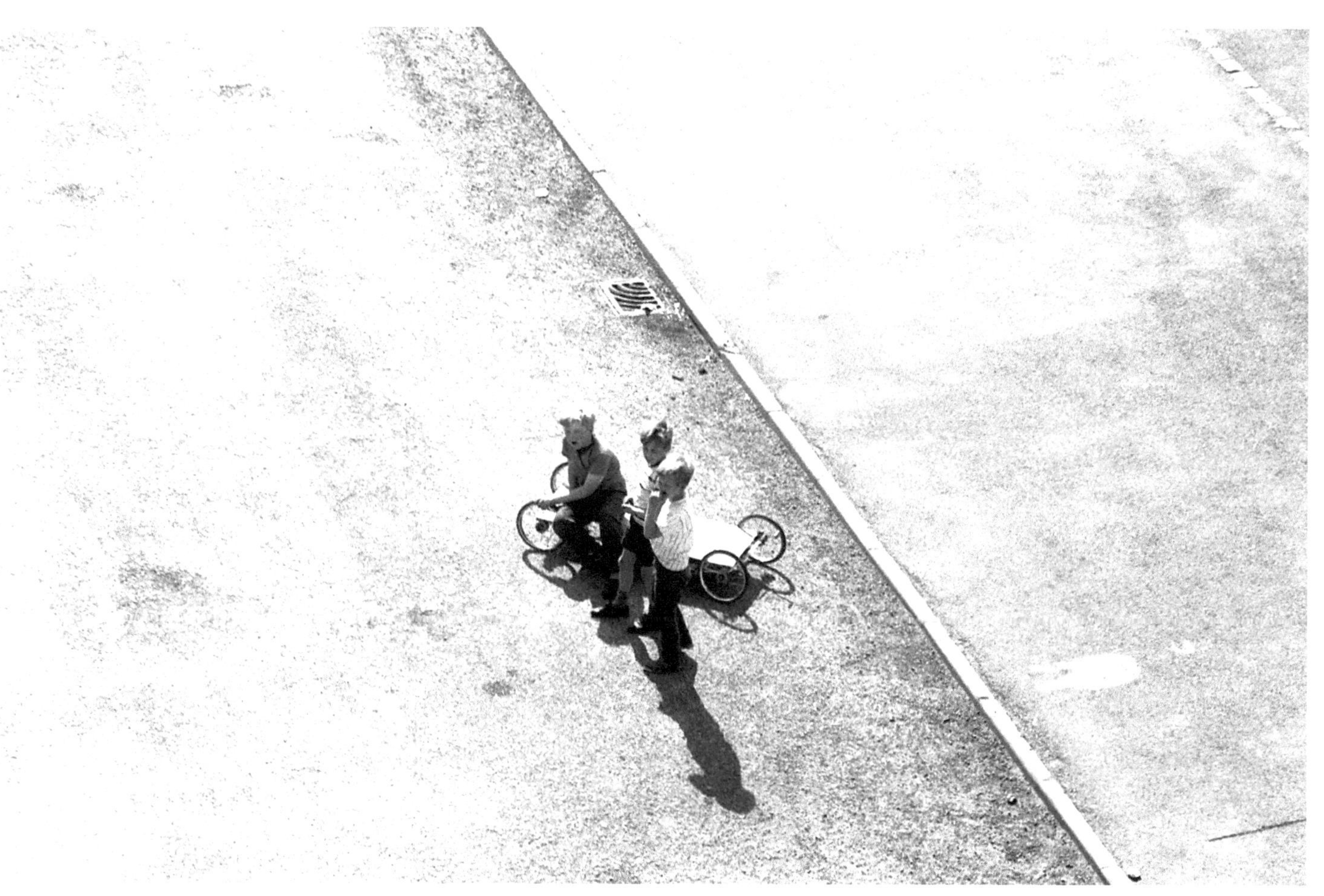

Some kids messing around with a home-made go-kart. This is the kind of thing we used to do as kids. There were no computers, no TV until teatime. This was taken from our kitchen landing on Long Henry Row.

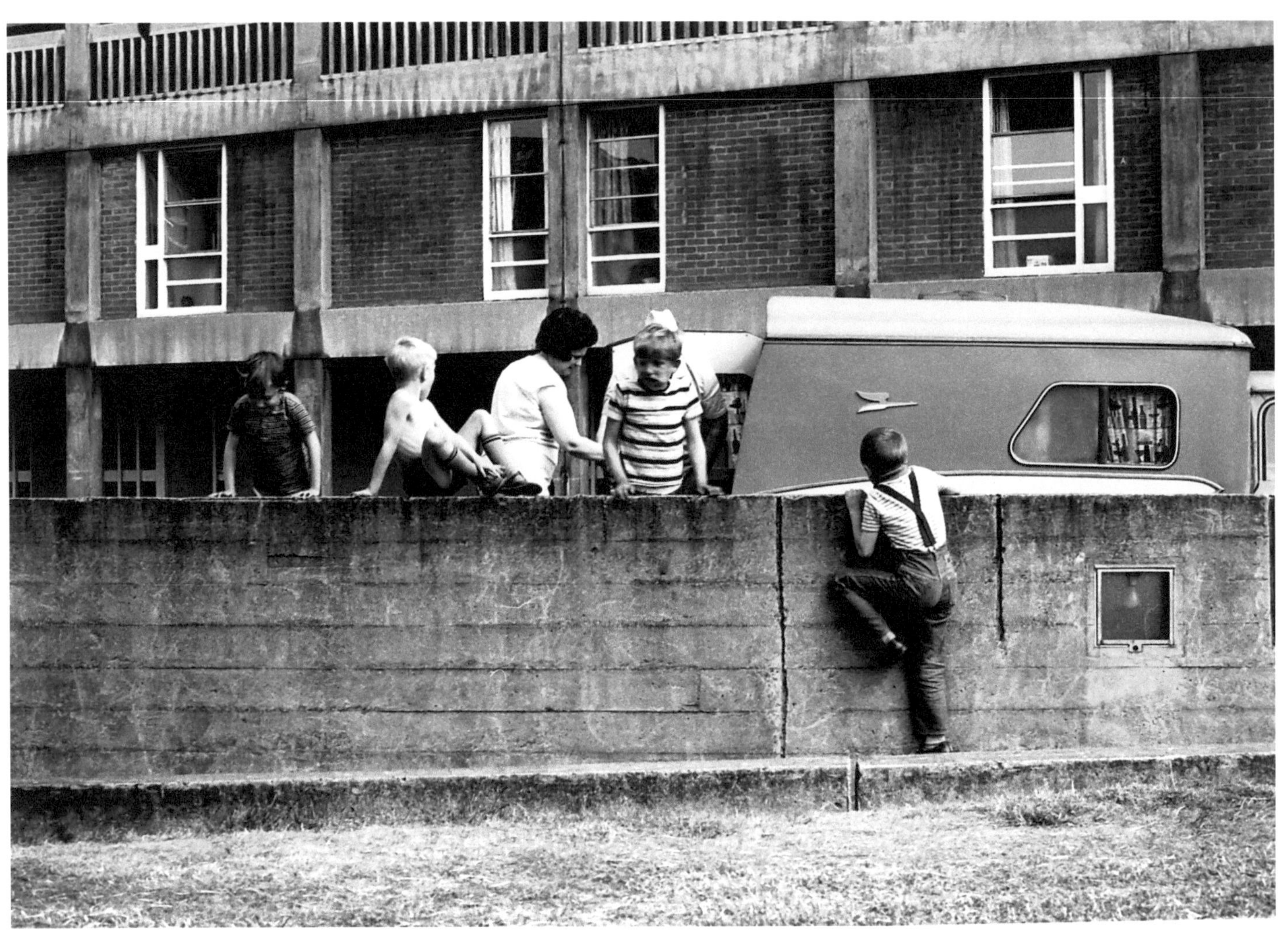

Kids playing on the estate, next to some sort of camper van. The lad in the stripey   t-shirt with the gobstopper in his mouth is Tony Pierpoint. That was the only way you could shut him up.

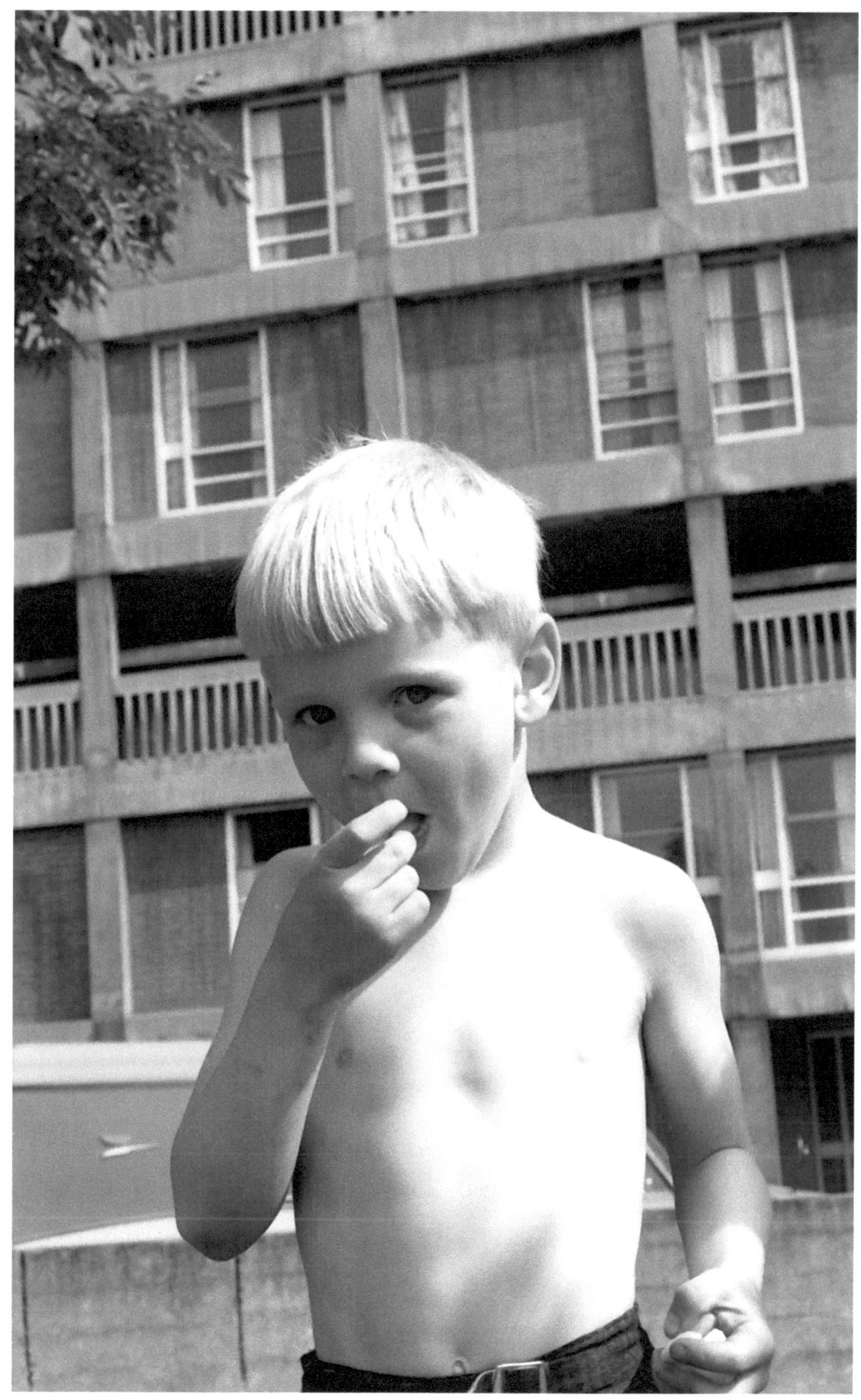

This is Steve Nemeth known a "Nemy" who is in the previous and the next picture too. You wouldn't want to eat those mint imperials that he has in his hand.

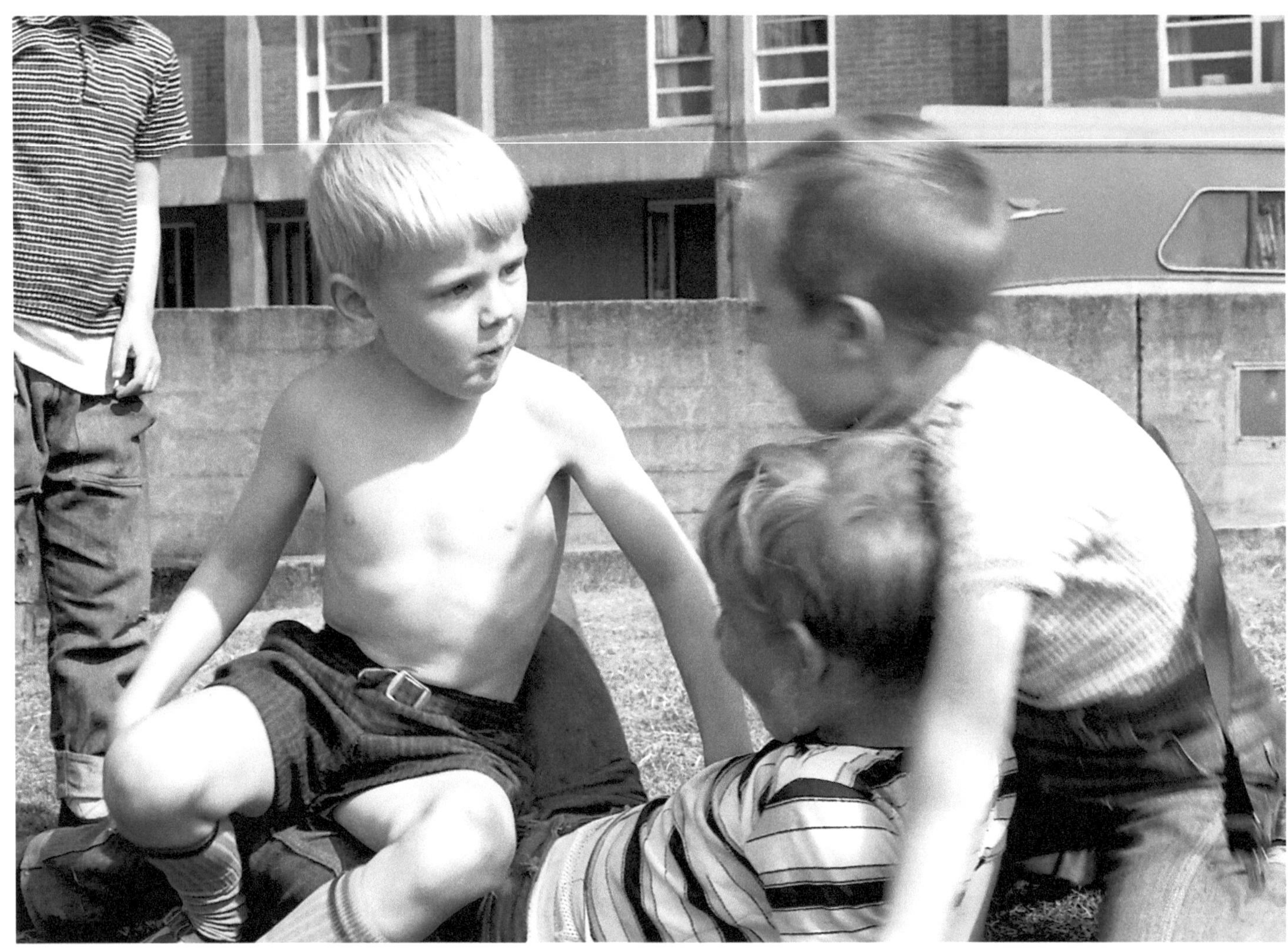

Steve was a lovely lad but a little bit of a varmint. One of his catchphrases was: "you're a big fat hairy melon!" He's now a taxi driver for a well-known Sheffield firm. Looks like he's gobbing off as usual.

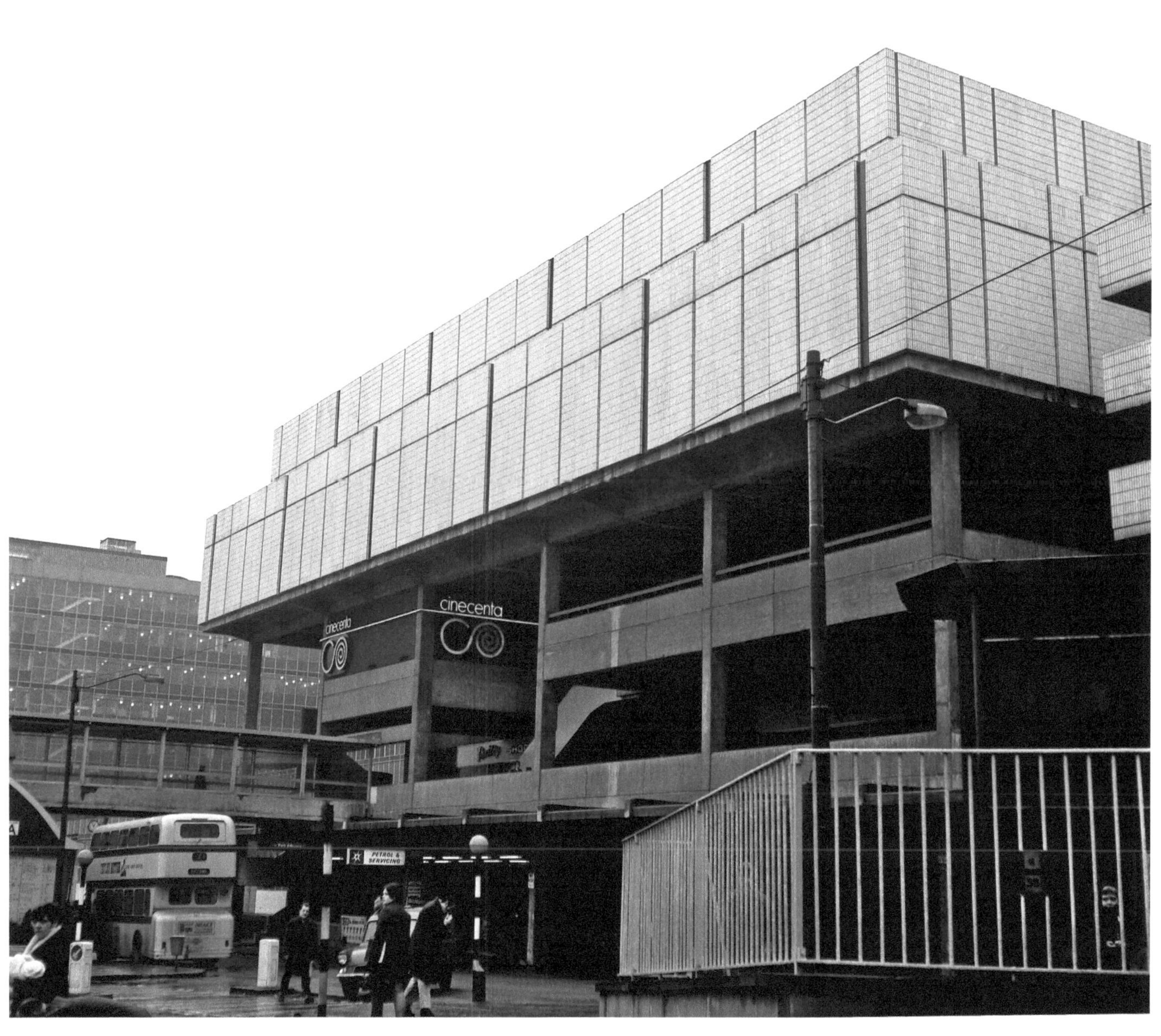

The Top Rank and Cinecenta taken from Pond Street. Ever get that feeling you are being watched?

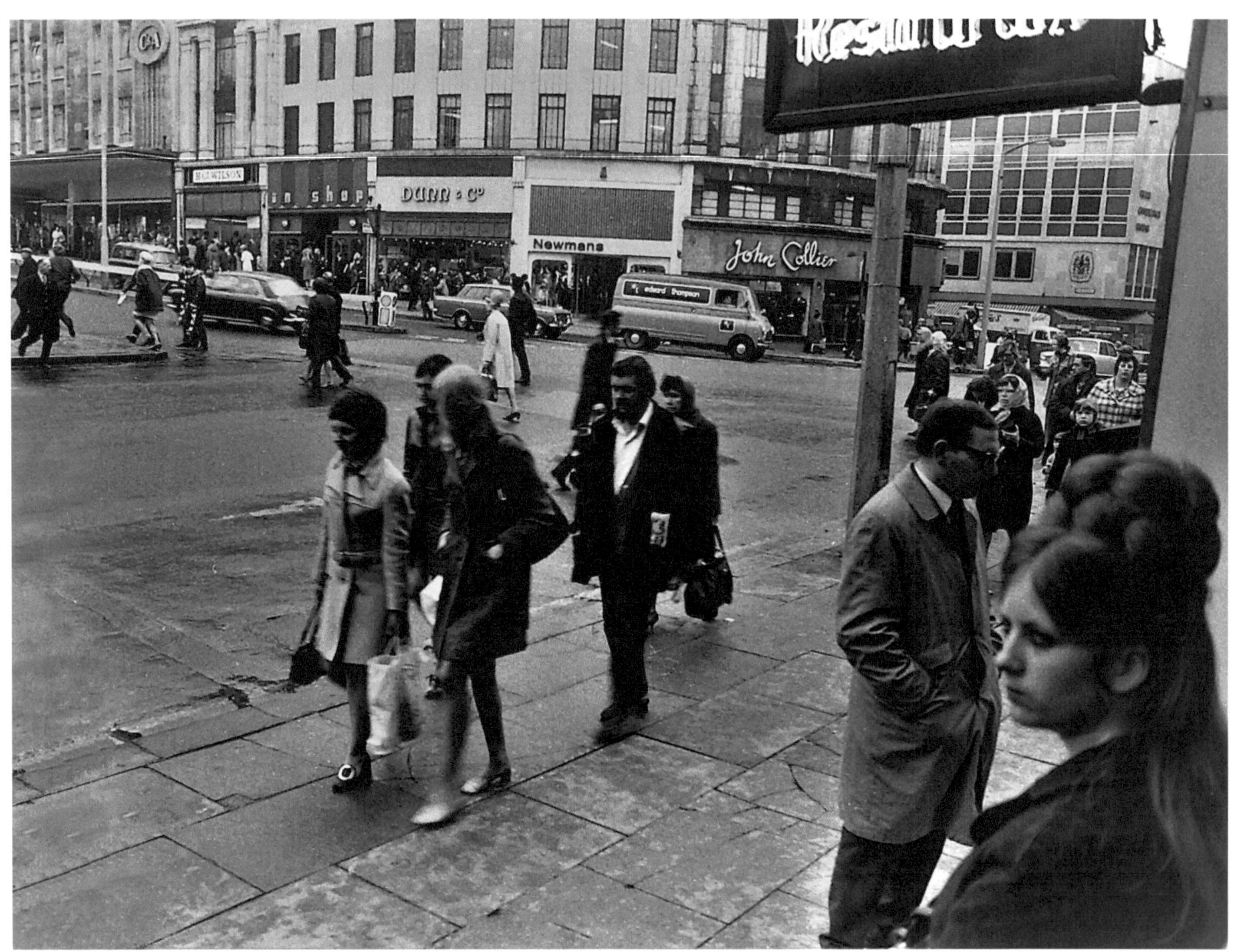

From the steps of the Classic cinema in Fitzalan Square looking towards Haymarket. C&A, and other disappeared high street names, Dunn & Co and John Collier, in the background. Two lads have just crossed the road on their way to the match, scarfs tied around their wrists.

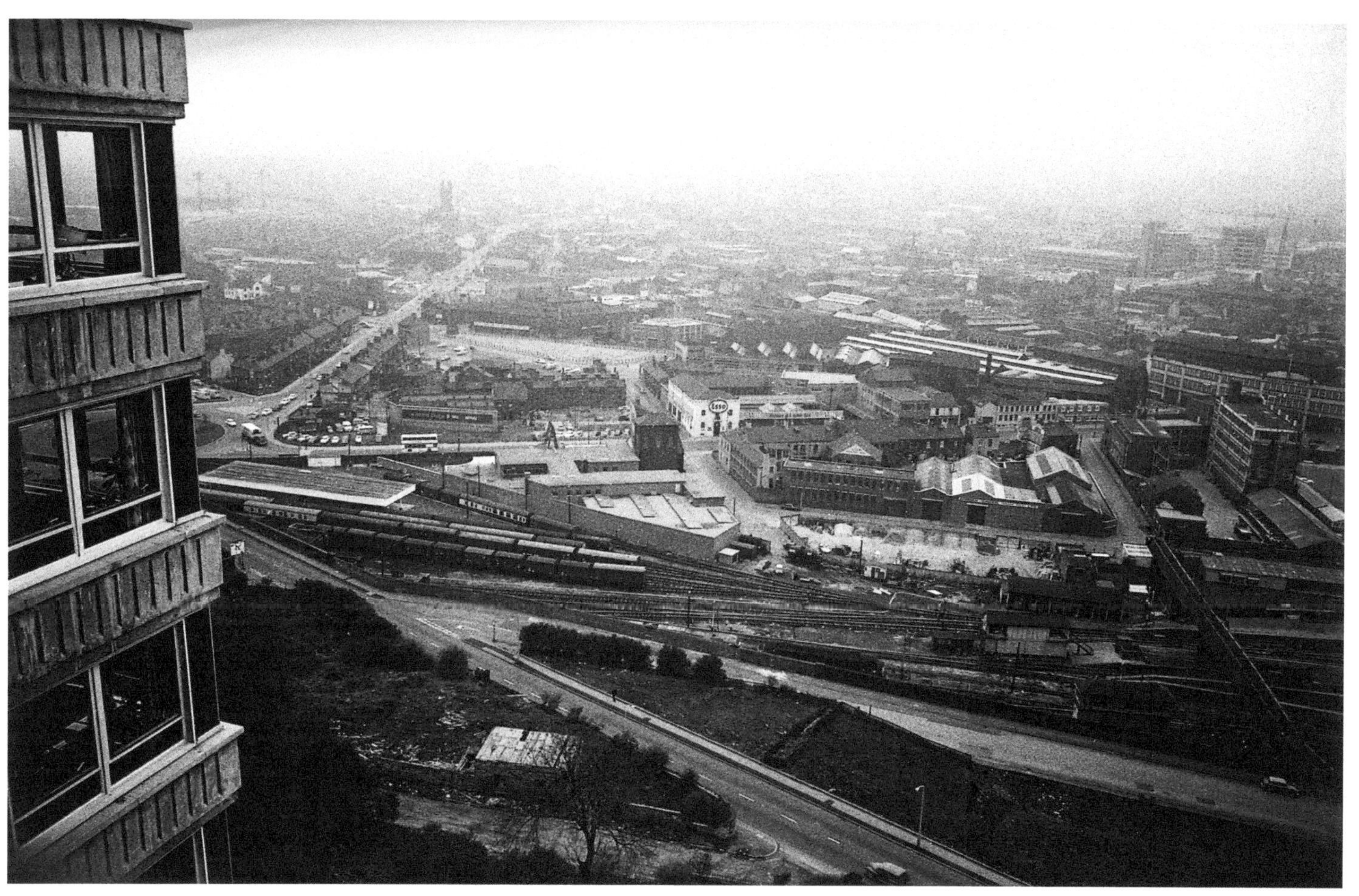

Taken from Claywood flats in 1970. Midland Station sidings in the foreground and St Mary's church and the floodlights of Beautiful Downtown Bramall Lane can just be made out through the haze. With a name like Mick Jones — I could hardly have been anything but a Unitedite could I? To balance things out a bit I have to confess that both my Dad & Granddad were Wednesdayites.

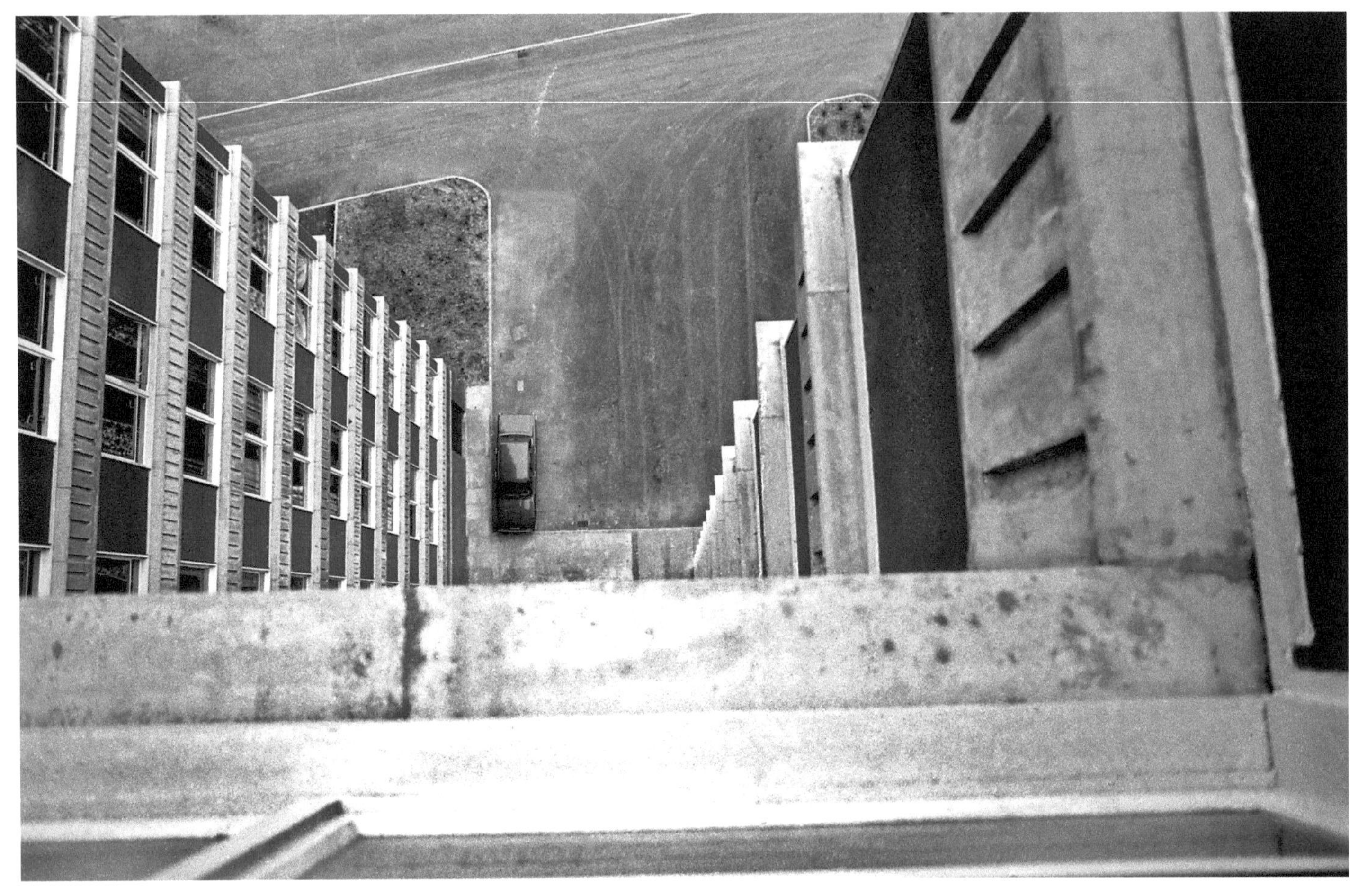

Looking down from Claywood flats. You had to have a head for heights. Just over 30 years later they were demolished; it seemed such a waste.

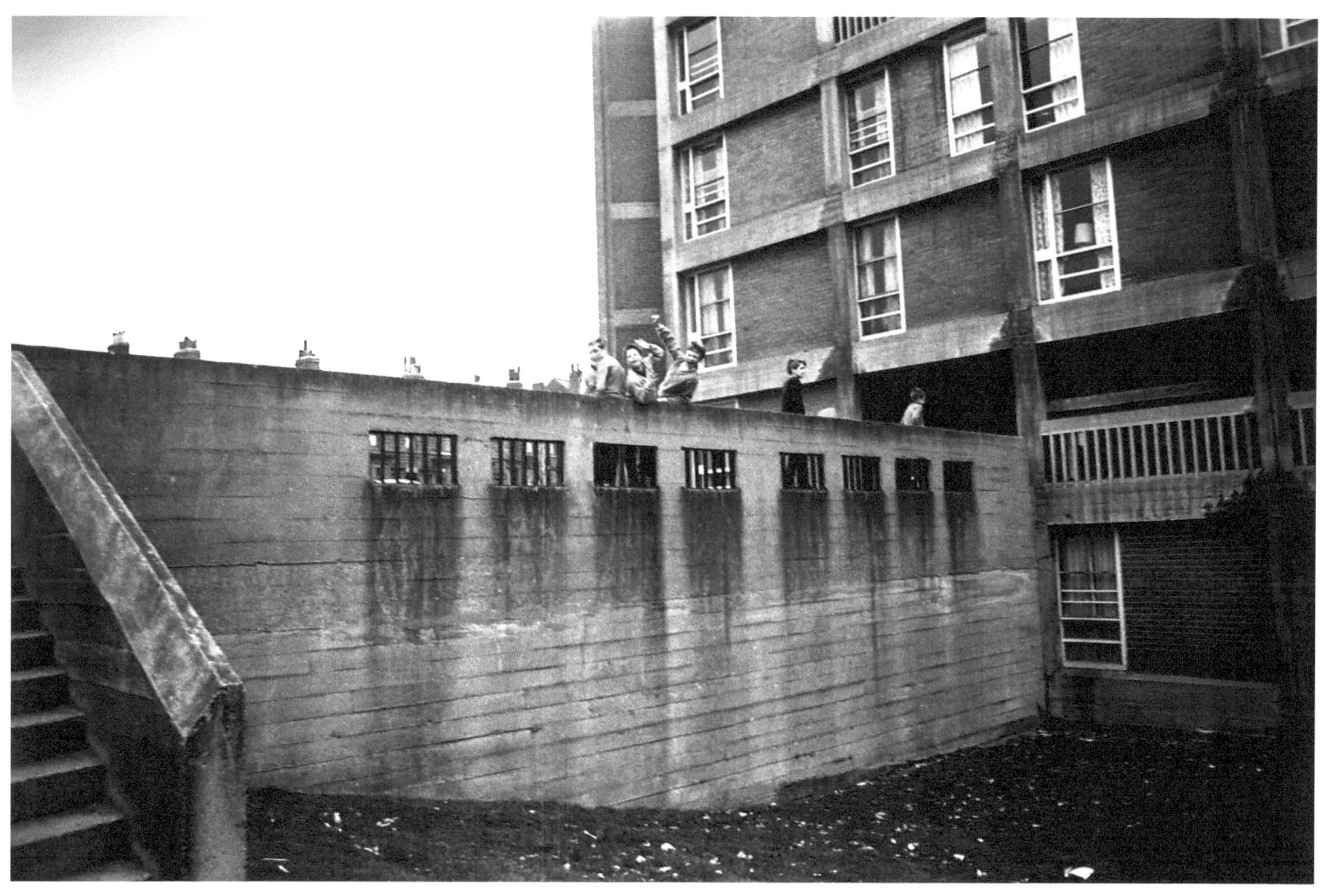

Playing up for the camera on Park Hill. Looks like the porters had forgotten to clear the litter up. To be fair though, Park Hill in the 60s was kept very clean and tidy by the porters.

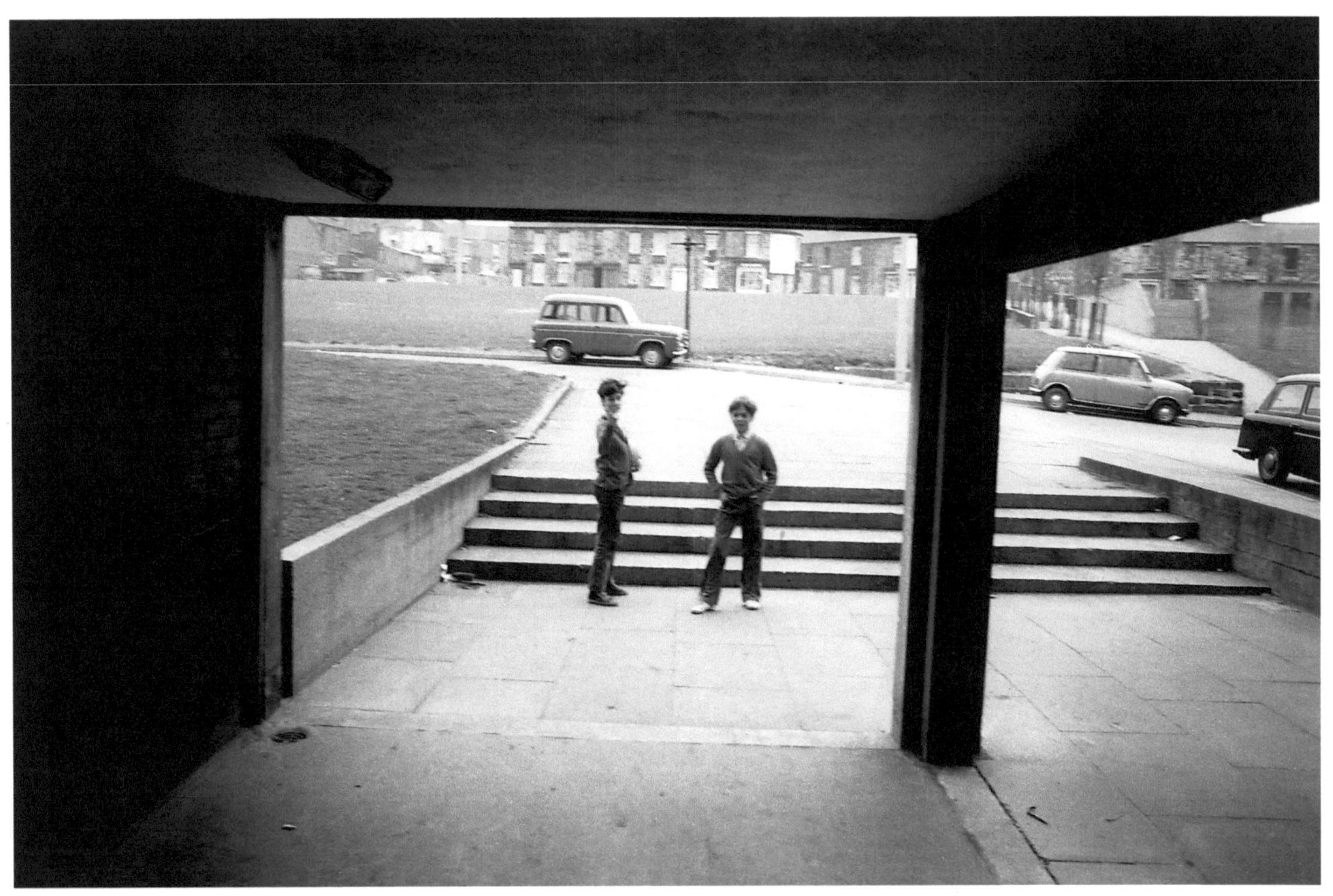

Ben Roe and Dave Foster with Talbot Street shops in the background. One of the shops was Simmonites Newsagents. I had a paper round there but packed it in after a few weeks because I couldn't get up in the morning.

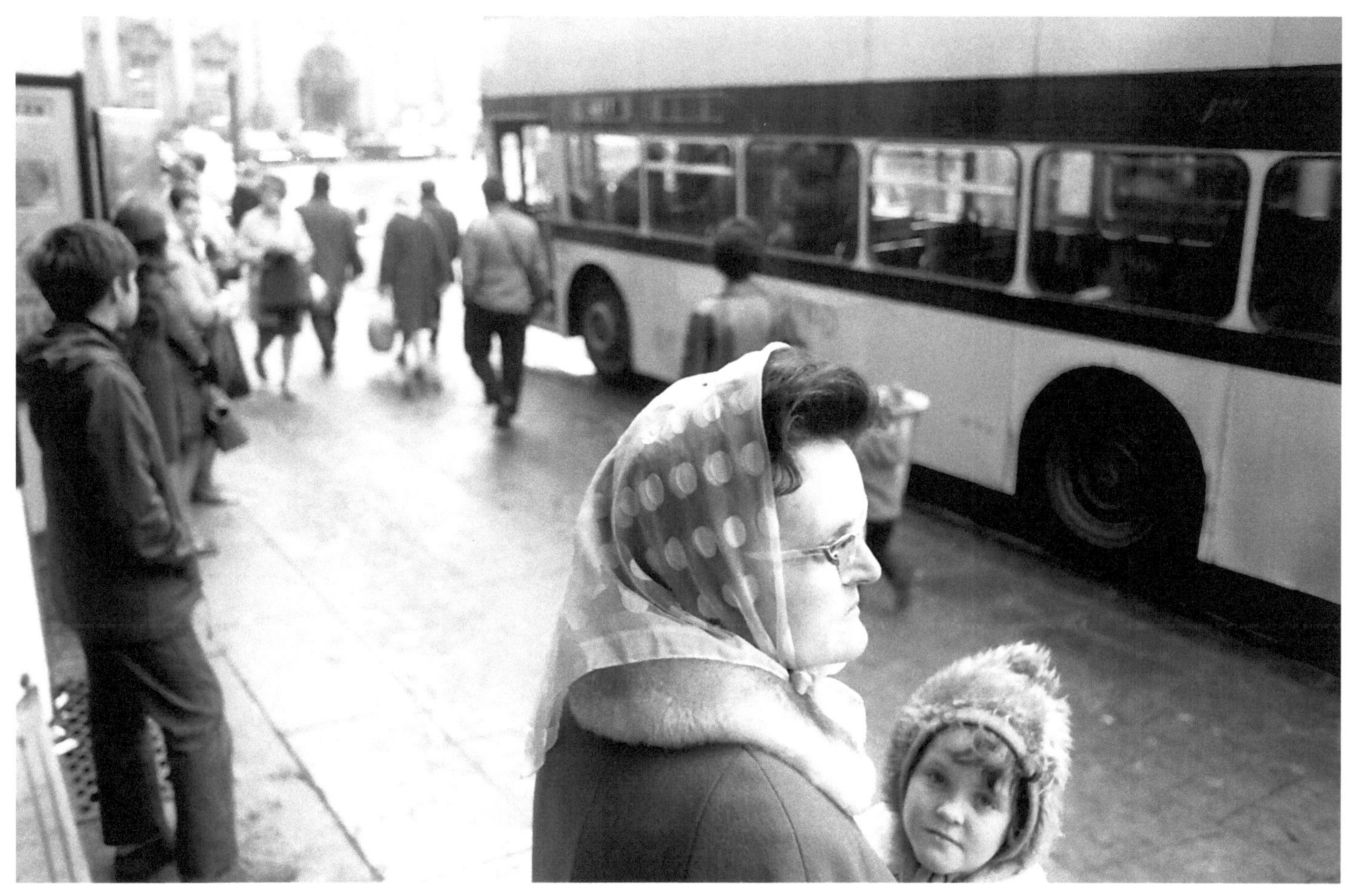

From the steps of the Classic cinema. The young girl will be in her late 50s now.

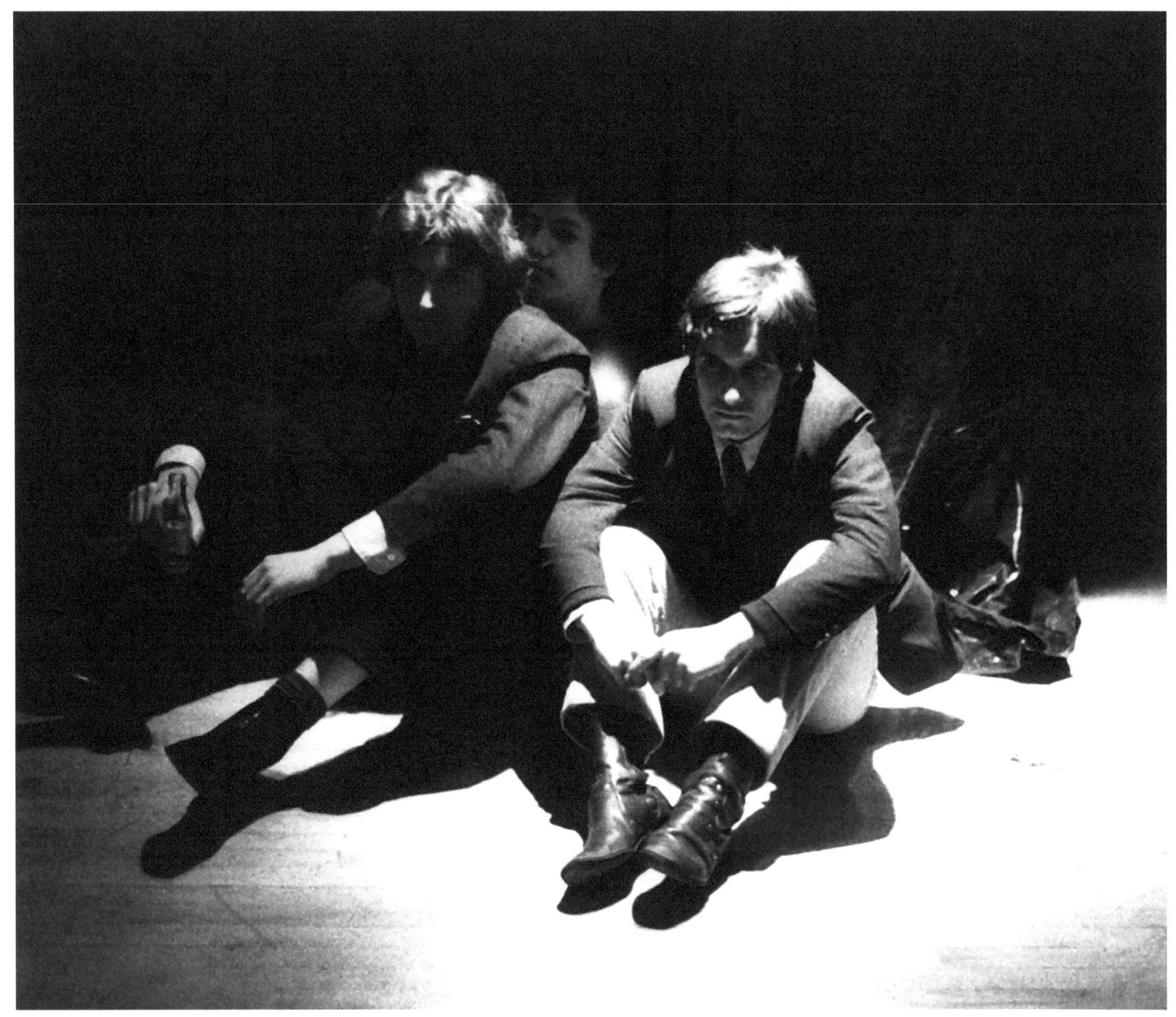

Left to right: Tom Lynch, John Columbine and Mick Aspinall — all mates from school. Taken at the Student's Union on Glossop Road — we used to go there quite a bit because the beer was subsidised: 1s 4d a pint for cider or 1s 8d for Newcastle Brown. The bar was always packed so we'd buy 3 or 4 at a time. I never had much money so I'd live on bread and dripping all week and save the rest of my dinner money for the weekend. My mum never found out, or she would have given me a right clip.

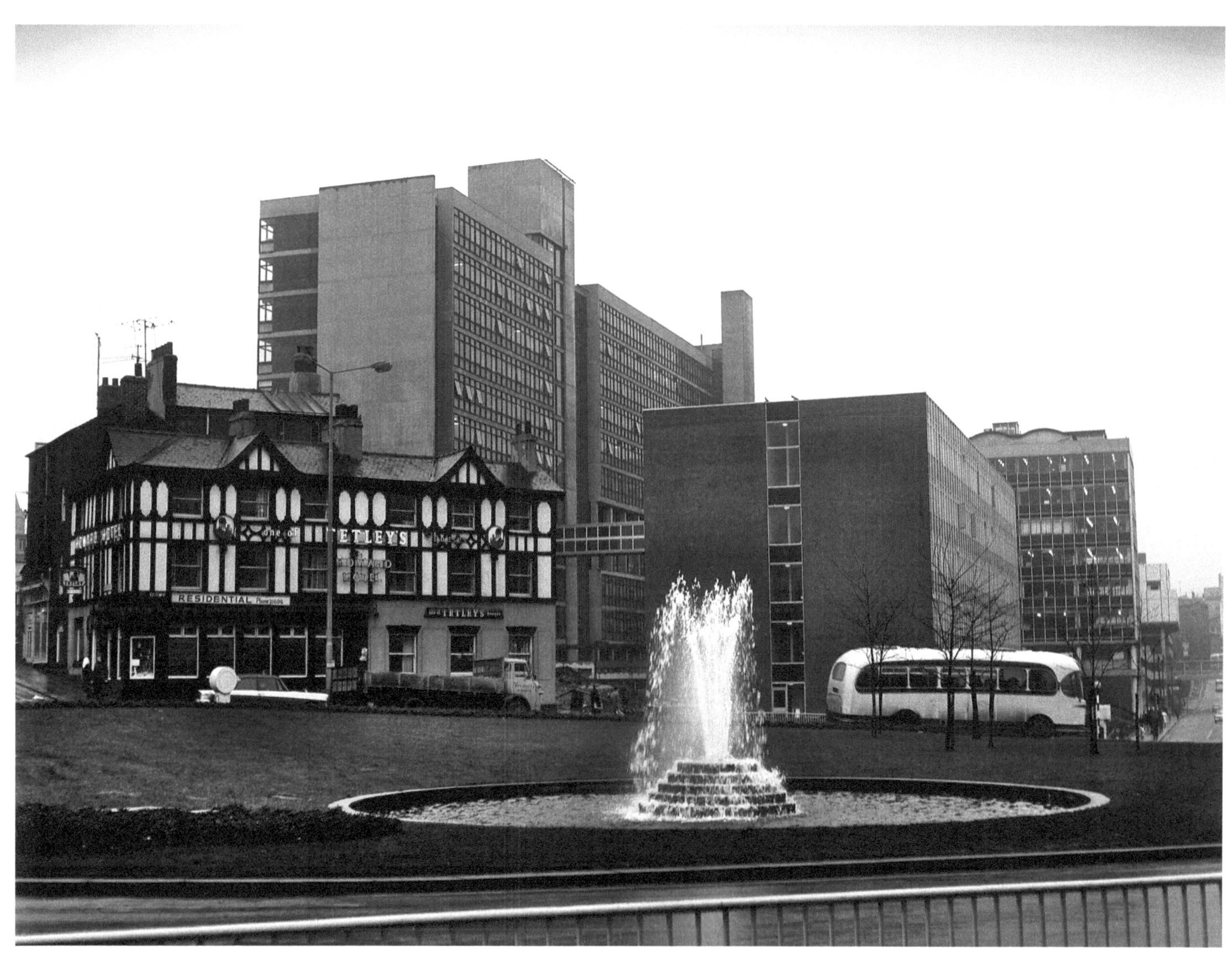

Late 69, bottom of Howard Street, with a single decker bus, or "Charabanc."

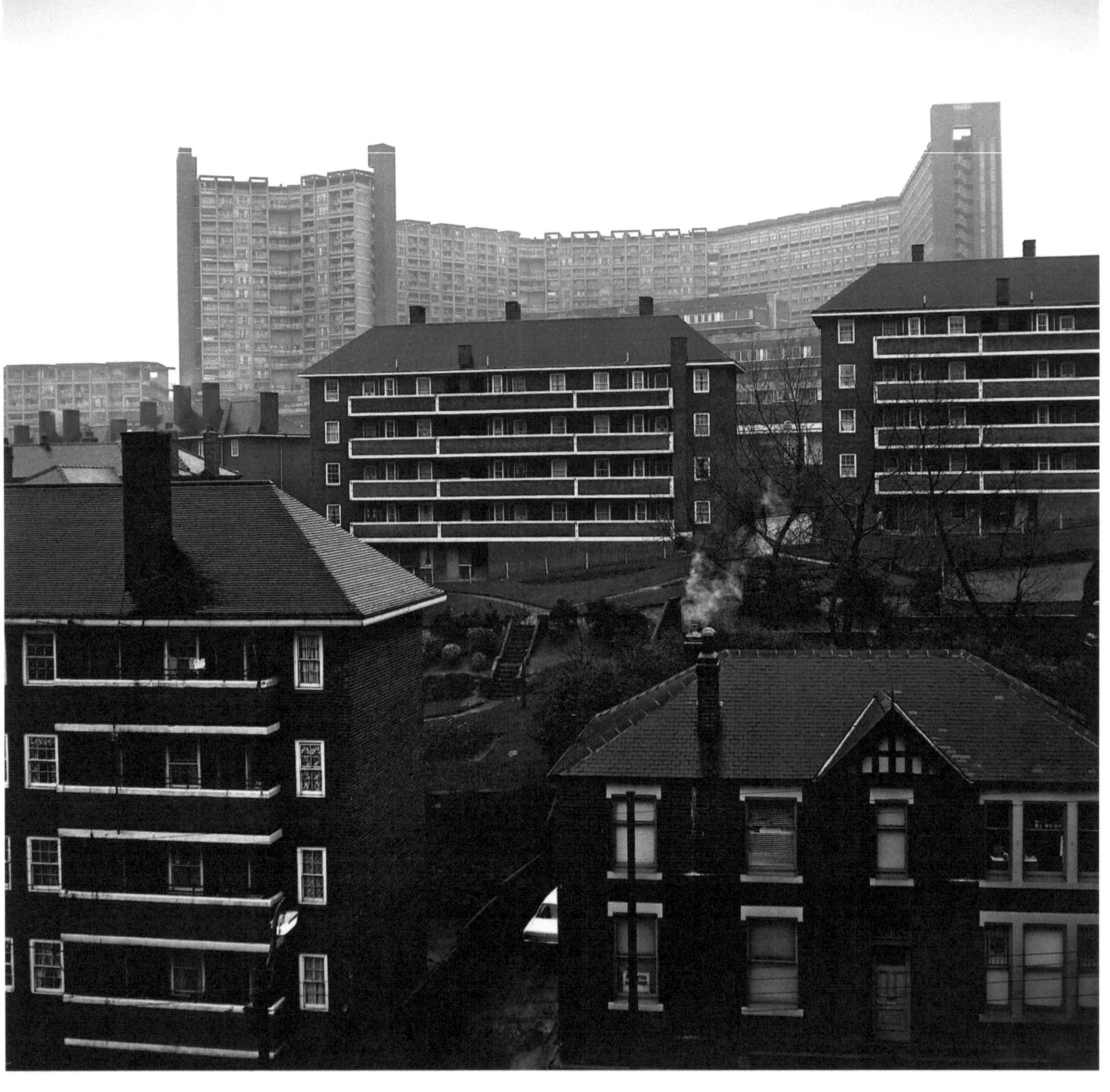

Taken from outside our bedroom window. I loved this view. The building in the front on the right was our local doctors. It's a long story involving being sent away to an open-air school in Woodford Green for my chest — but in short, I'd have been dead if my mum hadn't ignored the advice she got there!

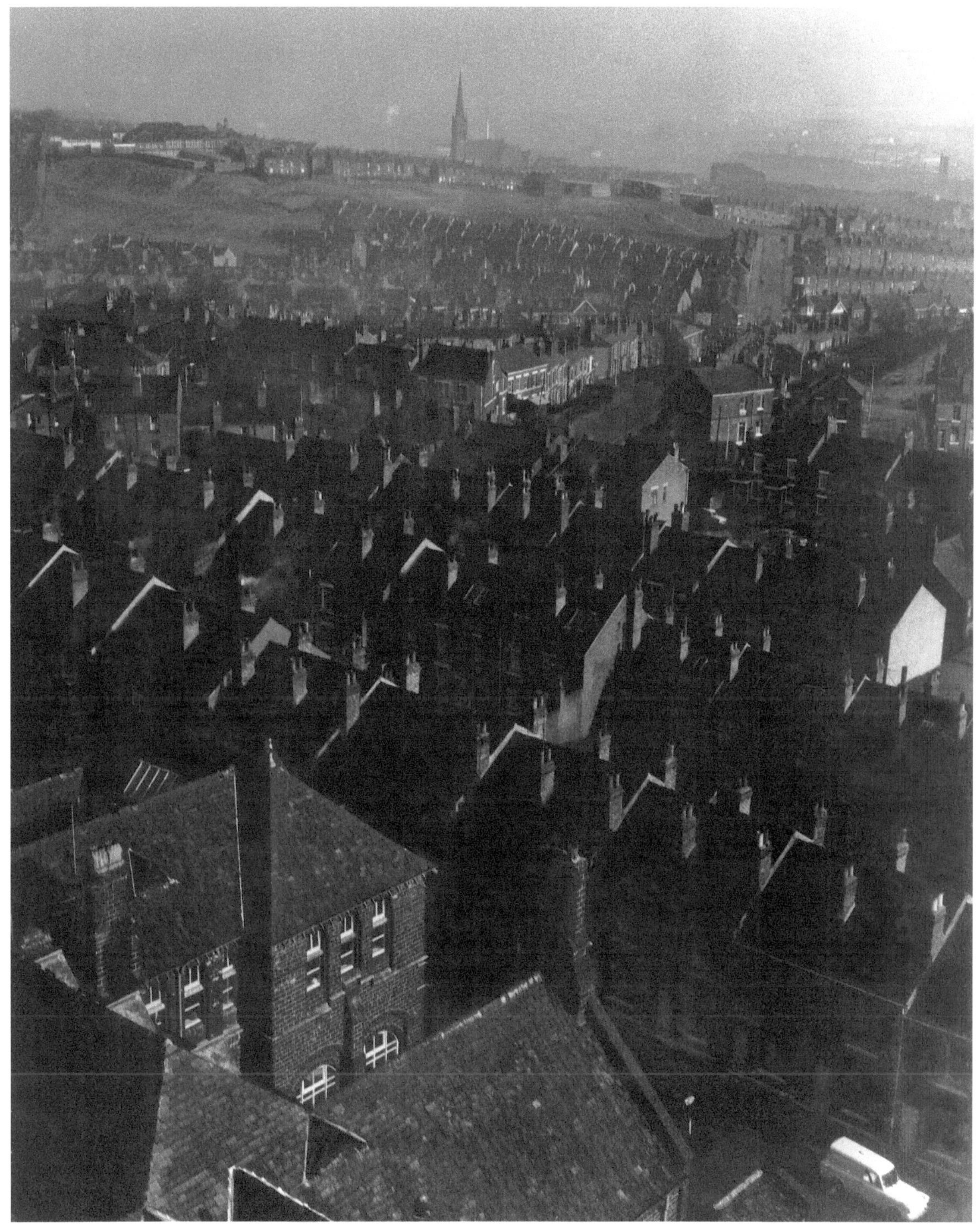

The view from my grandparents flat on Andover Street, with Pye Bank School where my Granddad went. He always bragged about being the "cock of the school."

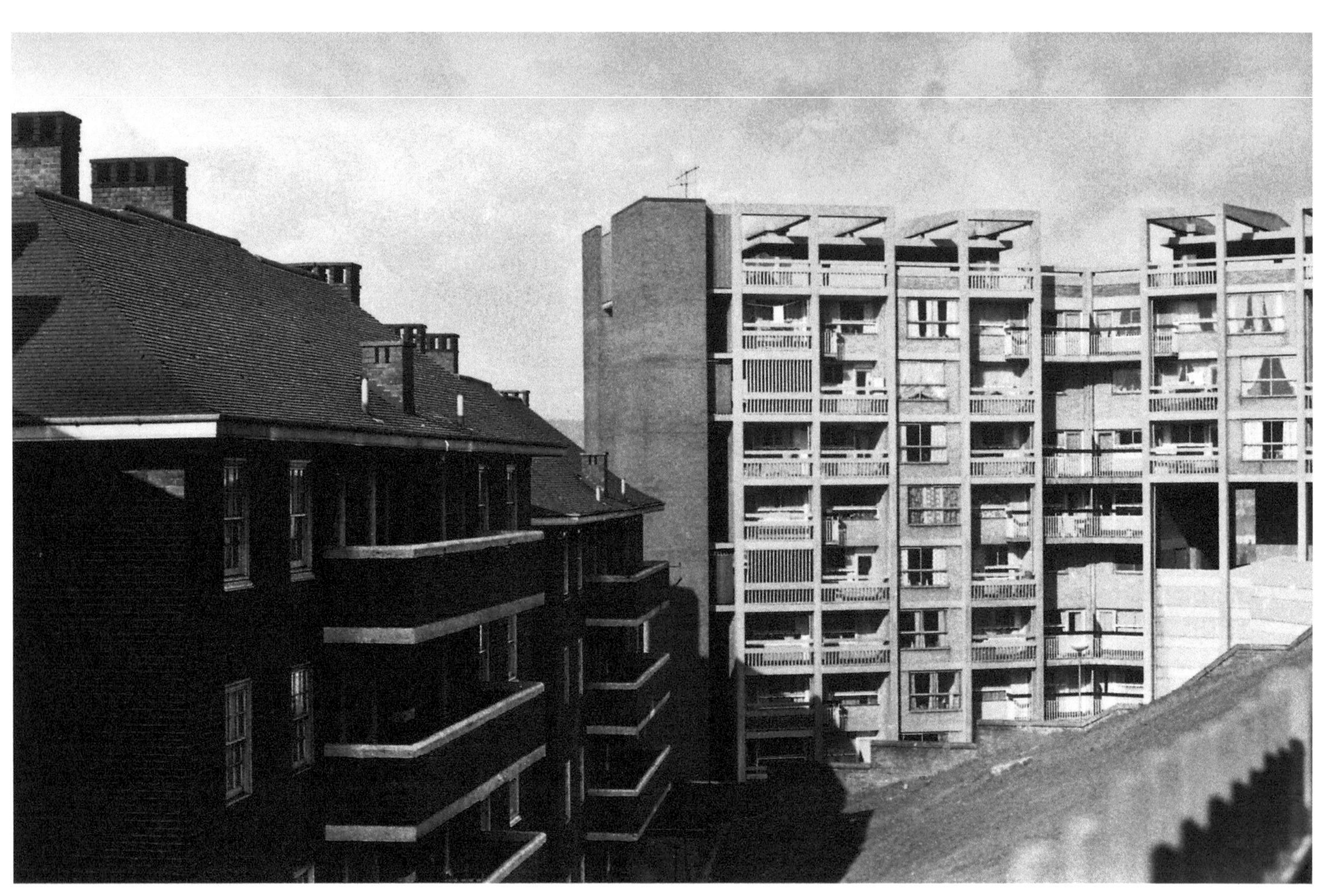

Bernard Street and Hyde Park Flats.

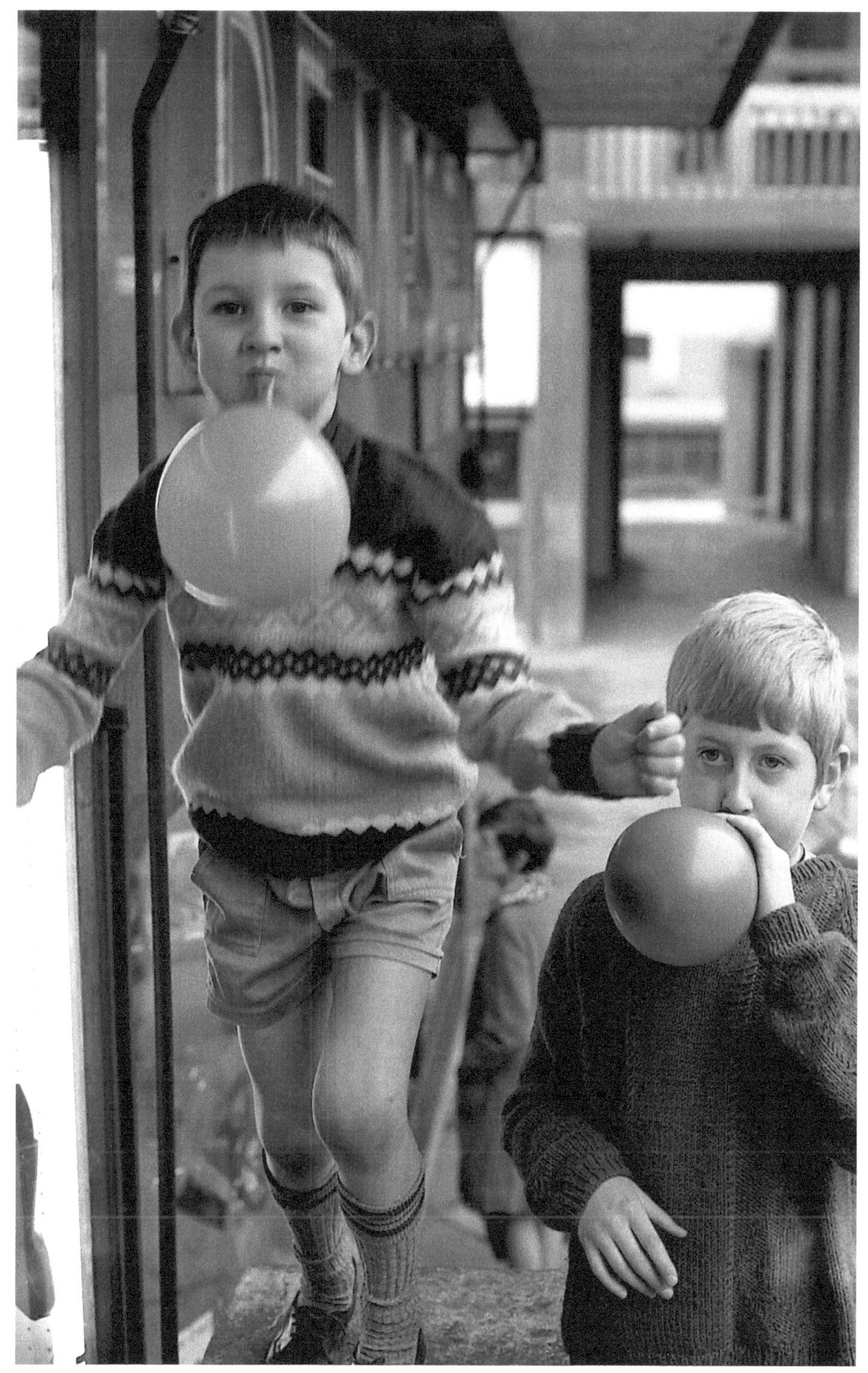

Neil Andrews and Alan Balderson messing about with balloons outside Dempsey's on Park Hill Flats. Most residents bought their shoes from Dempsey's. Plastic sandals were all the rage for the young 'uns, Doc Martens for us big lads.

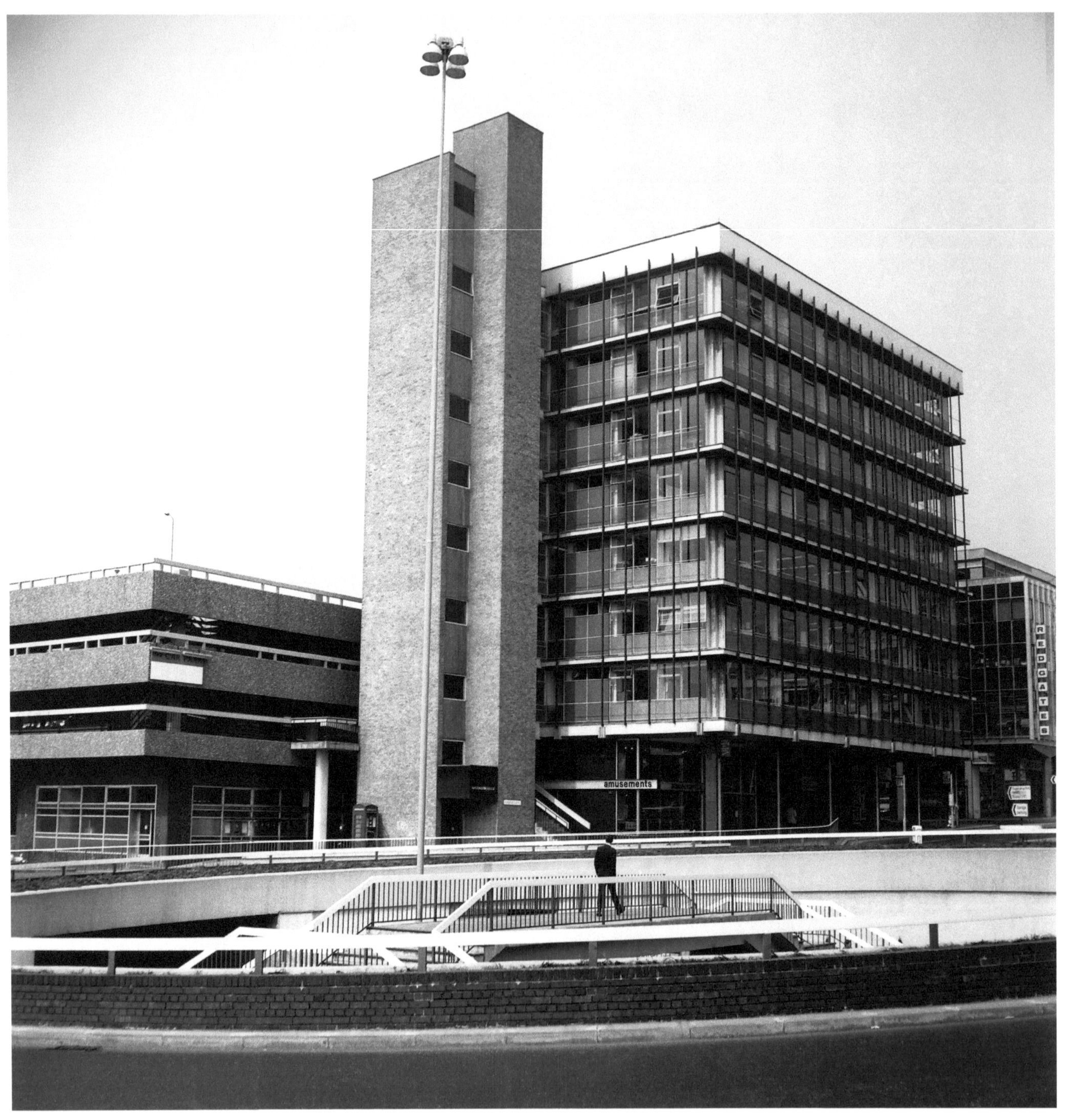

Arundel Gate with Furnival Gate and Redgates to the right. We used to go to the slot machine place on the corner and to the Pump Tavern a bit further down on the way to the match.

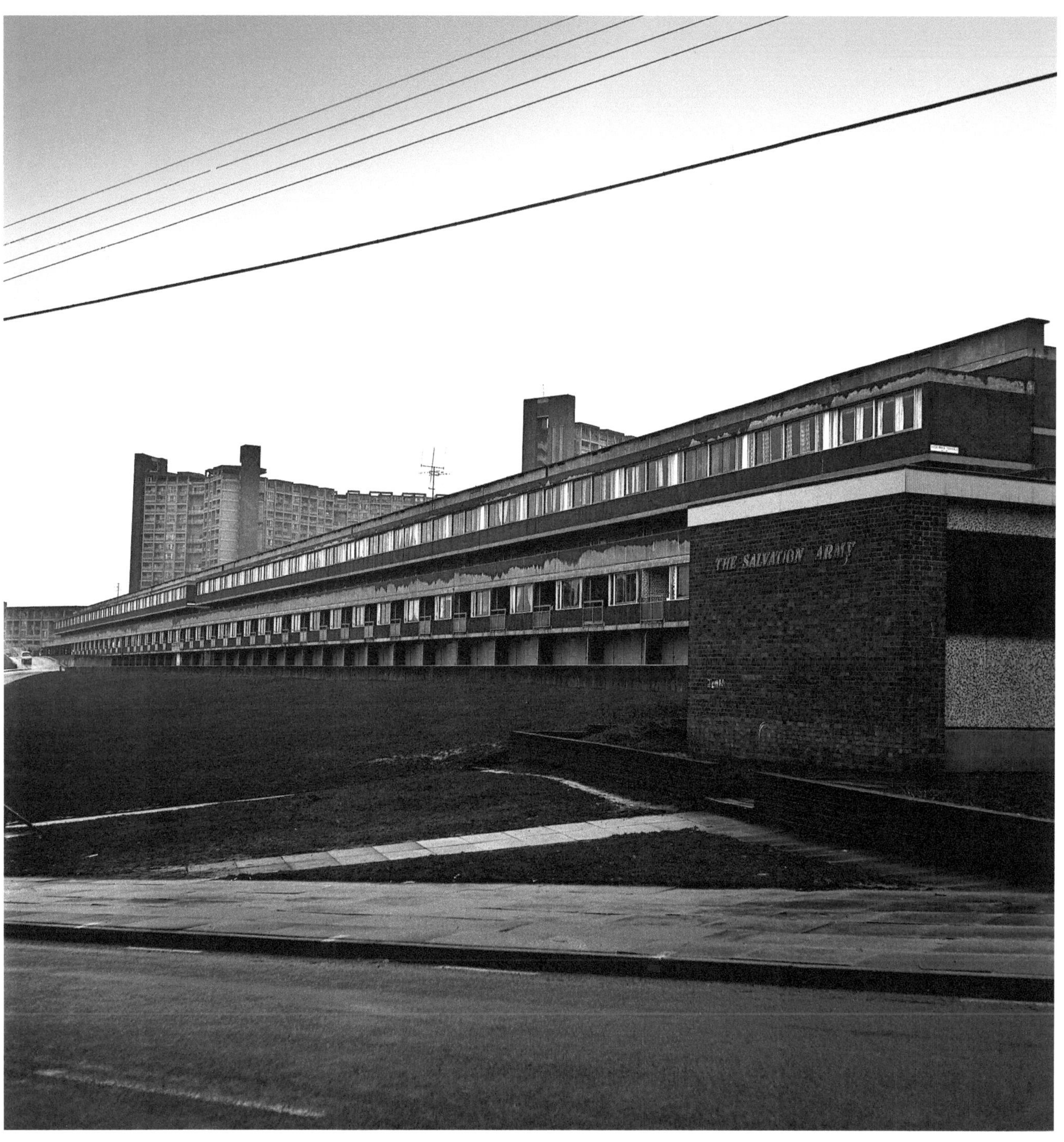

Hyde Park Terrace from the top of Duke Street, with the Salvation Army building. Their band used to play outside the Link pub every Sunday. The atmosphere was fab when they played at Christmas time.

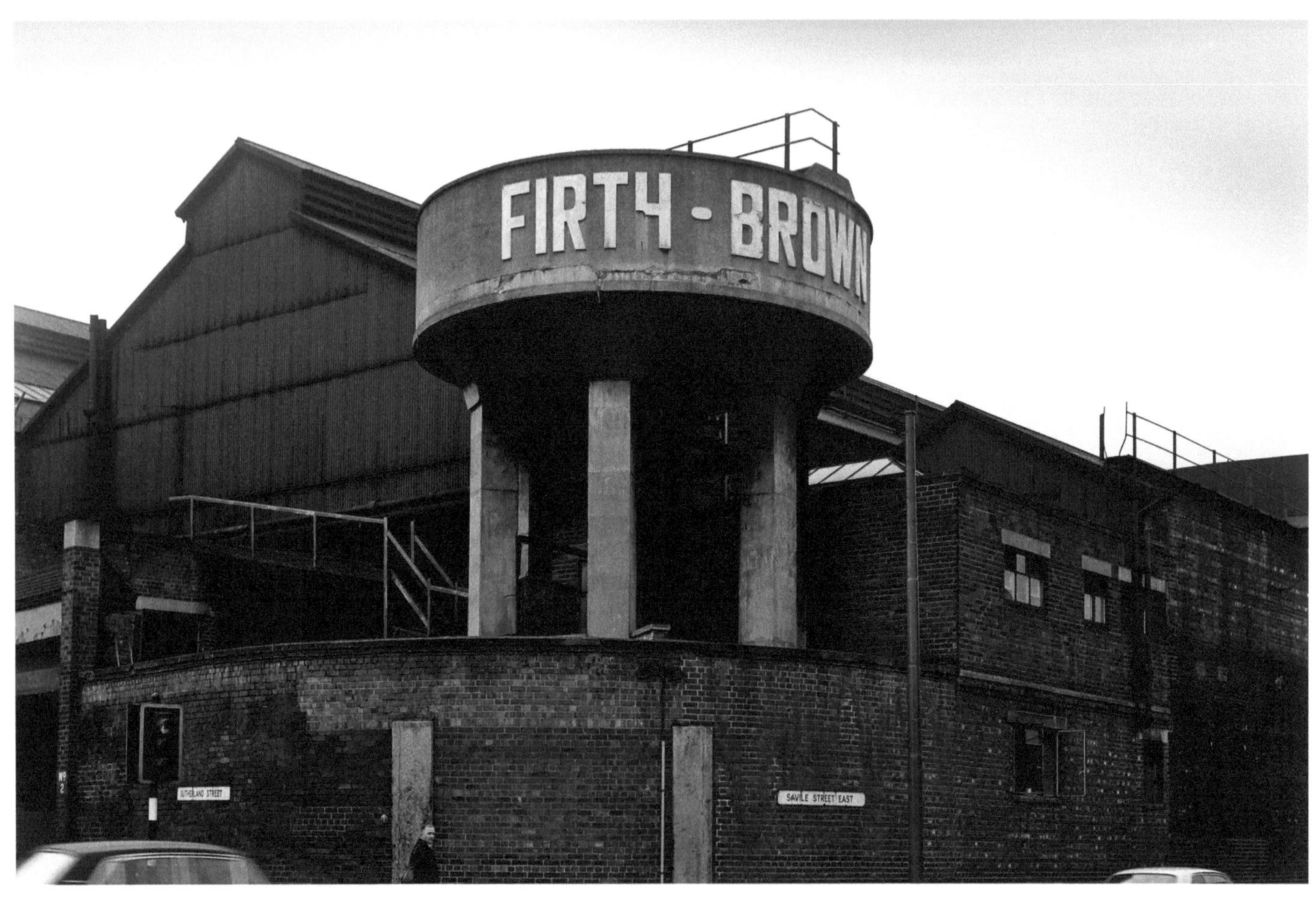

One of the photos taken to the college project brief of industrial areas. "Firty" Browns on the corner of Sutherland Street and Savile Street.

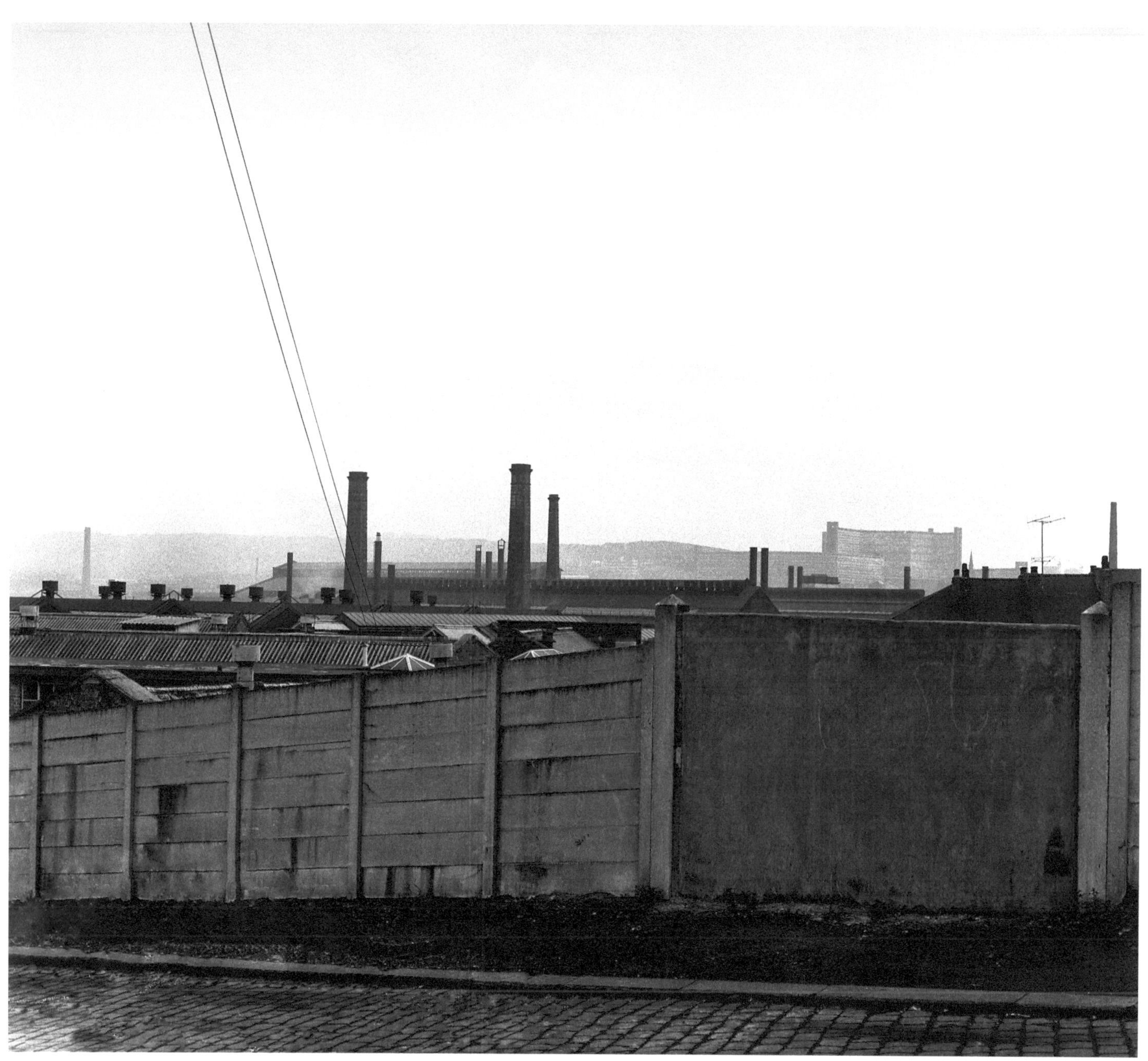

Taken from the top of Carwood Road in Pitsmoor with Hyde Park in the distance. I was born in Pitsmoor in a house we had to move out of — deemed not fit for human habitation. From there we were in a prefab for a short time and, after a few years on the Shirecliffe estate, "flitted" to Park Hill in late 1961.

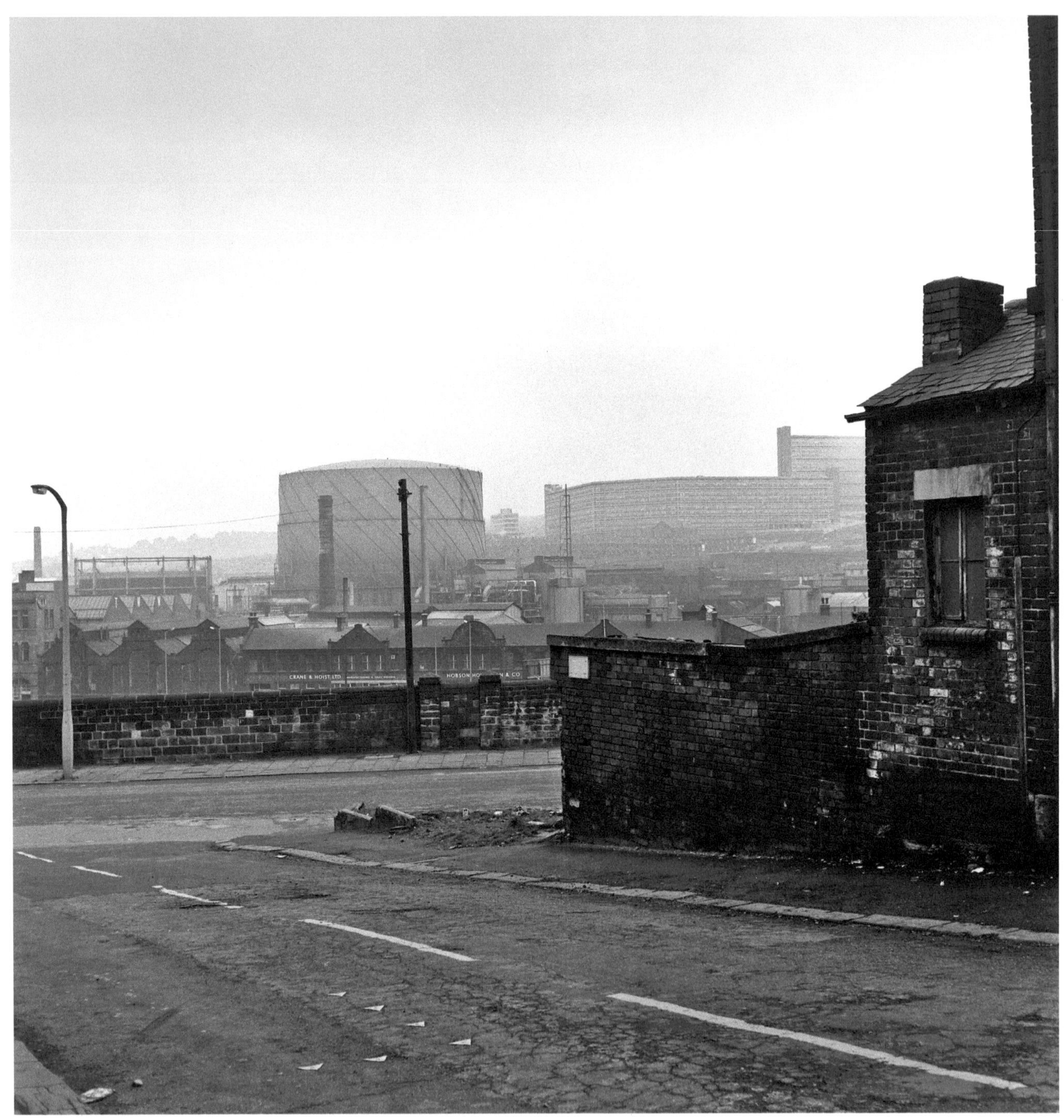

Spital Street looking towards Hyde Park and the Effingham Street gas works. This view is now blocked by the big Tesco. The building on Saville Street — over the wall on the left — with the three gables is now the Pentagon garage.

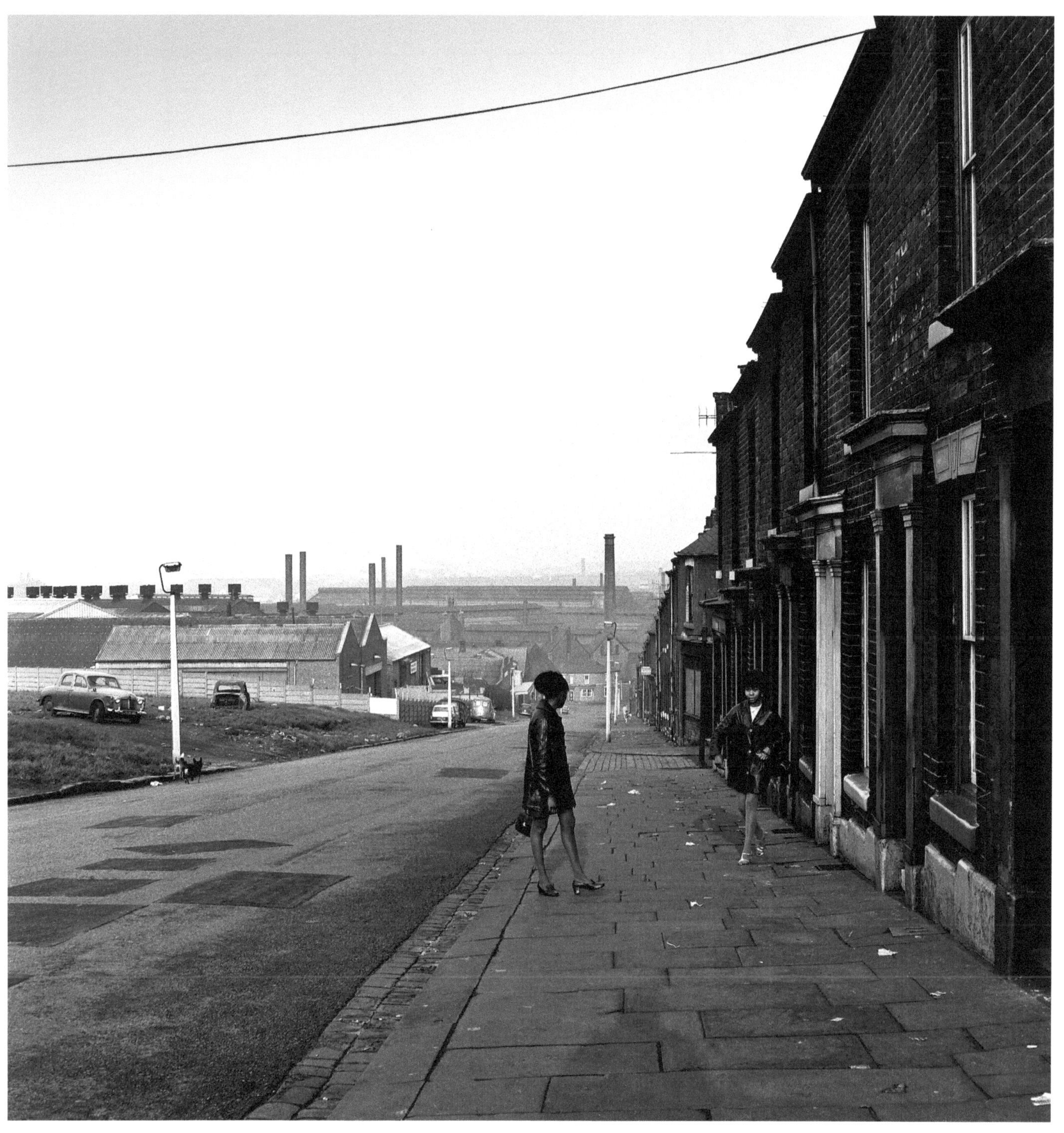

Ready for a night out. Lyons Street, Burngreave. I was just taking the view looking down the street. Well that's my story and I'm sticking to it.

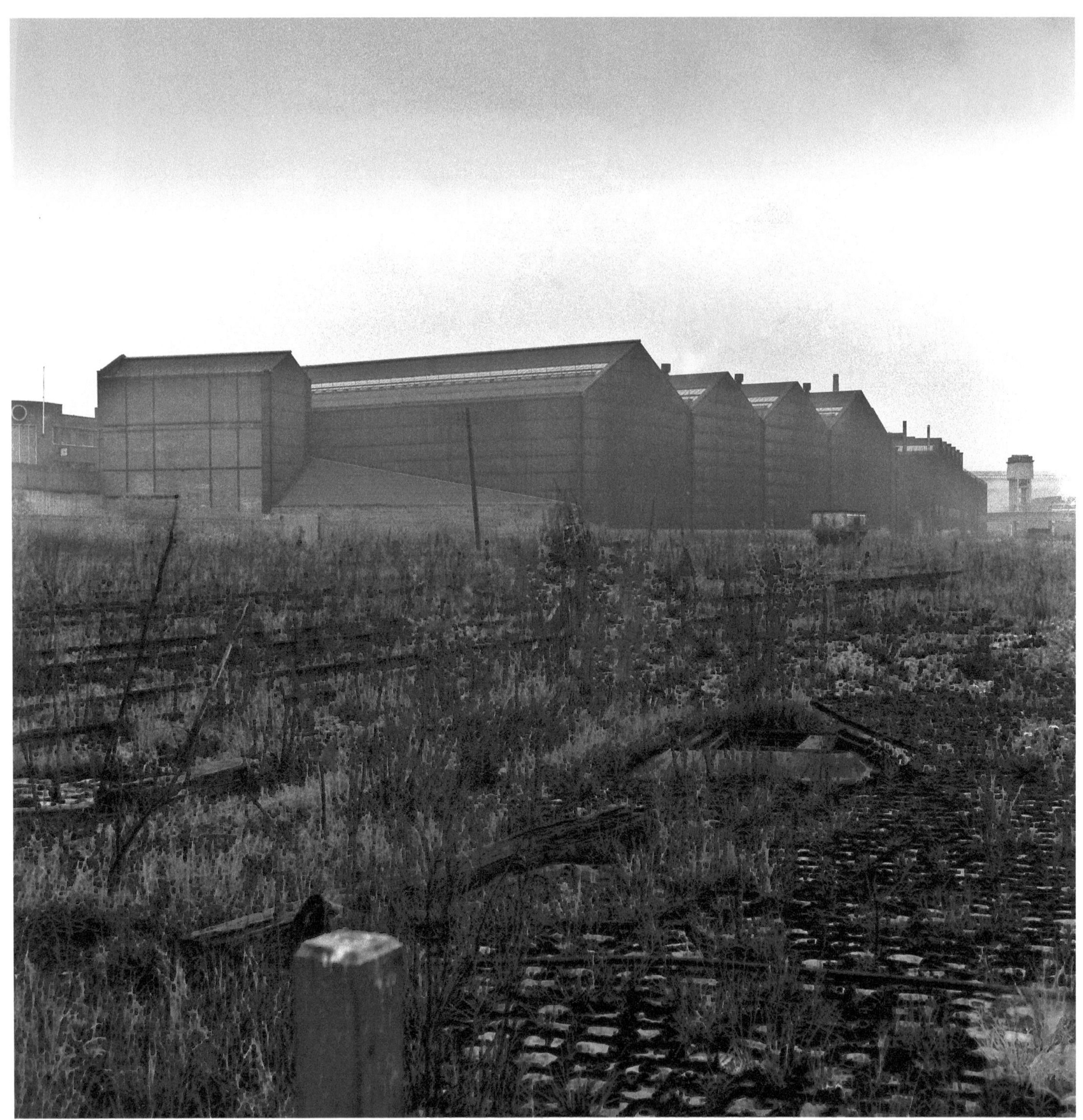

Wicker goods yard and Cyclops Works.

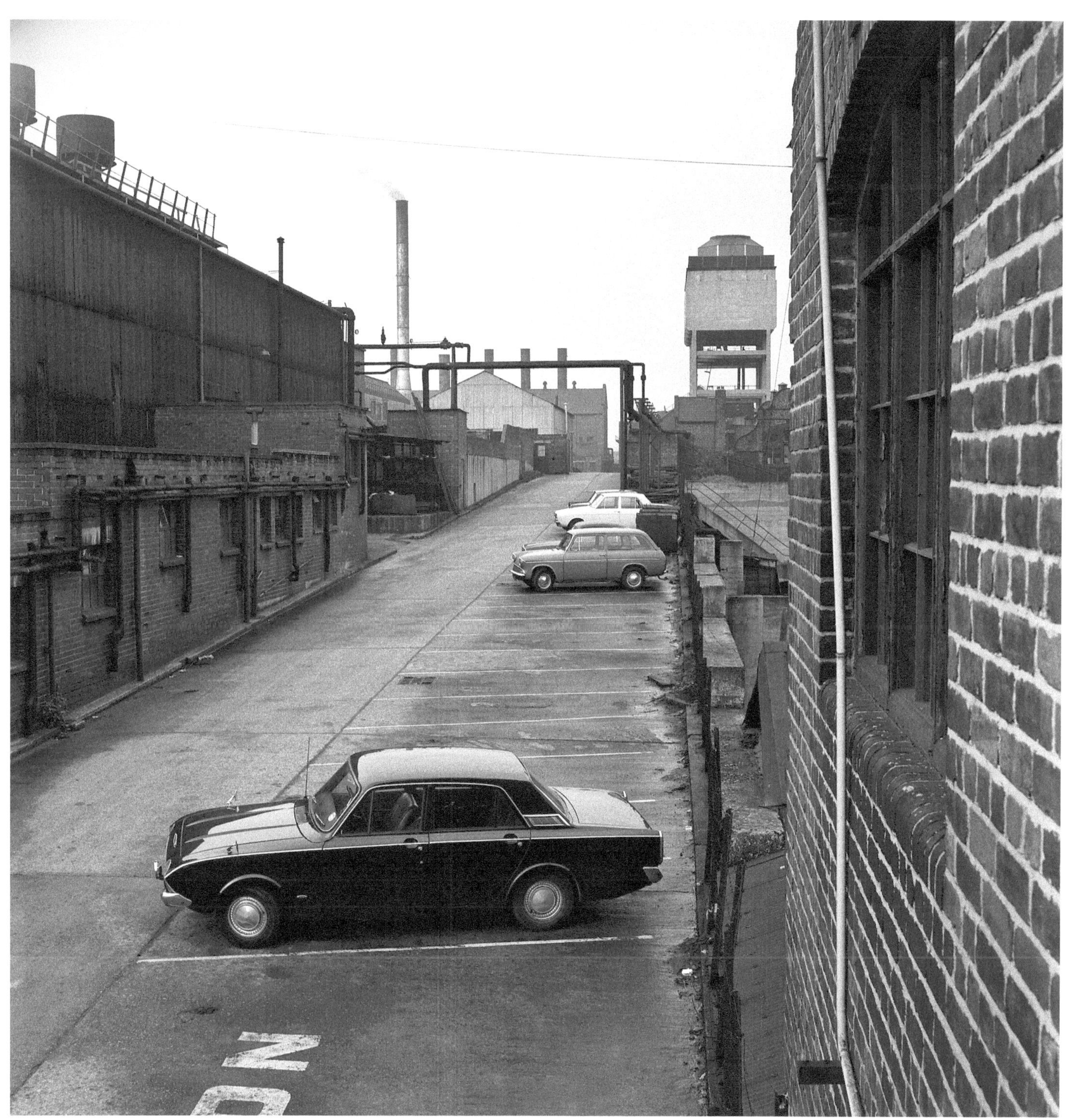

Firth Browns, early 1969, just off Carwood Road behind the Corner Pin Pub.

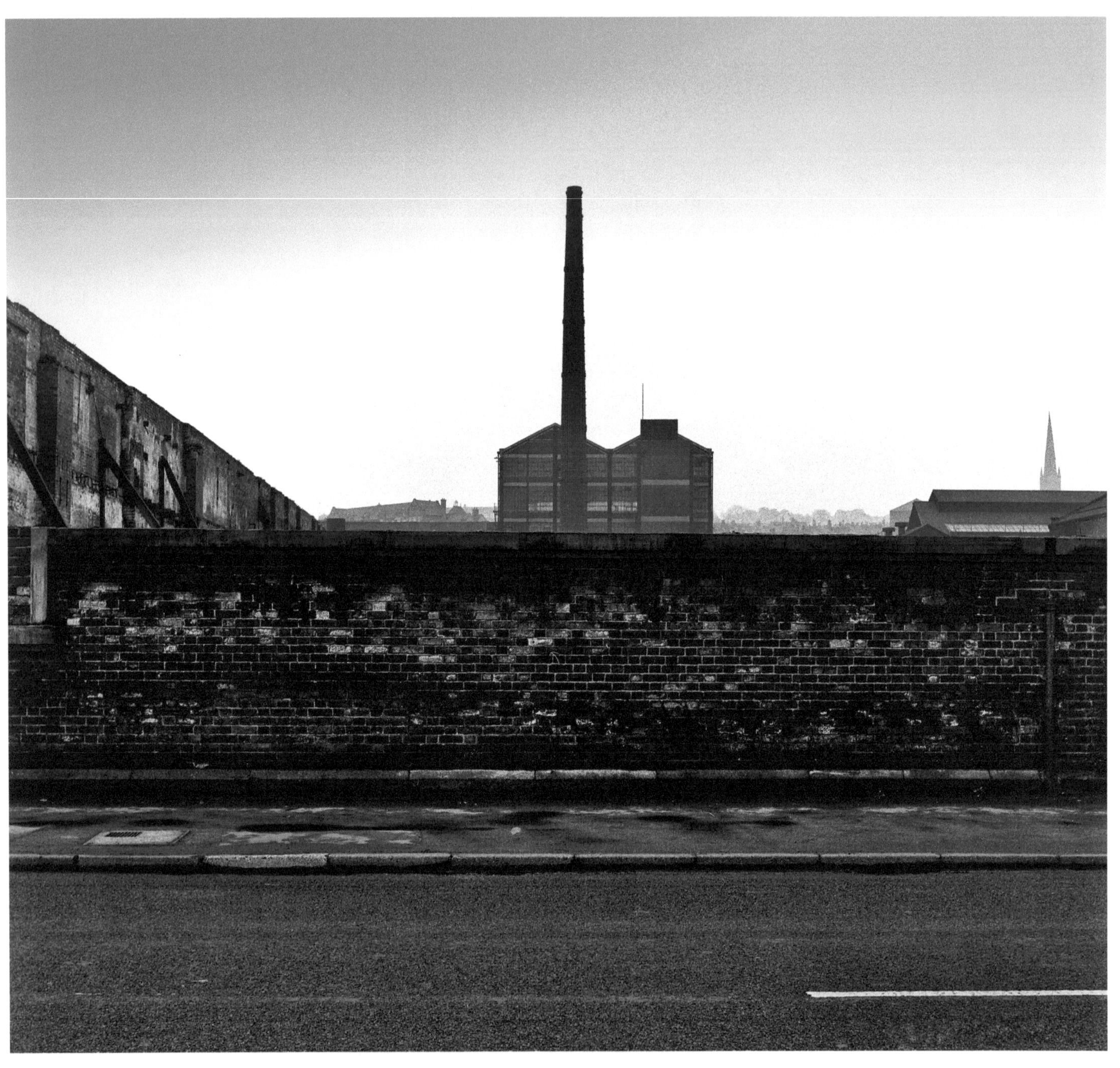

Carlisle Street. The church spire is All Saints (demolished in 1977) and, top left, you can just see Burngreave School.

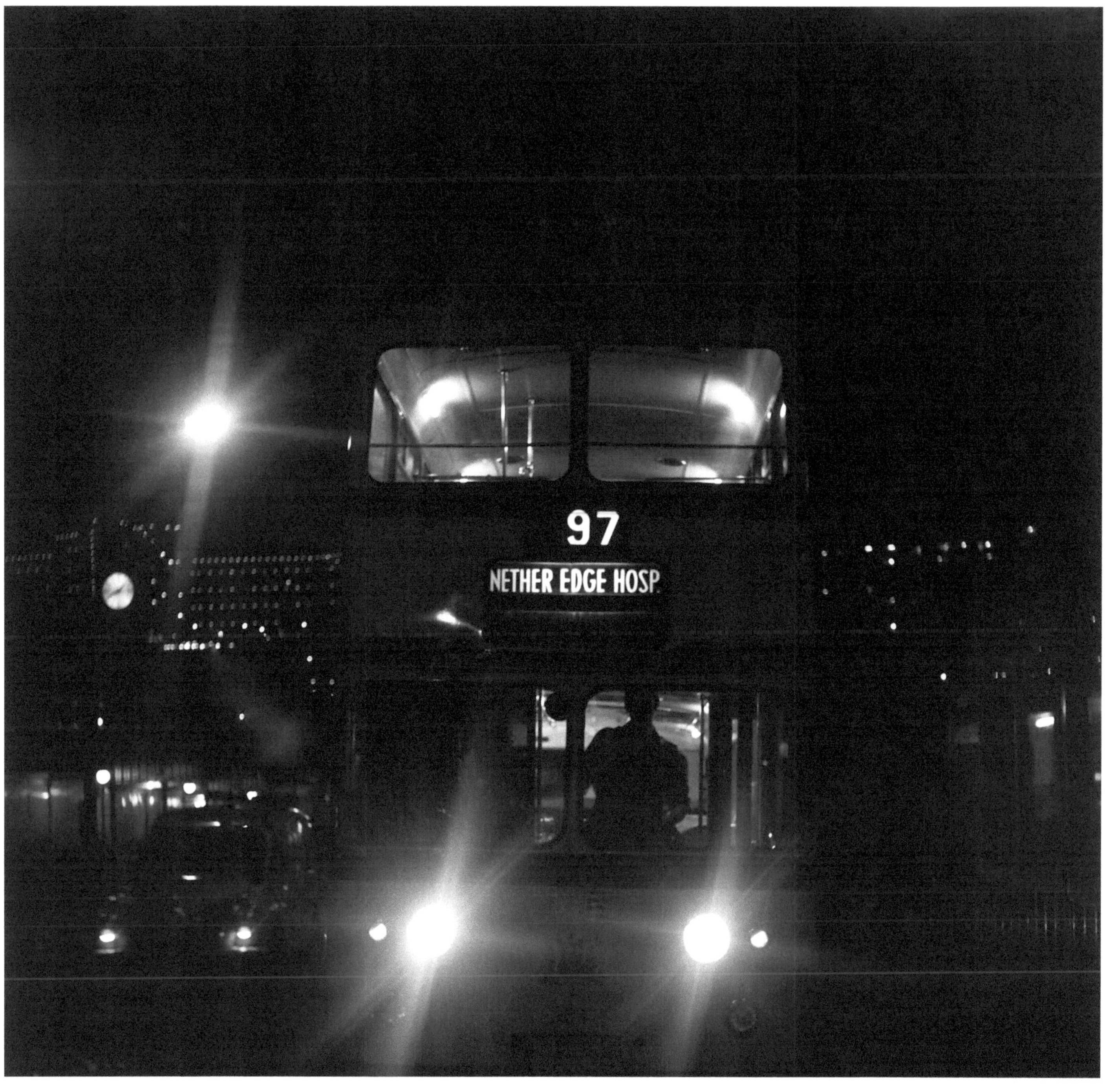

This was the bus we used to catch up to the Union Road annexe of the College of Art at Nether Edge. I took this photograph without a flash and was very fortunate it turned out as well as it did; the lights of Hyde Park and Park Hill in the background.

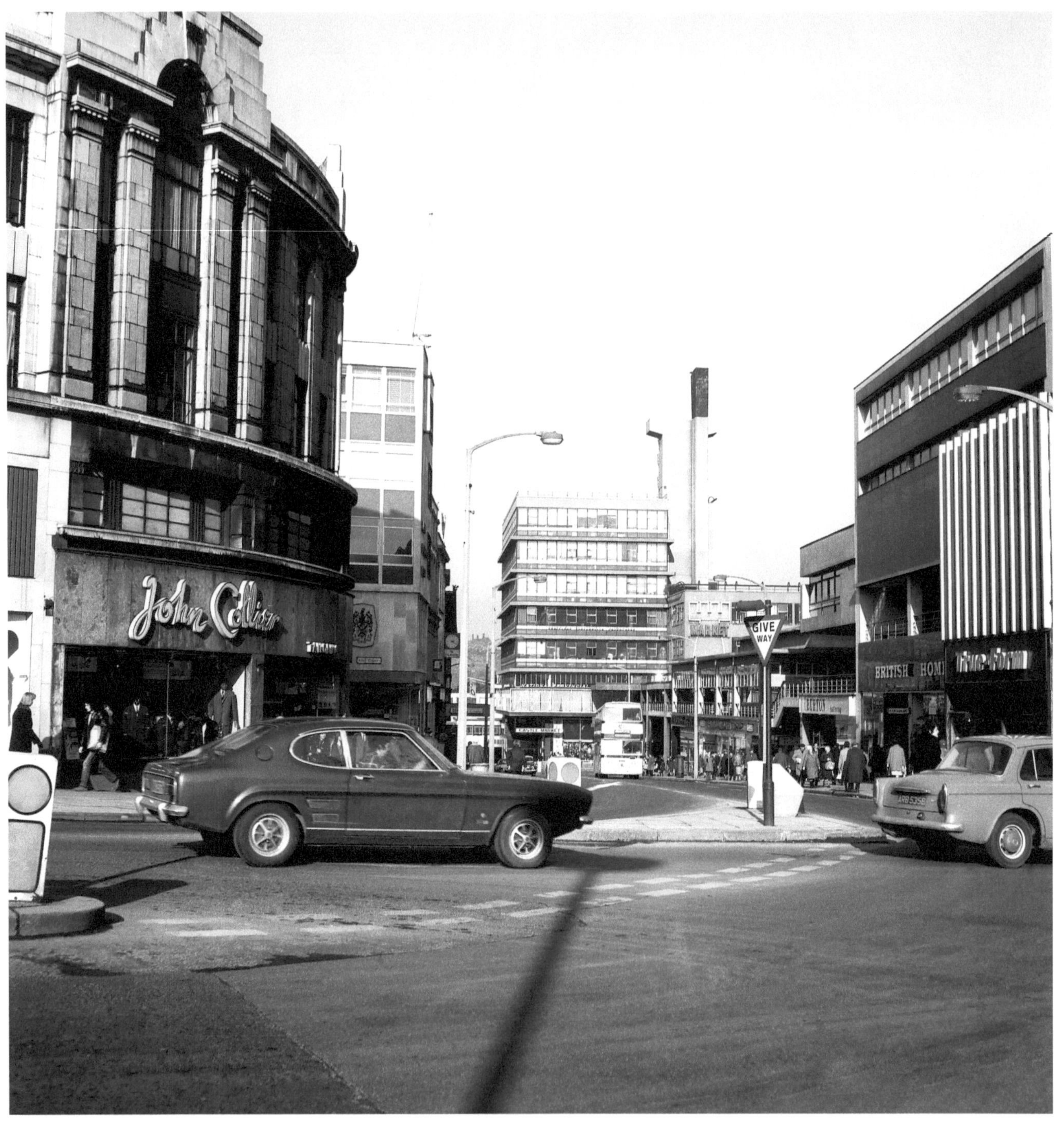

Haymarket: True Form Shoes, British Home Stores, Burtons, Woolworths and Castle Market. Woolworths later became Woolco — a posh Woolies. This was where I got my second job, as an advertising manager — shockingly really, because I blagged it. I earned good money for the 8 months I was there.

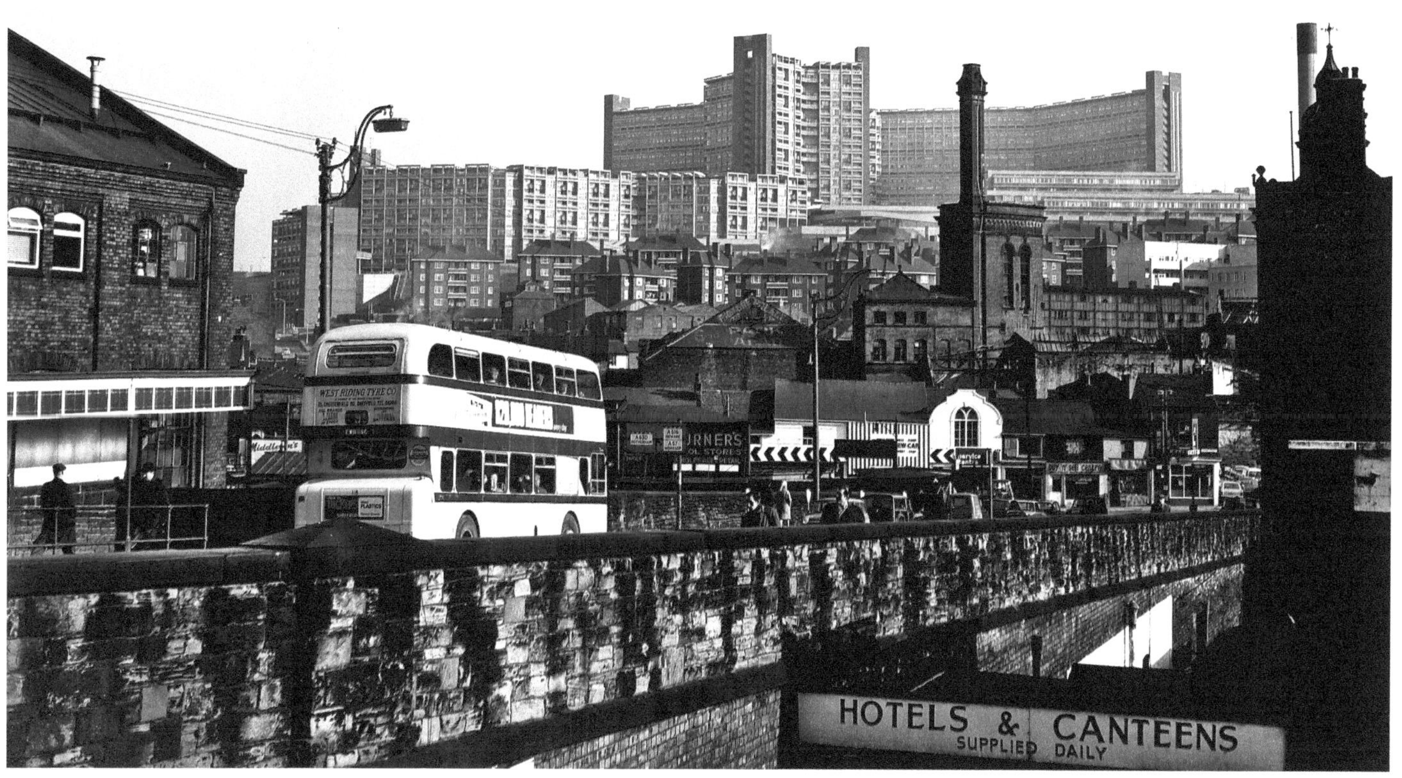

Taken from Commercial Street with Hyde Park on the hill, the chimney of the old William Greaves brewery in the middle distance, and the roof of Sheffield Park Picture Palace to the left. You can still see the Greaves name on some pub frontages and windows.

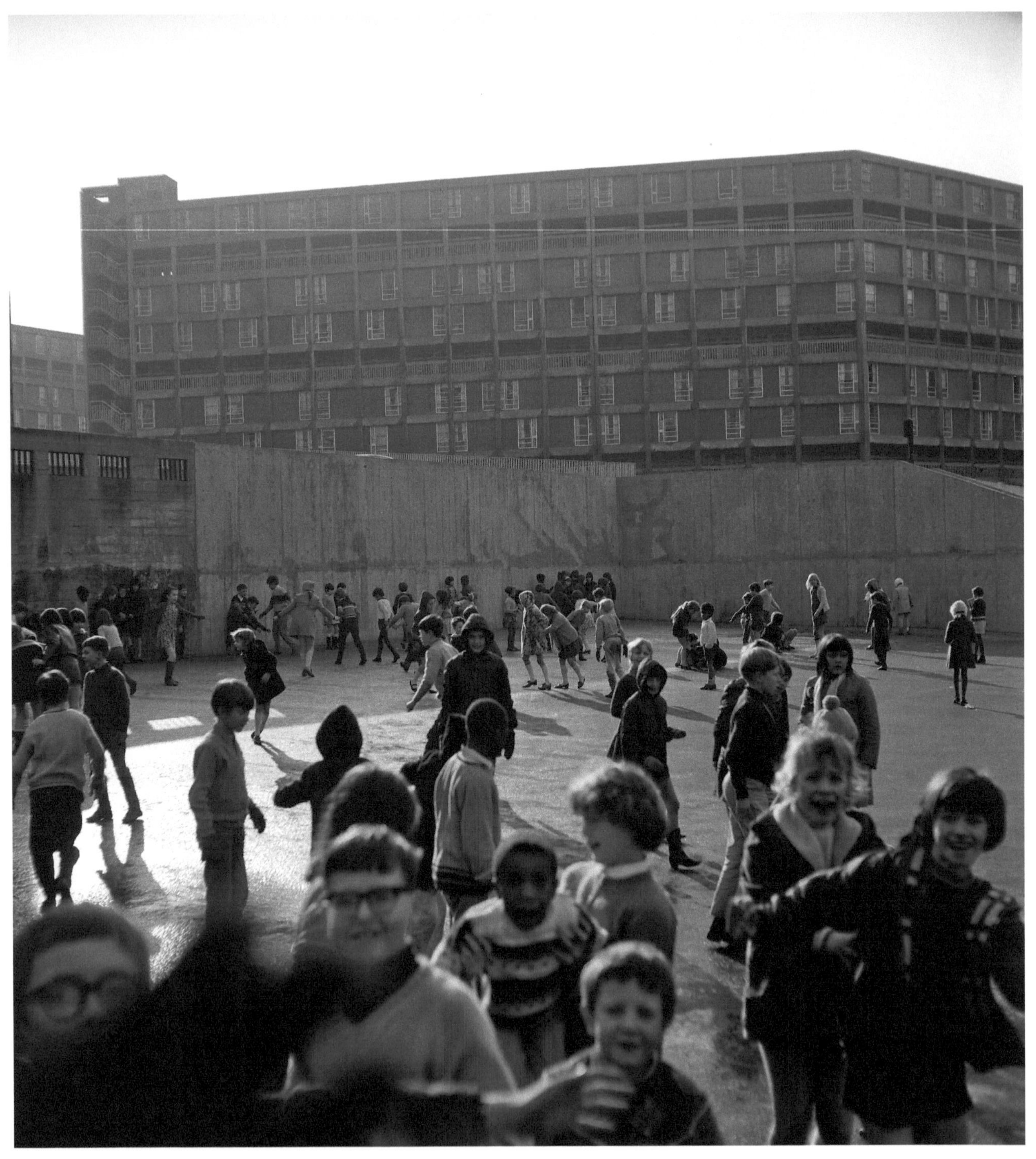

"Ere Mister — can you take us photo?" Park Hill — our block on the left. When school was closed we'd play football here for hours.

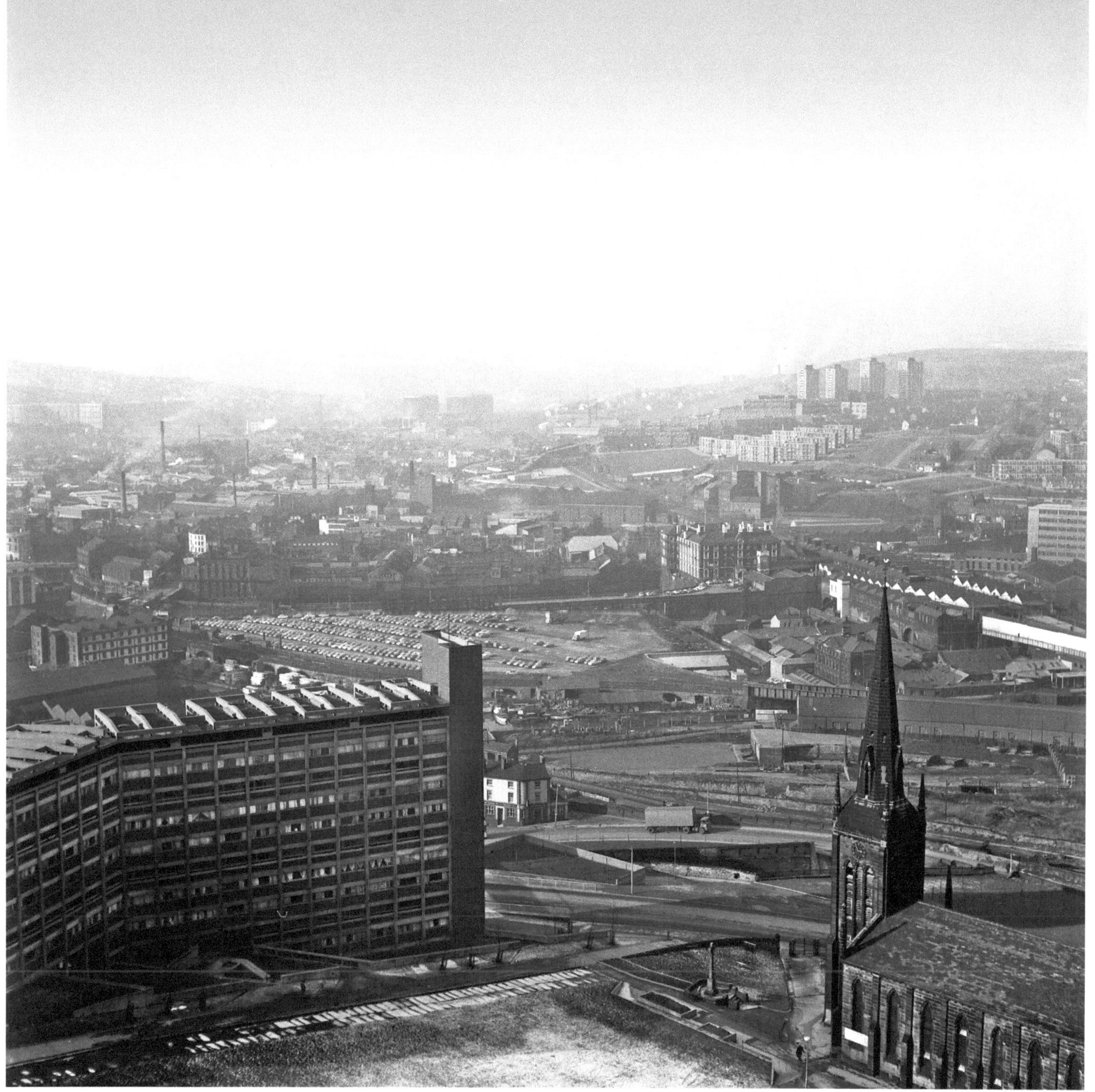

Winter 1969: you can just make out snow on the hills in the distance. St John's church in the foreground, the canal basin, Victoria Station and the last of Sheffield's old forest of chimneys. Just below the flats to the left of the church are the grave stones laid out in 2 straight rows.

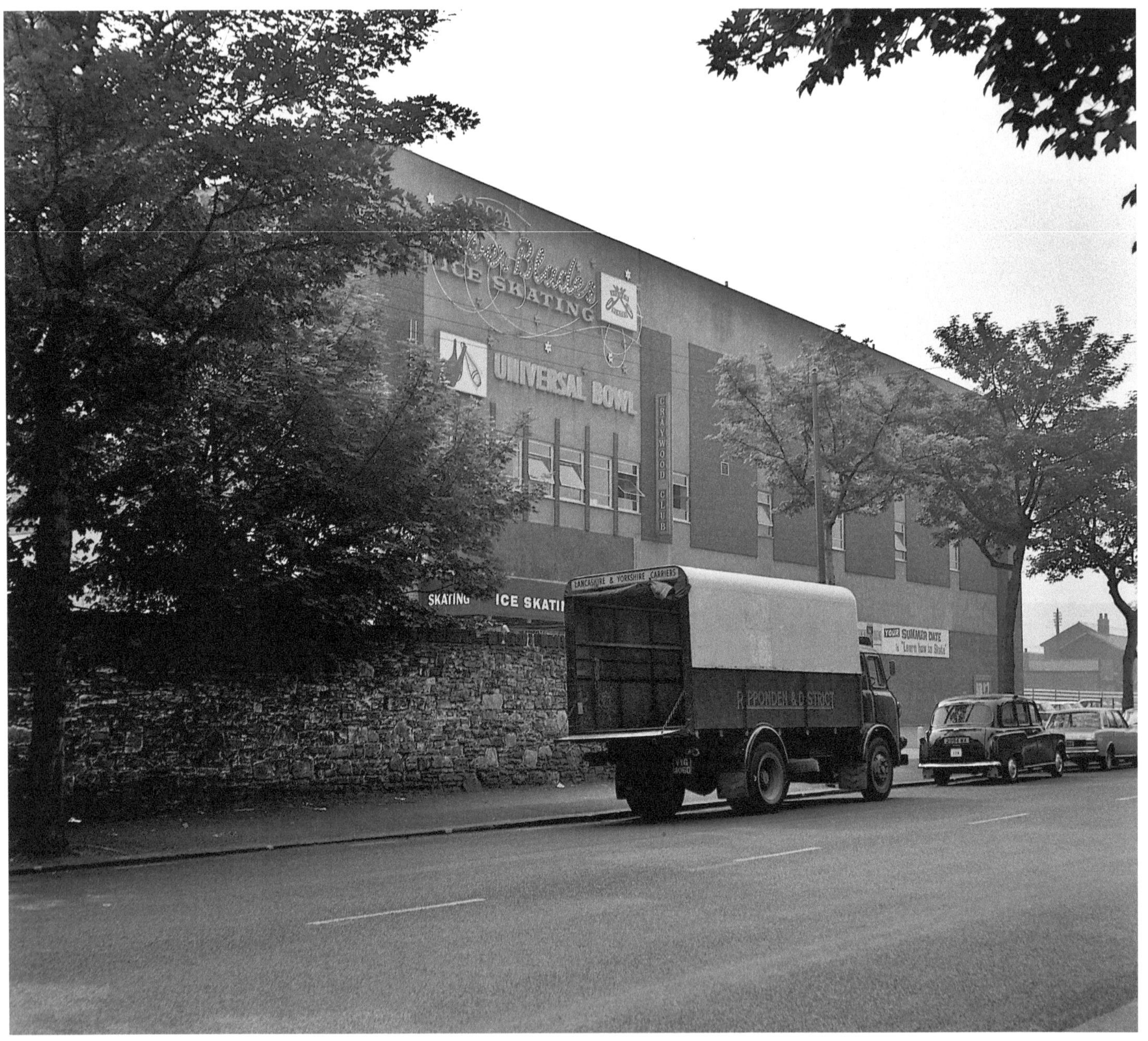

My second home: Silver Blades Ice Rink and the Heartbeat above it. The 1970 World Cup was shown on a colour TV they had in the back room — it was amazing to see football in colour. Silver Blades was *the* place when we discovered girls: skating round, checking them out, as the DJ played *The Letter* by The Box Tops or Traffic's *Hole in my Shoe.* There was a bowling alley here too — and it was only 5 minutes from Park Hill. The DJ at the Heartbeat was called "Mighty Atom."

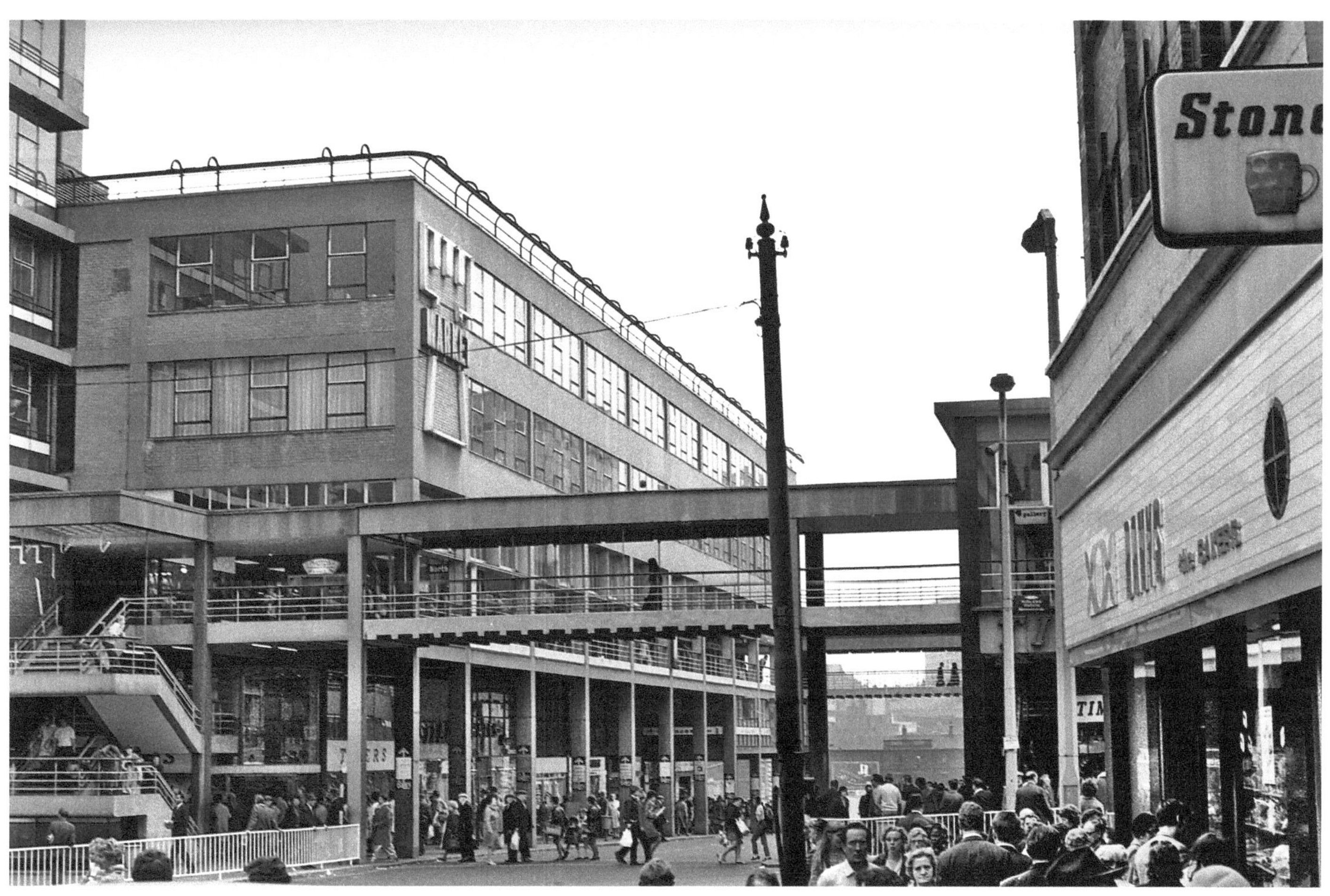

Haymarket, Exchange Street and Castle Market. We loved looking at all the different birds and animals in Mace's Pet shop, which was on the left. If dad won on the horses he'd give us 10 bob and we'd run up to Woollies and buy Airfix models and packs of their little soldiers.

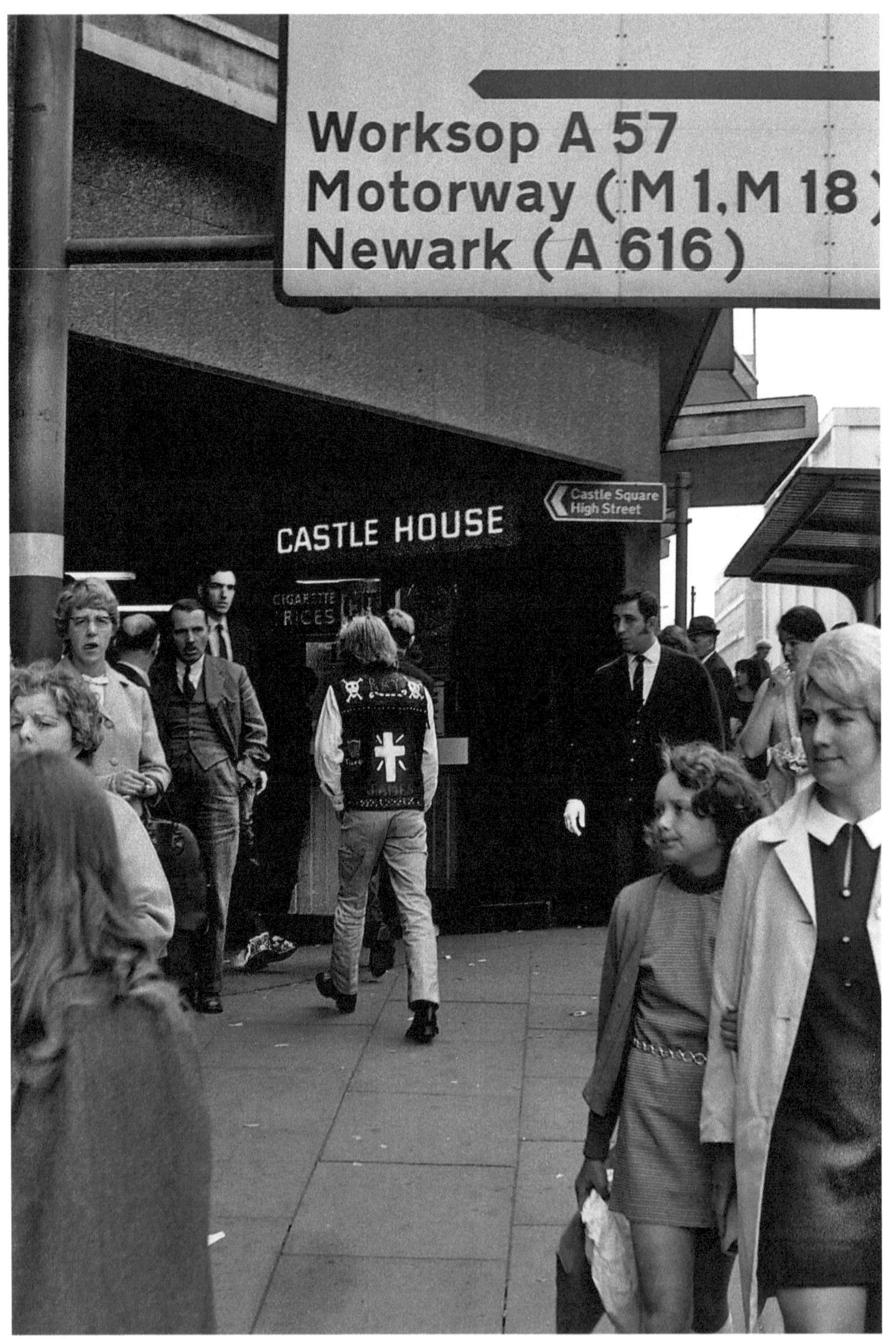

The Castle House route into the Hole in the Road from Angel Street. I still love looking at all the different fashions we wore in those days.

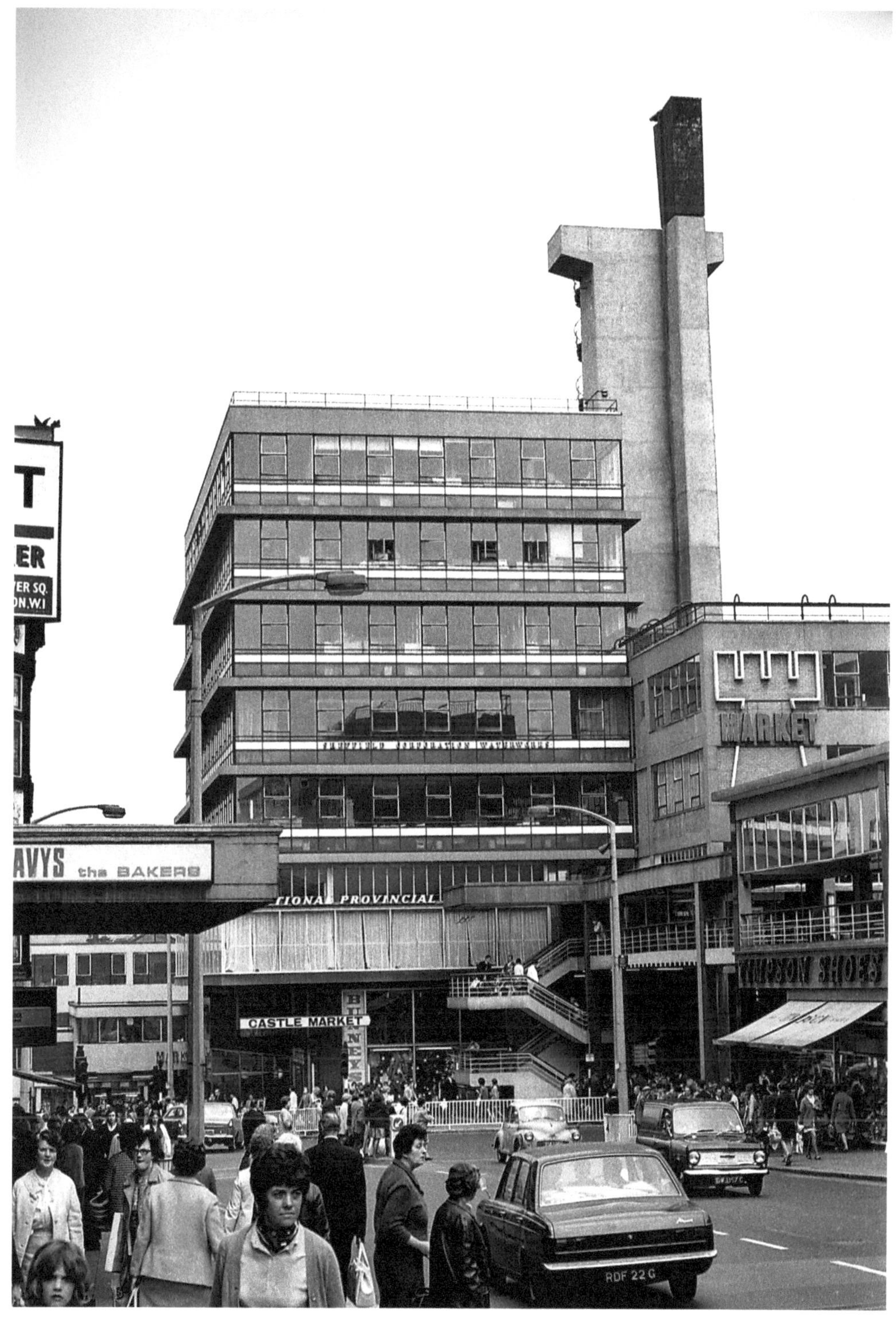

Castle Market and the Sheffield Corporation Waterworks office.

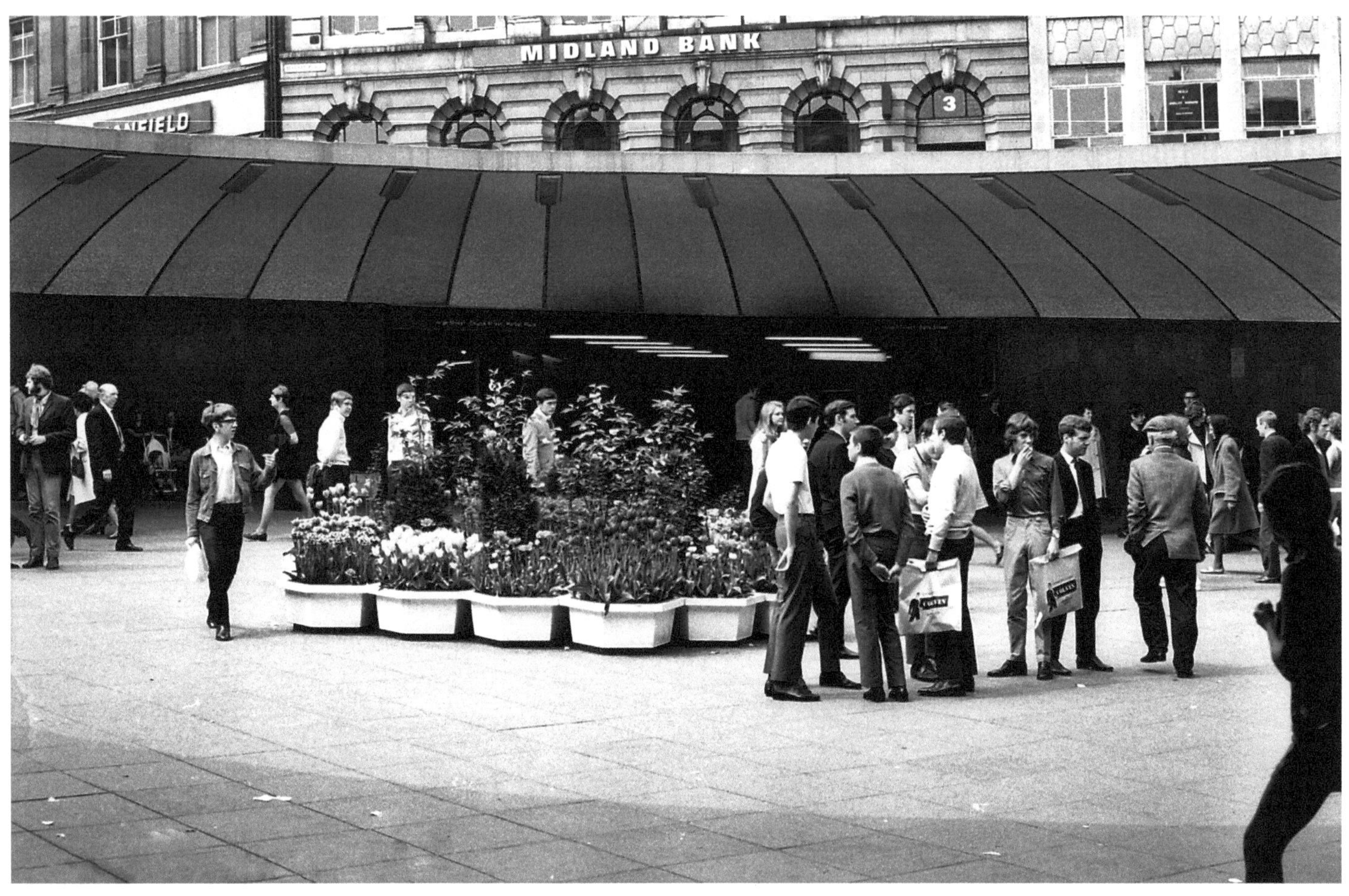

The Hole in the Road in Spring 1970. It hadn't been built long then. It was the place where everyone met up: mods, rockers, skinheads — or if you had a girlfriend you'd meet by the fish tank. The Midland Bank behind is now the Banker's Draft pub.

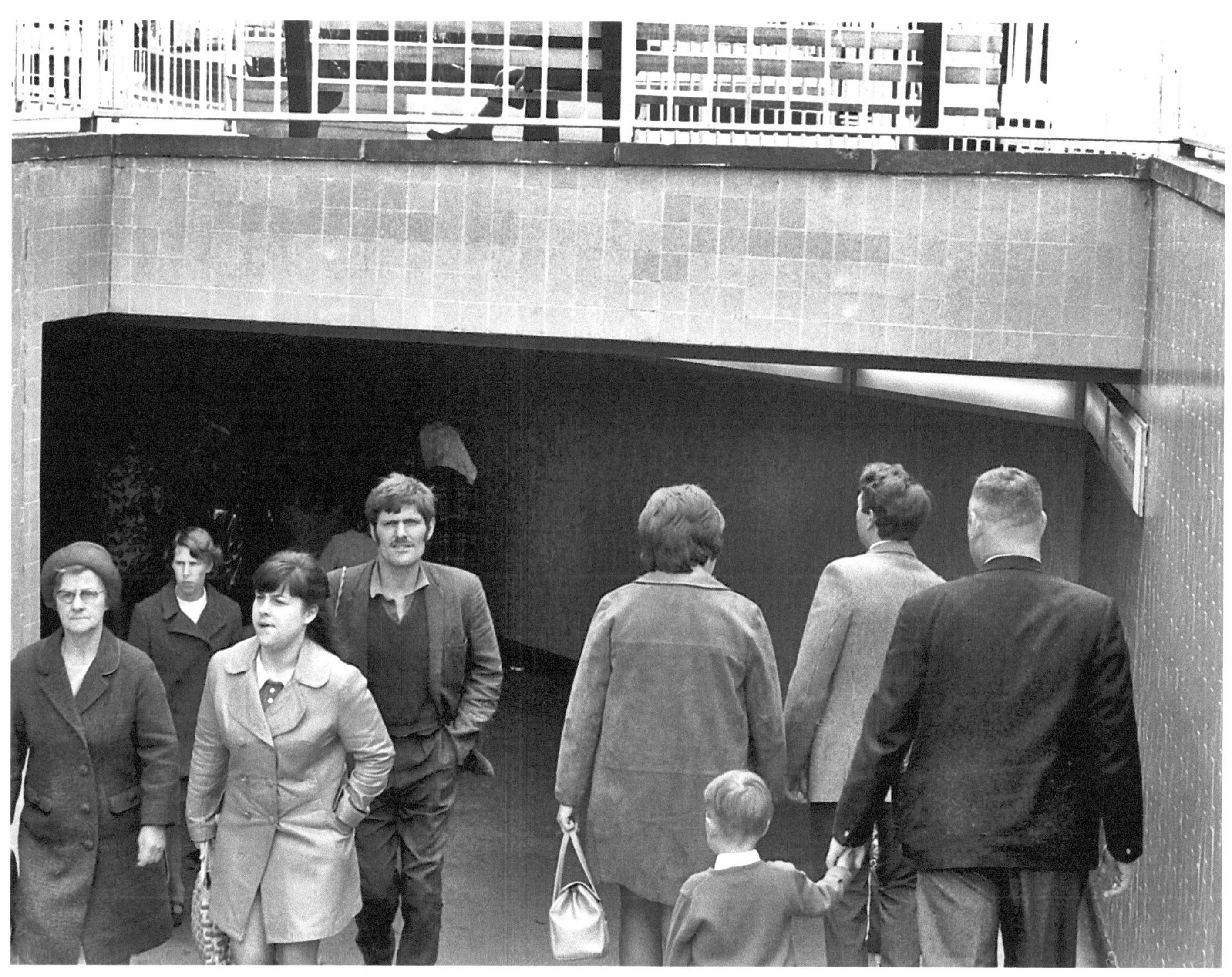

Coming out of the Hole in the Road. The man in the middle is George Lee — someone on Facebook recognised him as their uncle.

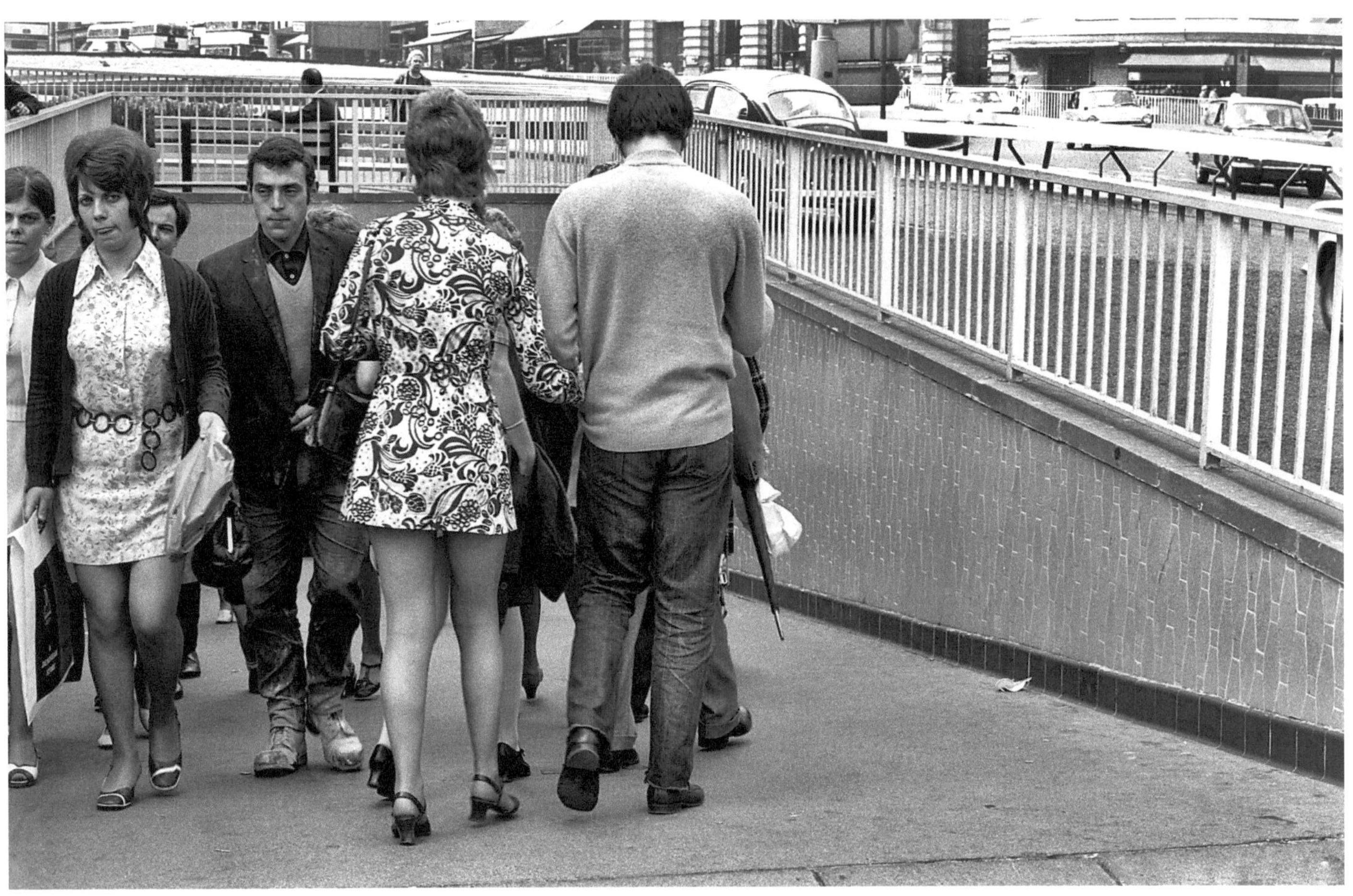

Hole in the Road entrance from High Street. Being a young lad I daresay the miniskirt was one of the attractions of the photo. Those chain belts worn by the woman on the left were everywhere at the time; even my 11-year-old sister had one.

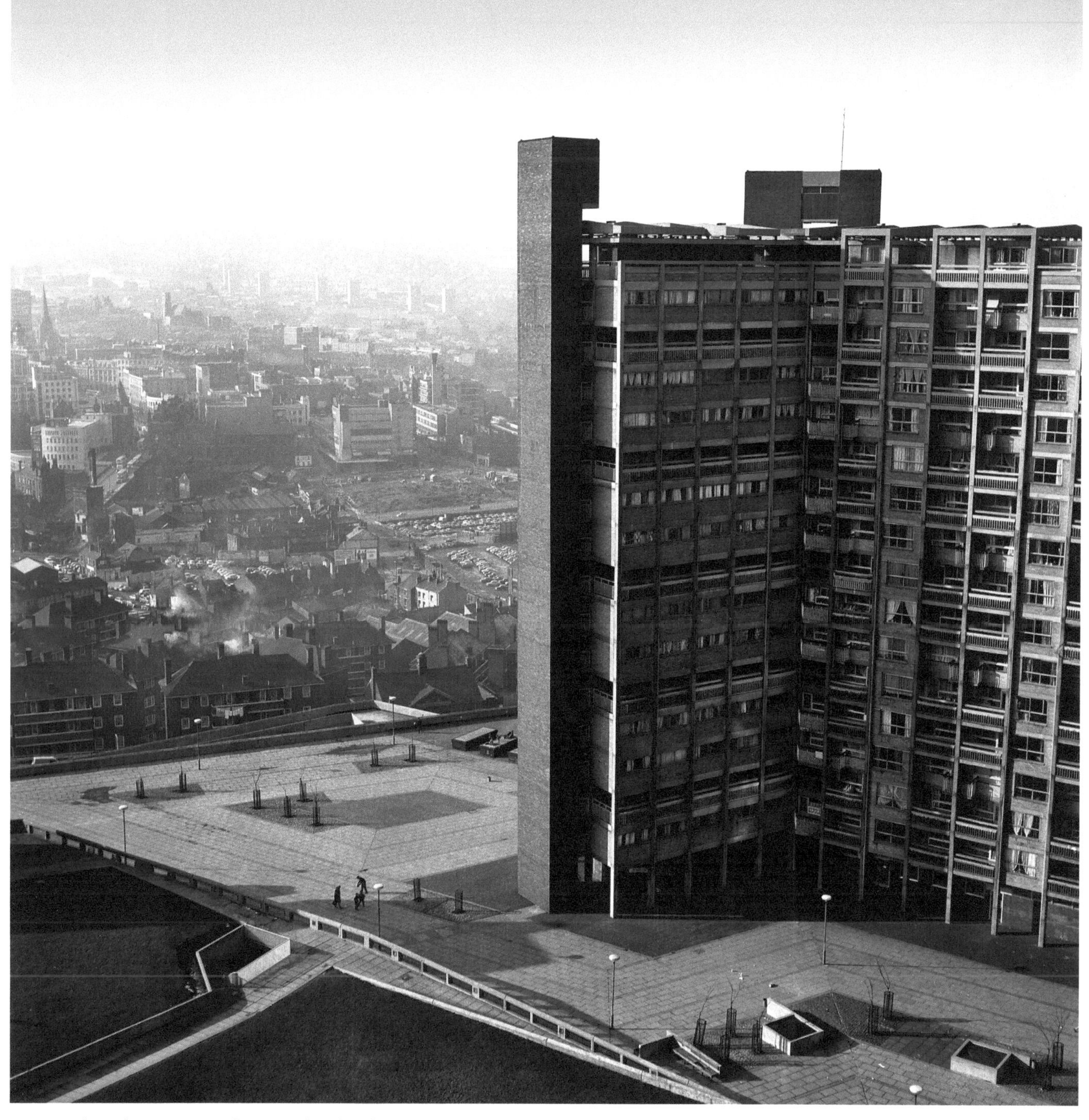

In the distance: the Cathedral and St Vincent's church. I went to St Vincent's school (... as did film star, Patrick McGoohan!) There is a bit of potato-famine-immigrant Irish blood in me: my great grandad Concannon ran a beer-off near there.

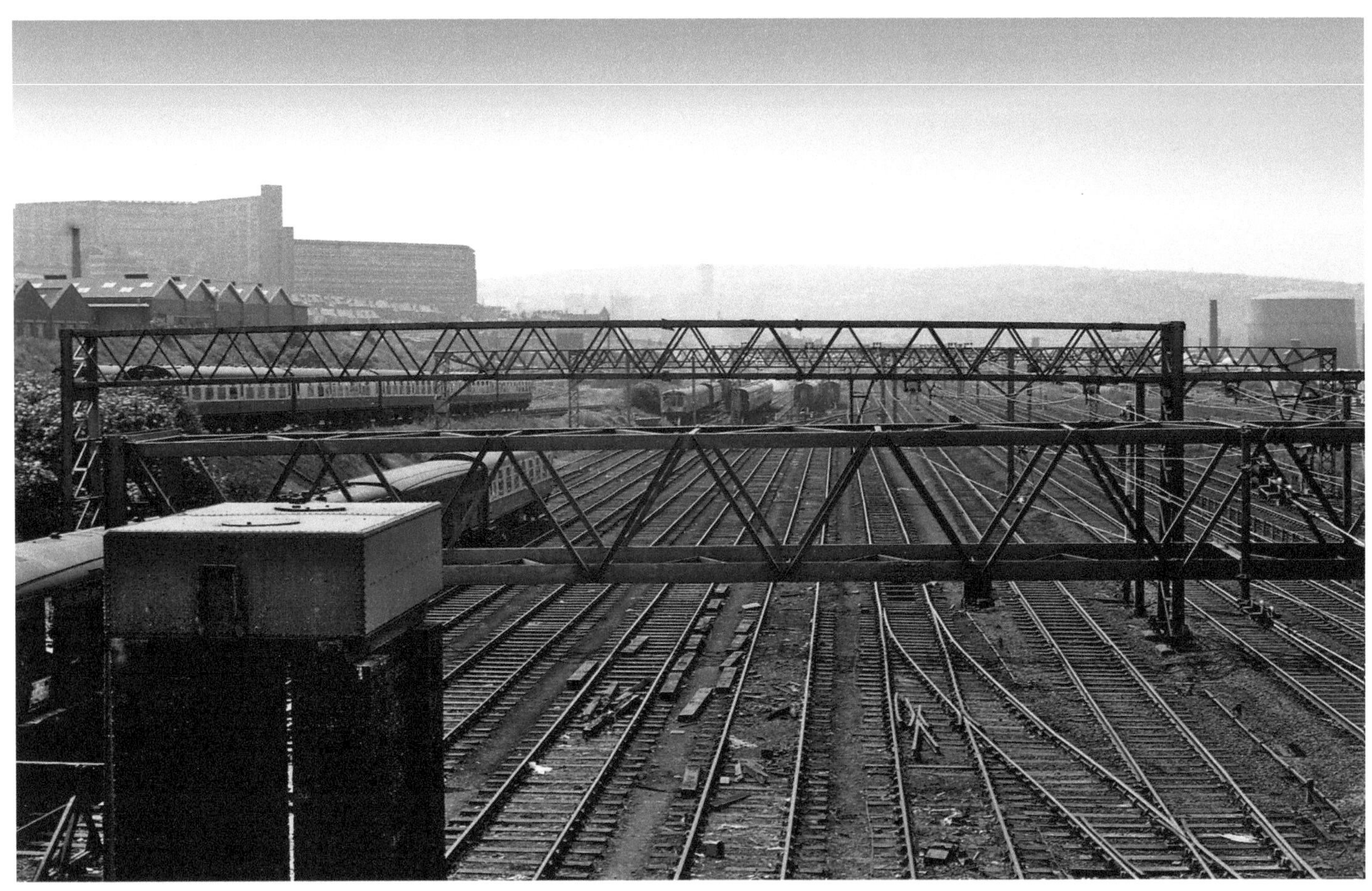

Nunnery sidings taken from Woodbourn Road. The tram depot and the Park-and-Ride are here now. Hyde Park flats in the distance. The building to the left with the chimney was the abattoir.

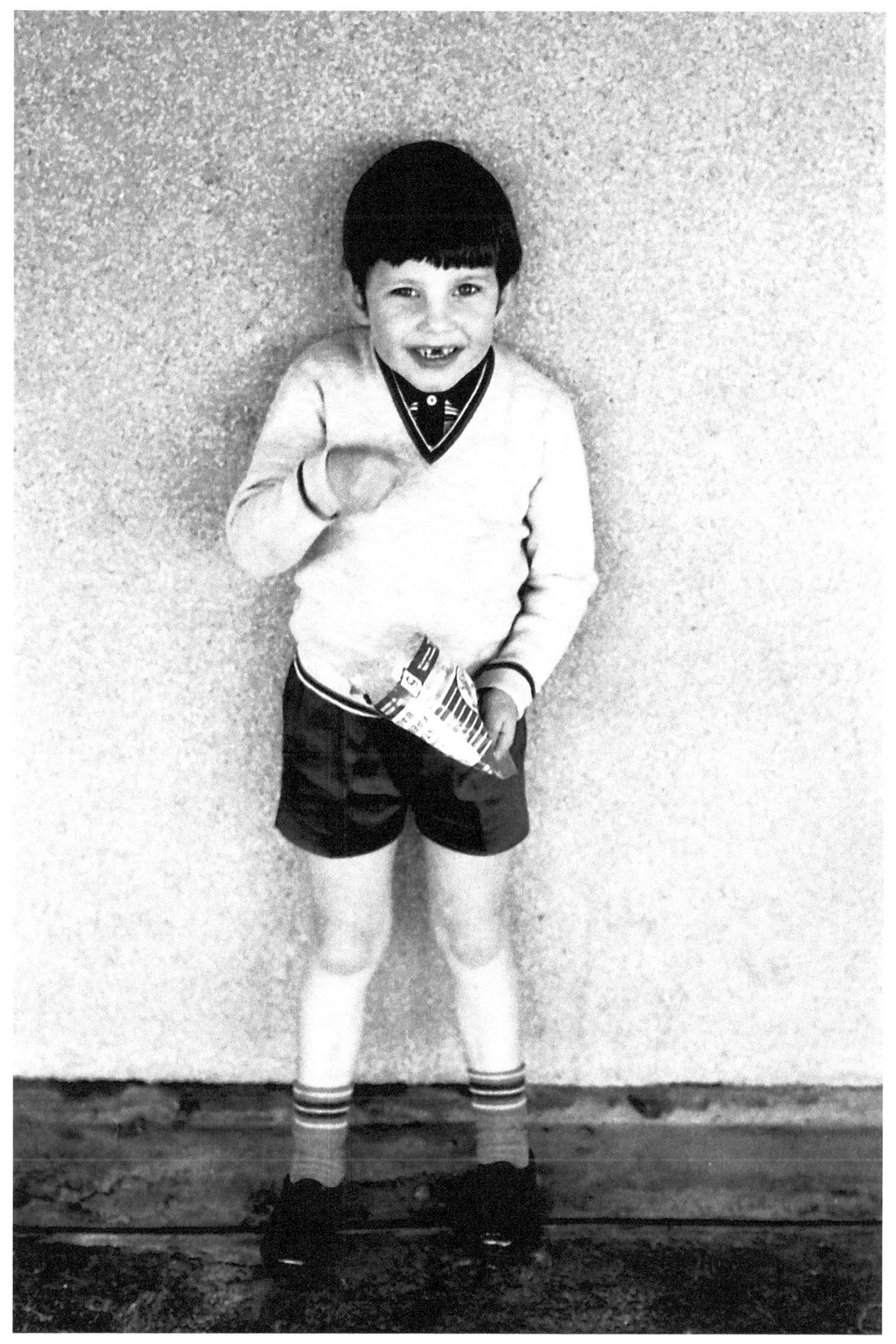

Paul Andrews, one of the neighbours' kids — an informal Whitsuntide shot. Paul is now an accomplished photographer; I'm not sure he picked any tips or tricks up from me.

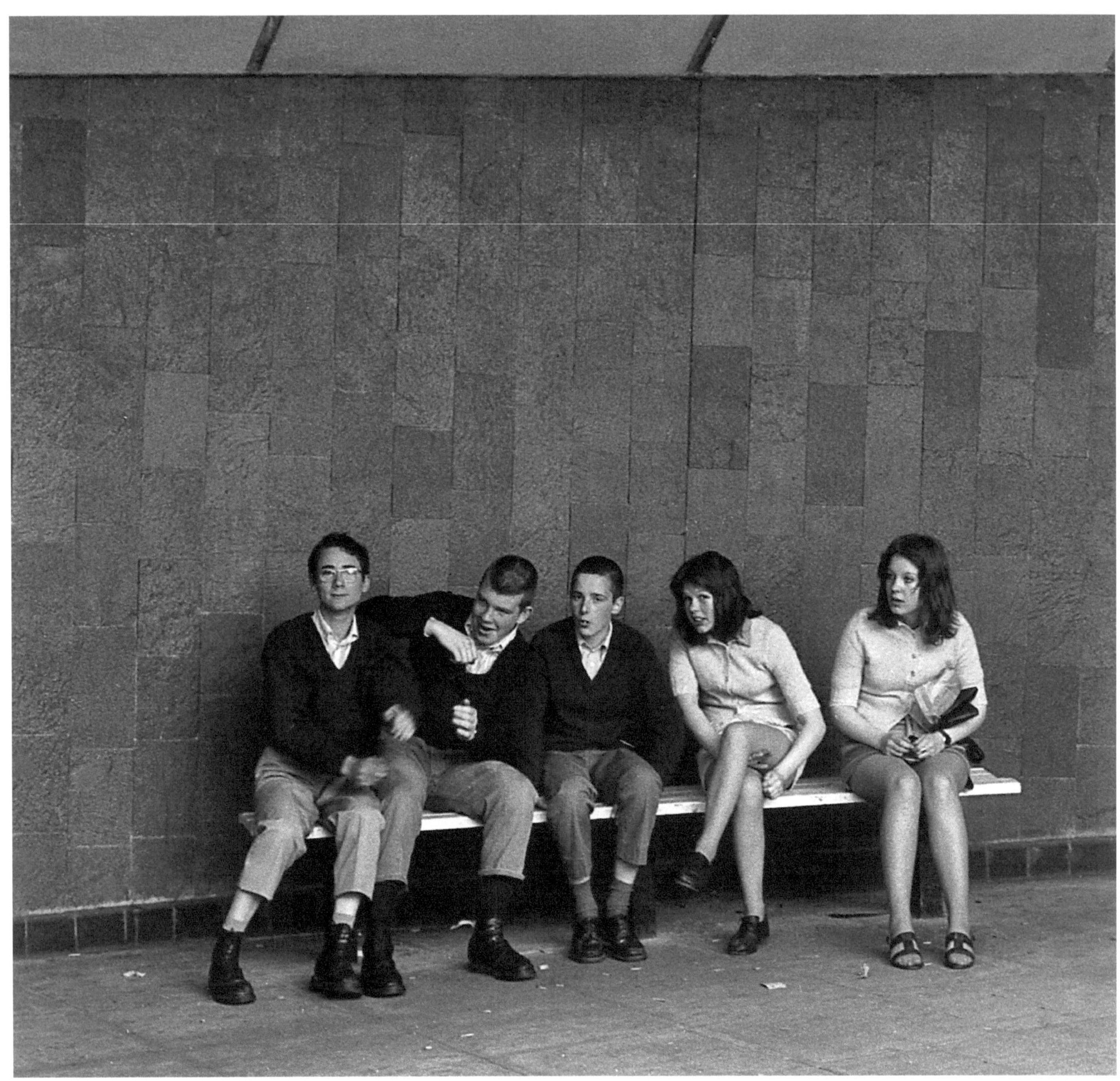

Hole in the Road: Steve Fox, Dave Haworth and Vinnie Golland, friends of mine — not sure who the two women were, but I suspect they were sisters. Sadly Steve Fox on the far left died a few years ago.

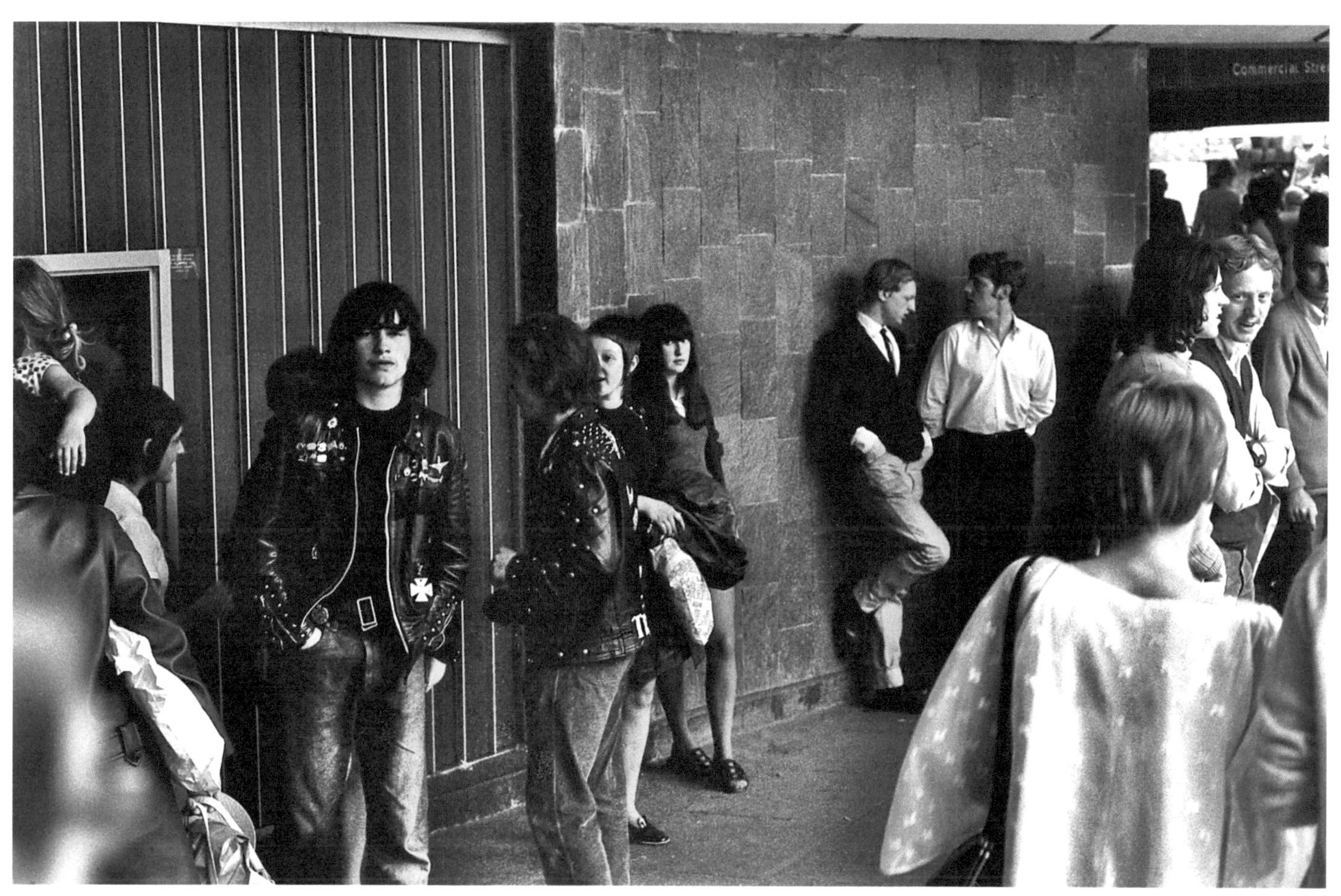

By the Hole in the Road fish tank. A rocker giving me a bit of a look.

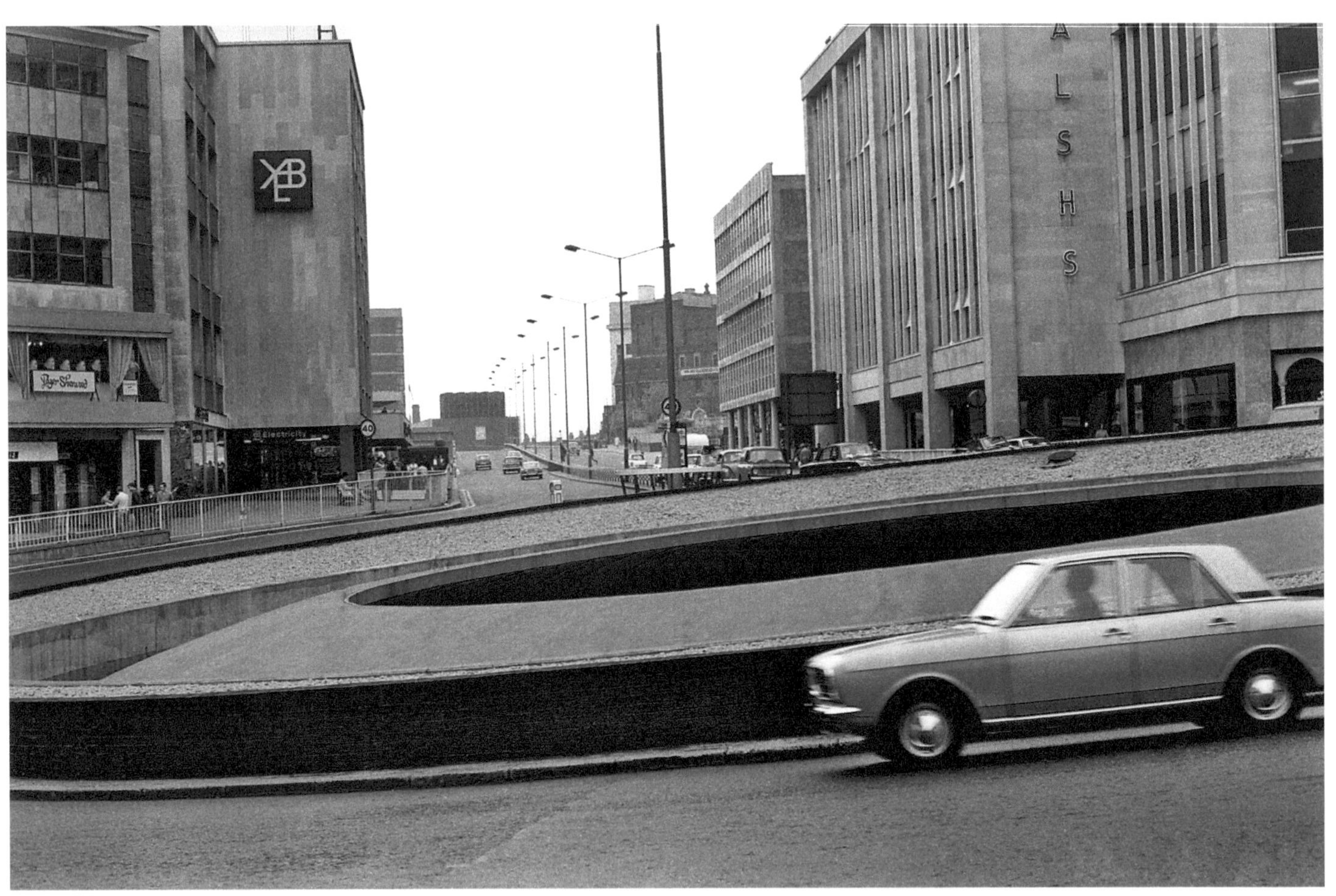

Looking towards Arundel Gate. Walshs on the right and Roger Sherwoods on left — it was *the* place to get your hair done — cost you a fortune. Later on my girlfriend, who eventually became my wife, drove a Mark II Cortina. The famous Hole in the Road had only been open for a couple of years.

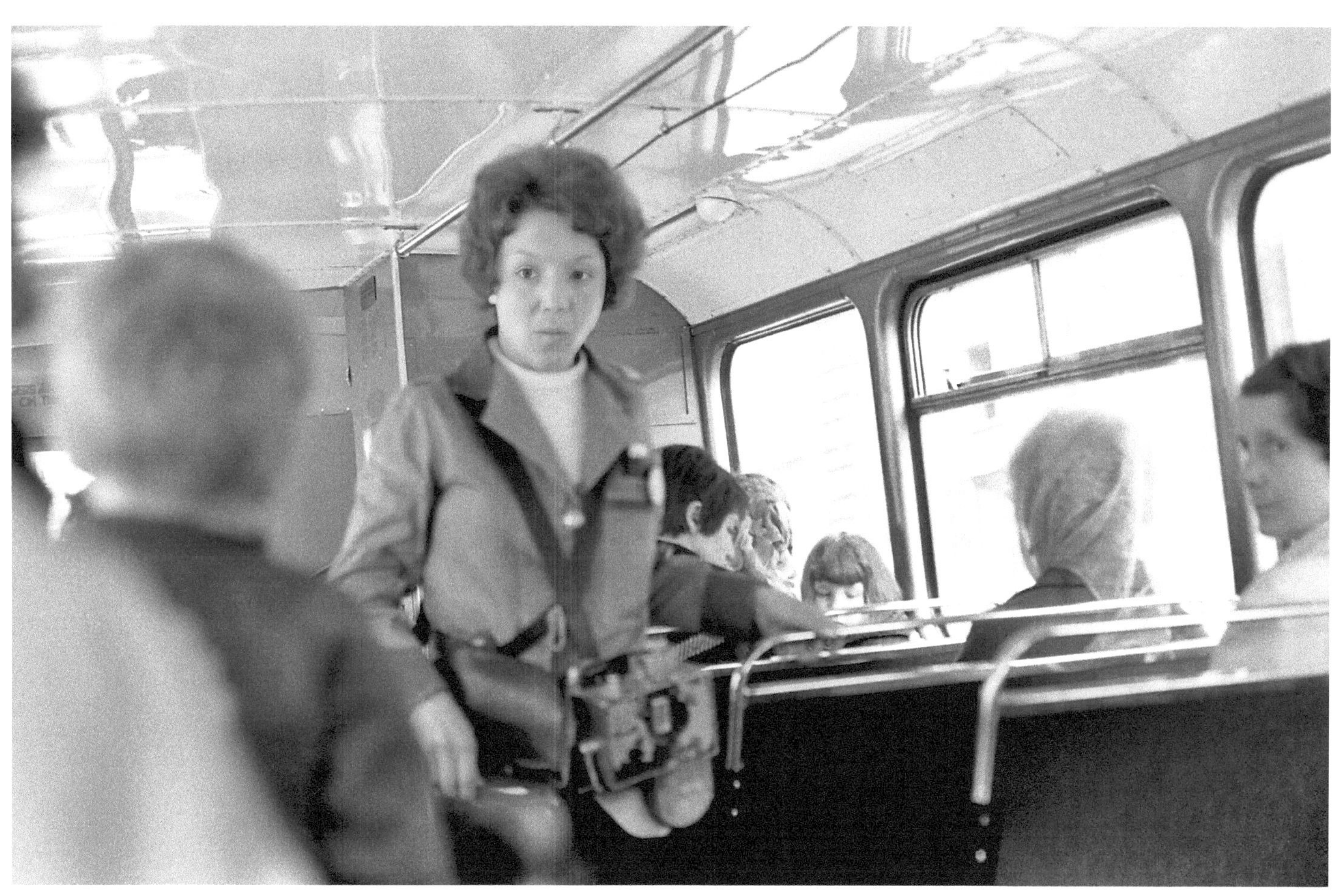

Bus conductor not looking too happy at being captured for posterity.

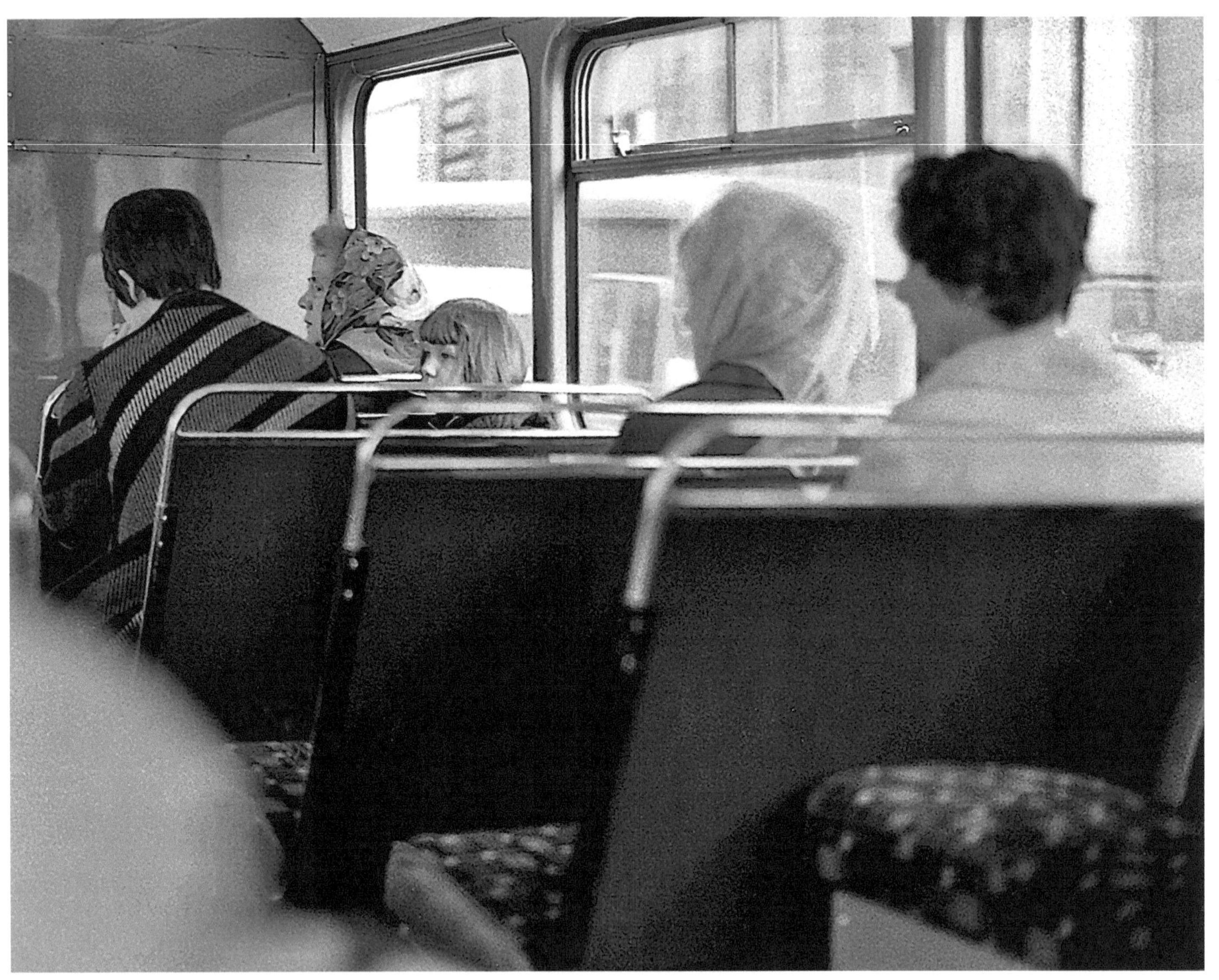

We are just about to set off from Commercial Street; you can just make out the Gas Board office building on the right.

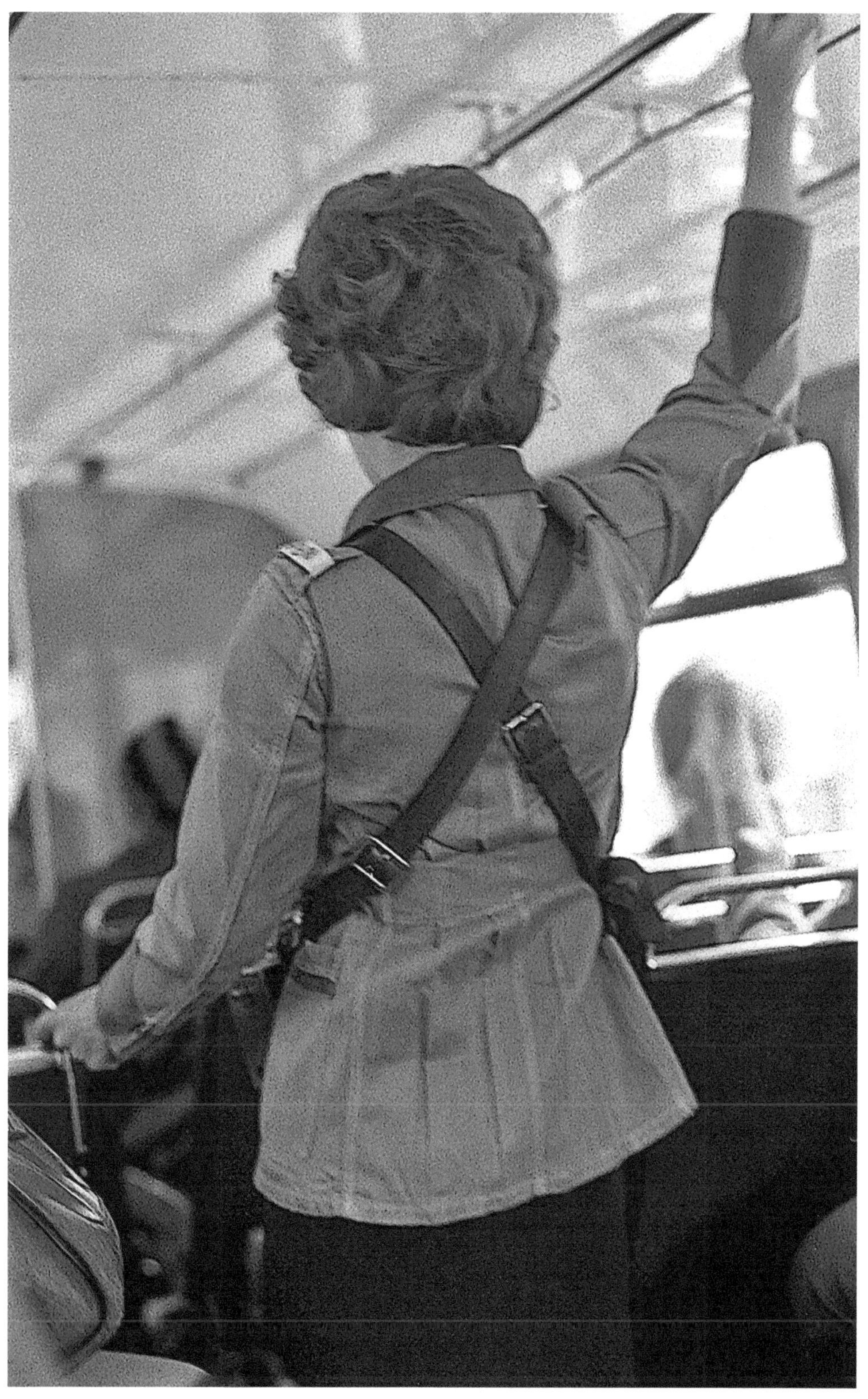

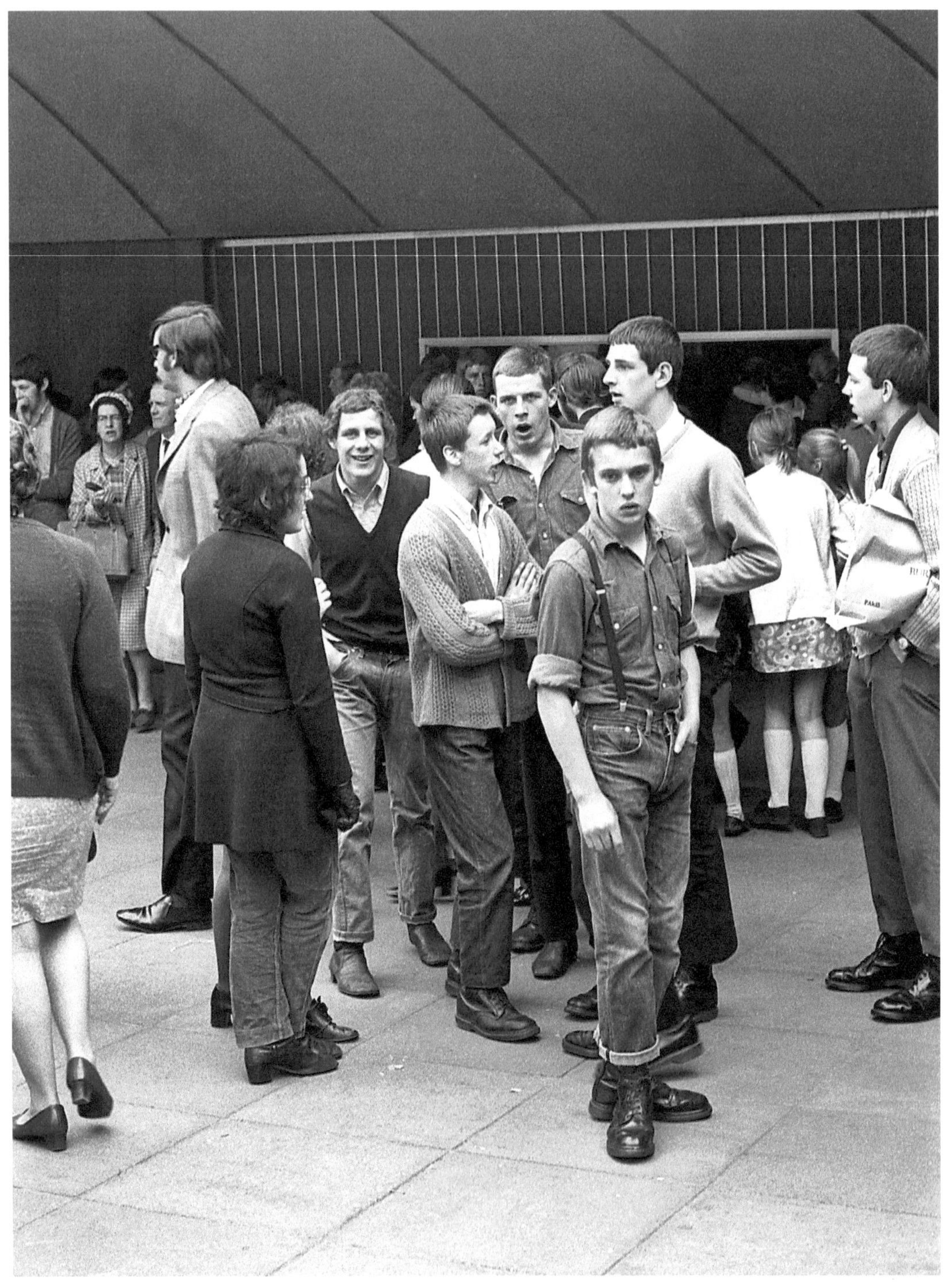

Skinheads and suedeheads at the Hole in the Road, May 1970. You can also see the famous fish tank. A number of the people have been identified in this image.

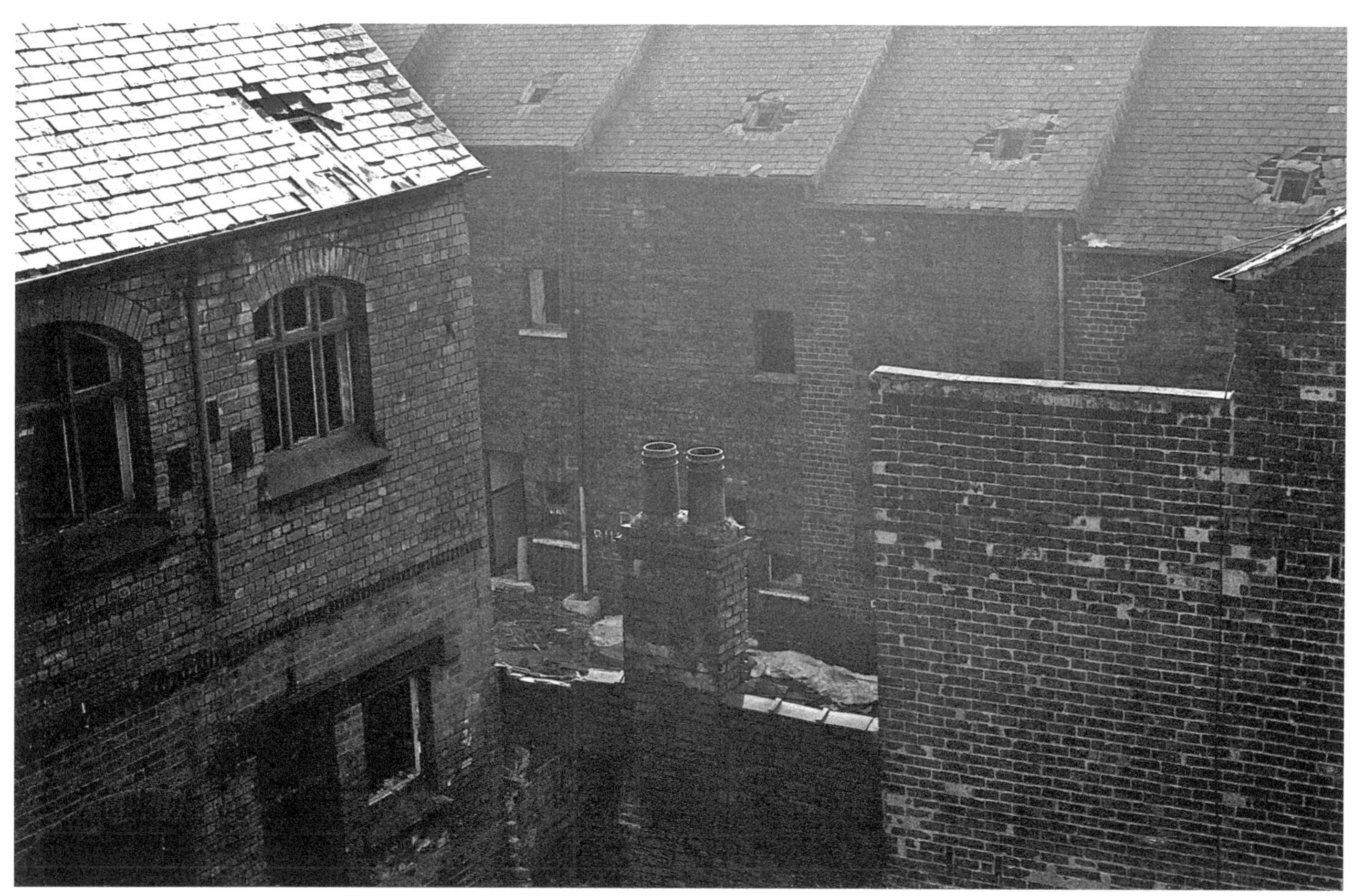

Somewhere in Heeley: taken for the "slum clearance" brief.

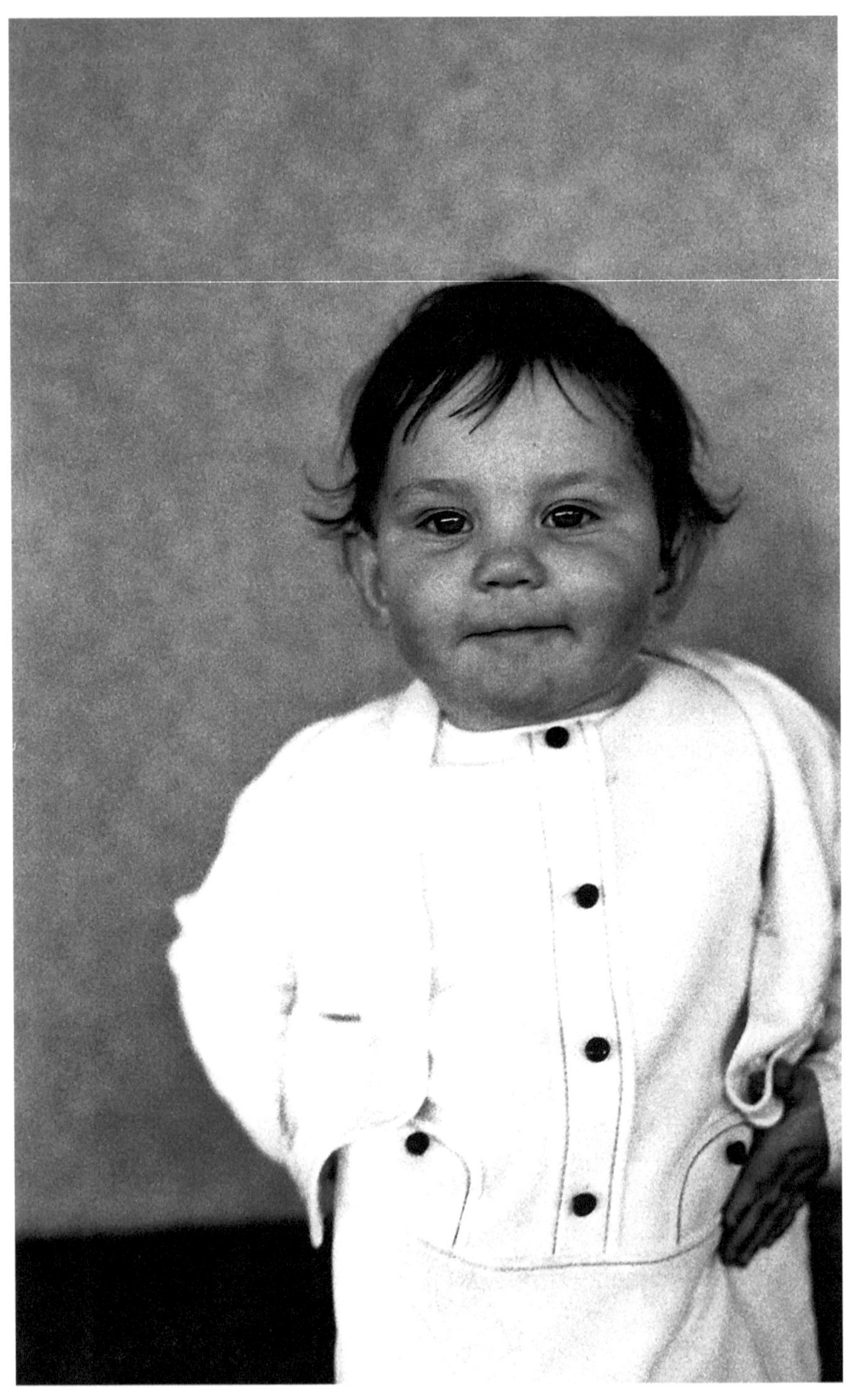

Lisa Andrews at Whitsuntide. My sister was about ten at the time and Lisa used to follow her around everywhere.

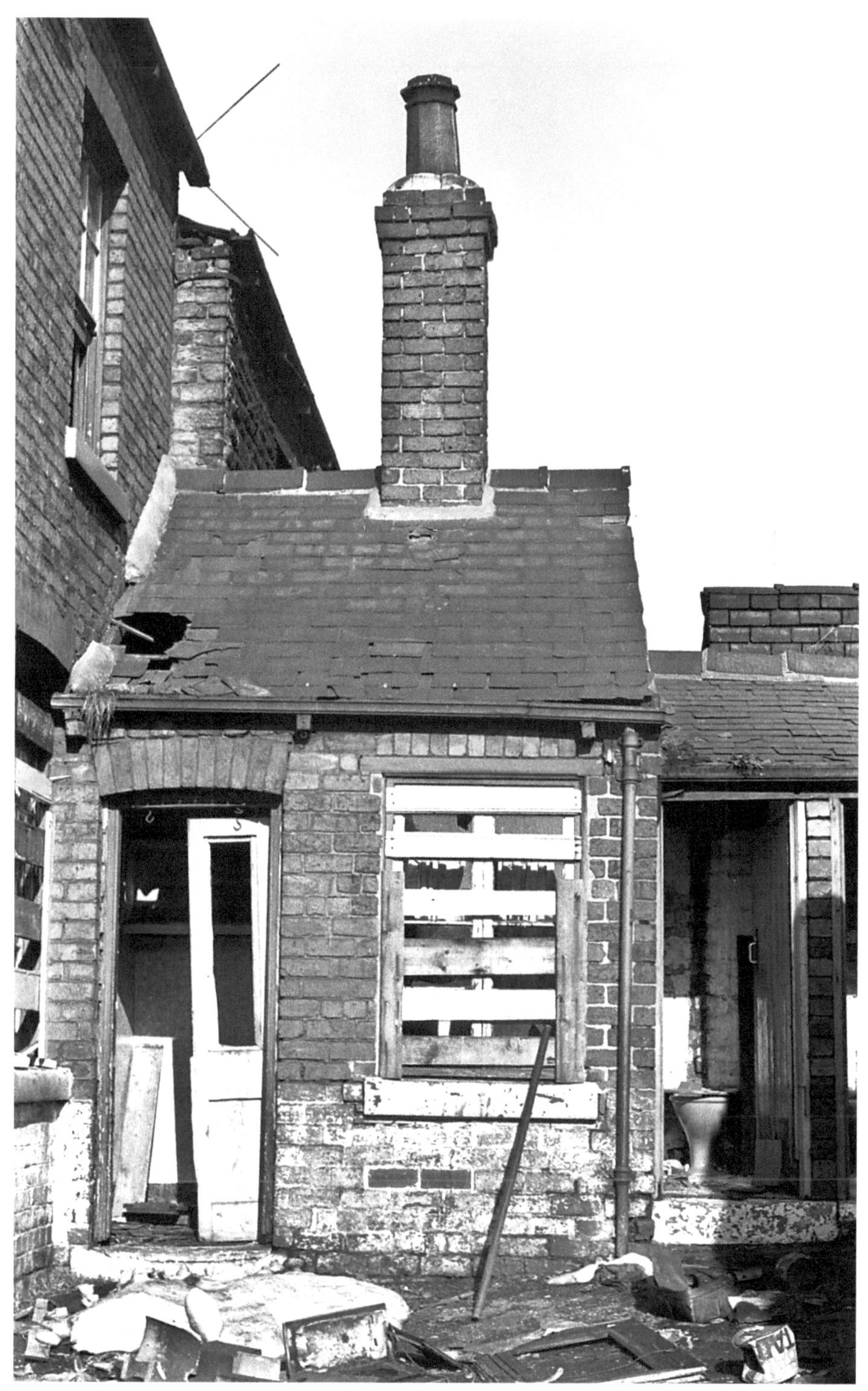

Heeley — the remains of what someone once called home.

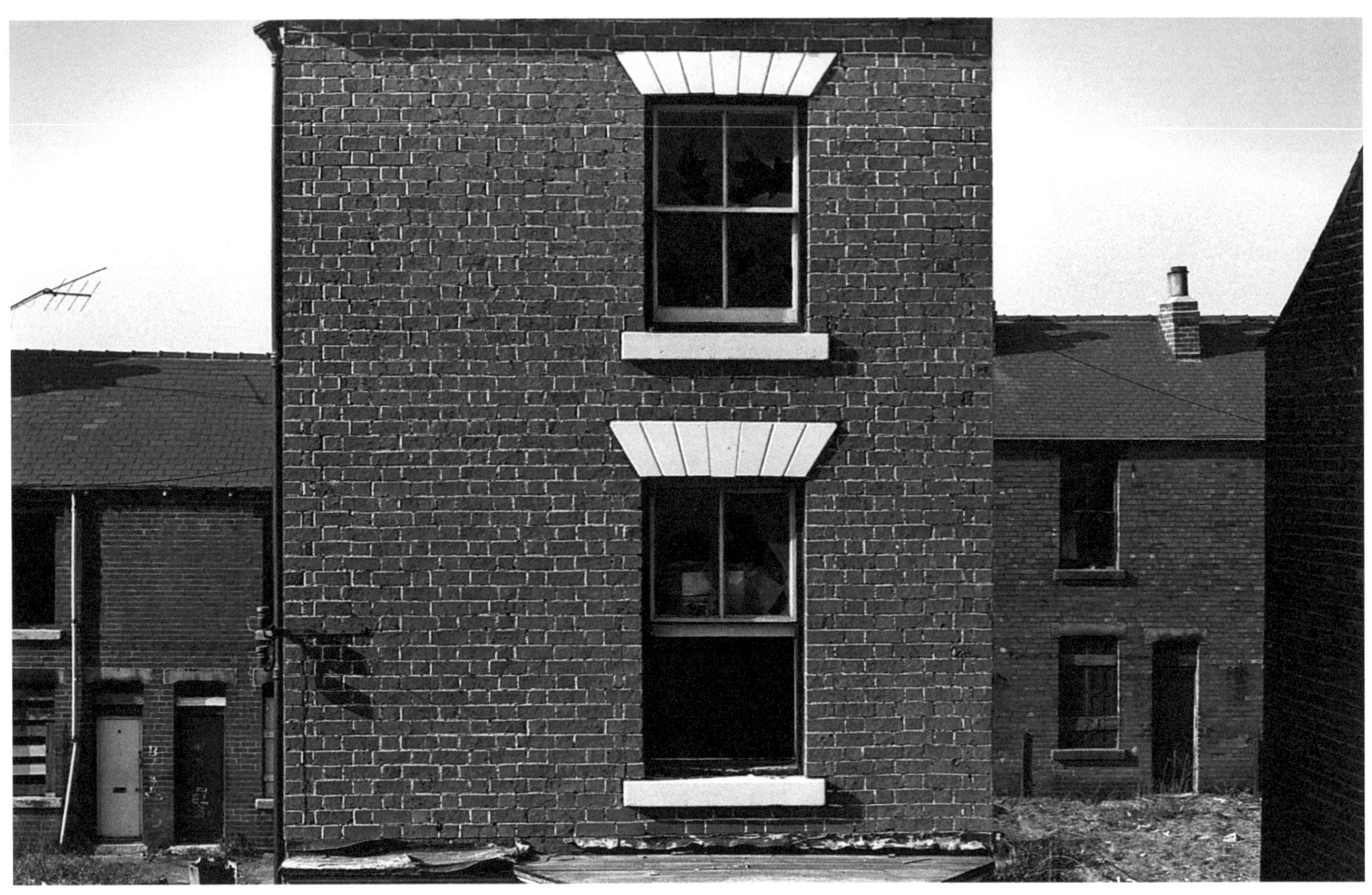

Windows and walls in Heeley.

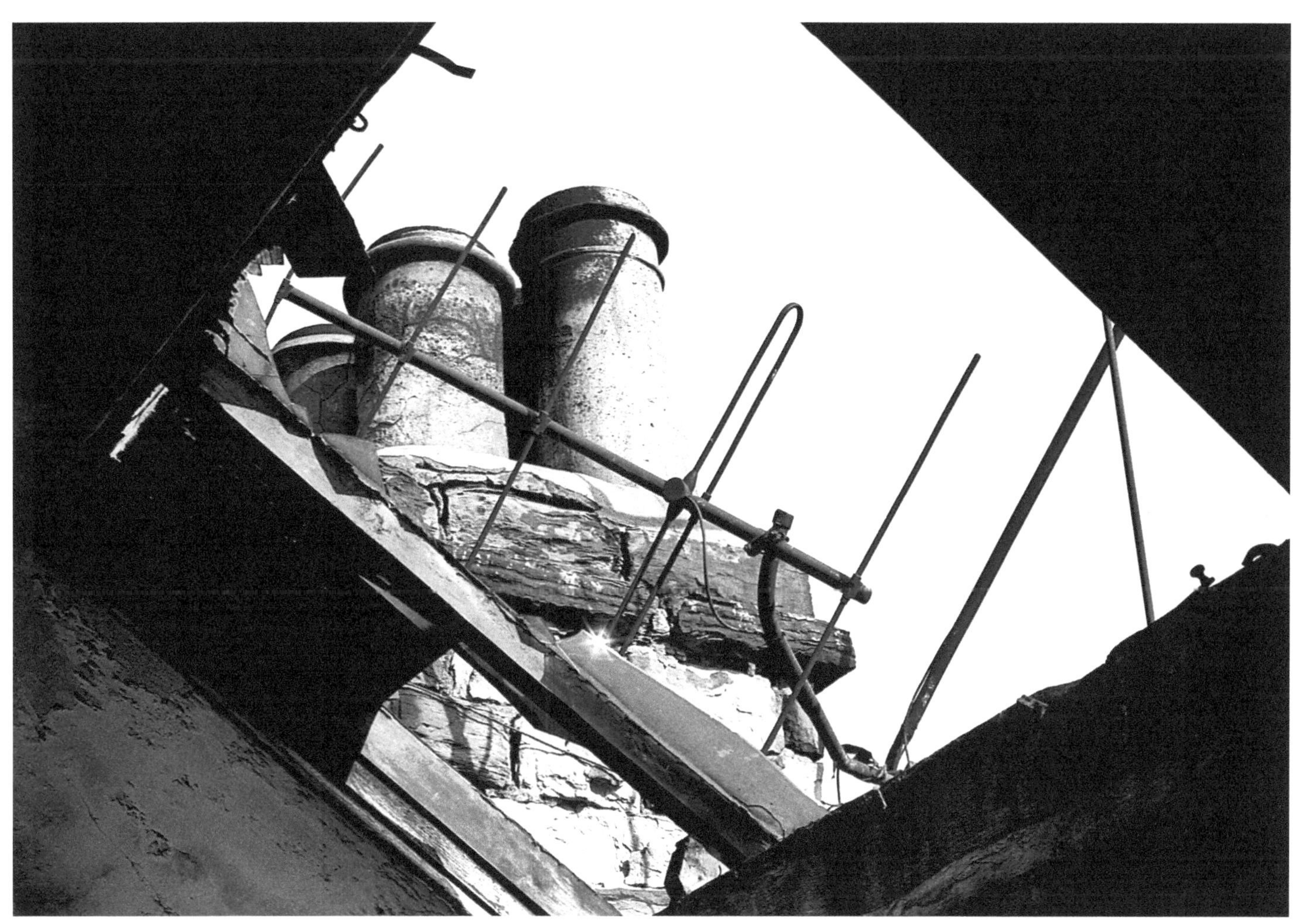

I love the glint on the broken skylight glass in this picture.

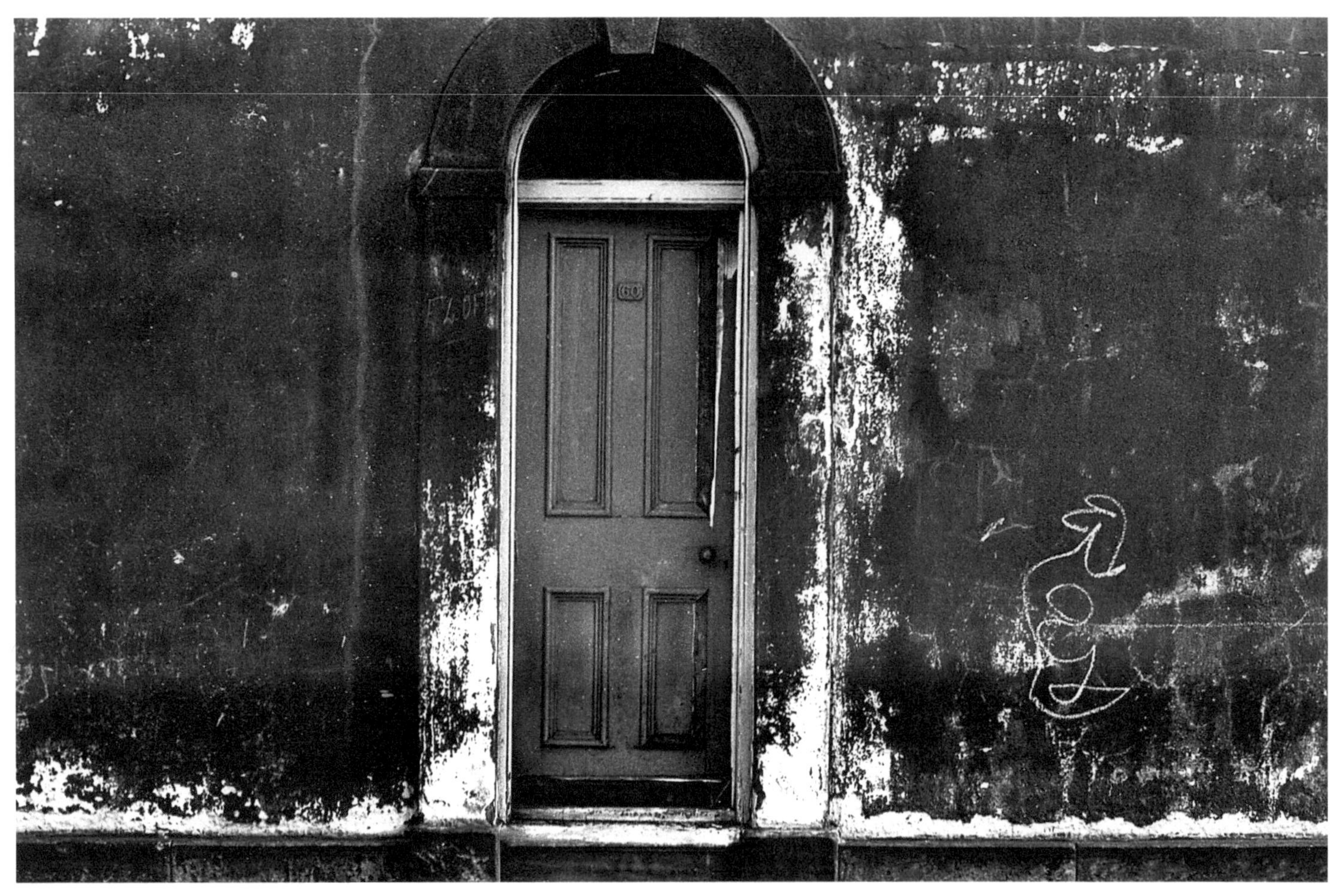

The tutors at college loved this one and made me blow it up to poster size for exhibiting in the college.

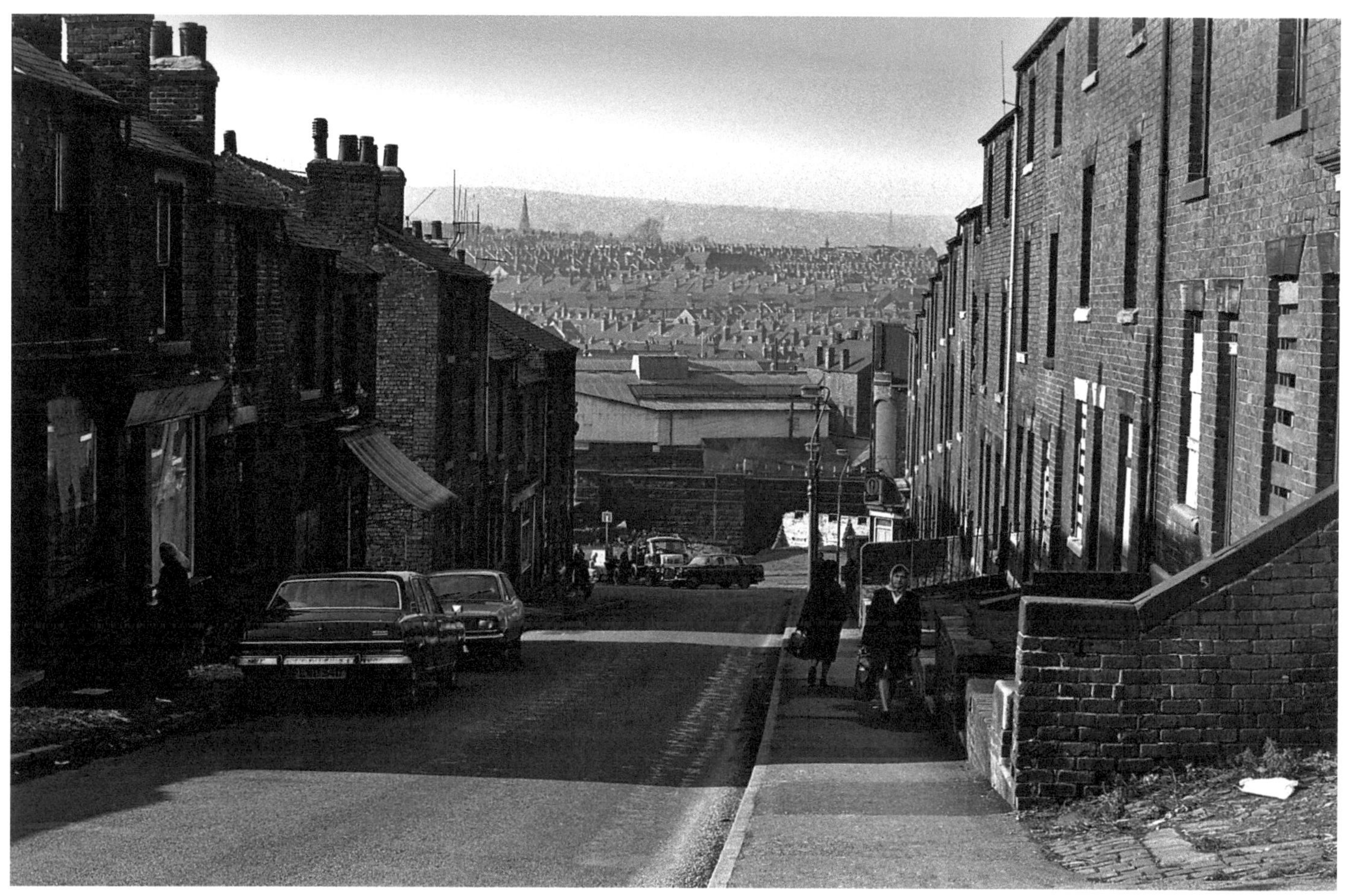

Bottom of Gleadless Road, Heeley. On the right at the bottom you can see the corner of the Sheaf View pub — one of the few remaining buildings. The spire of the chapel at the General Cemetery is on the horizon. This tells a story of a community as houses become derelict awaiting demolition whilst others remain.

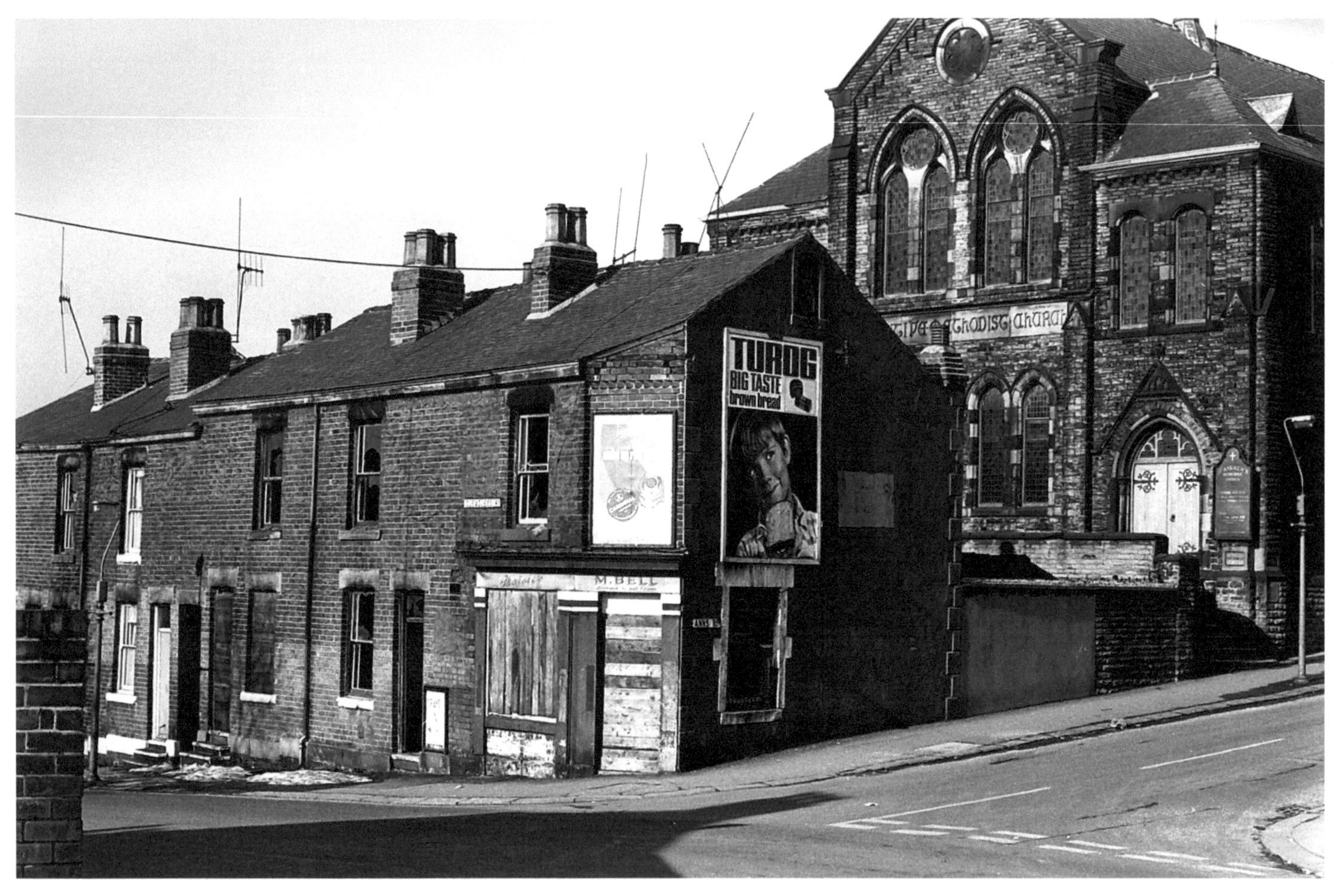

It looks like t' corner shop's shut, perhaps I'll try 'em again t'morra.
St Andrews Church on the corner of Gleadless Road and Ann's Road. It is now the Sheffield Chinese Christian Centre and stands pretty much alone.

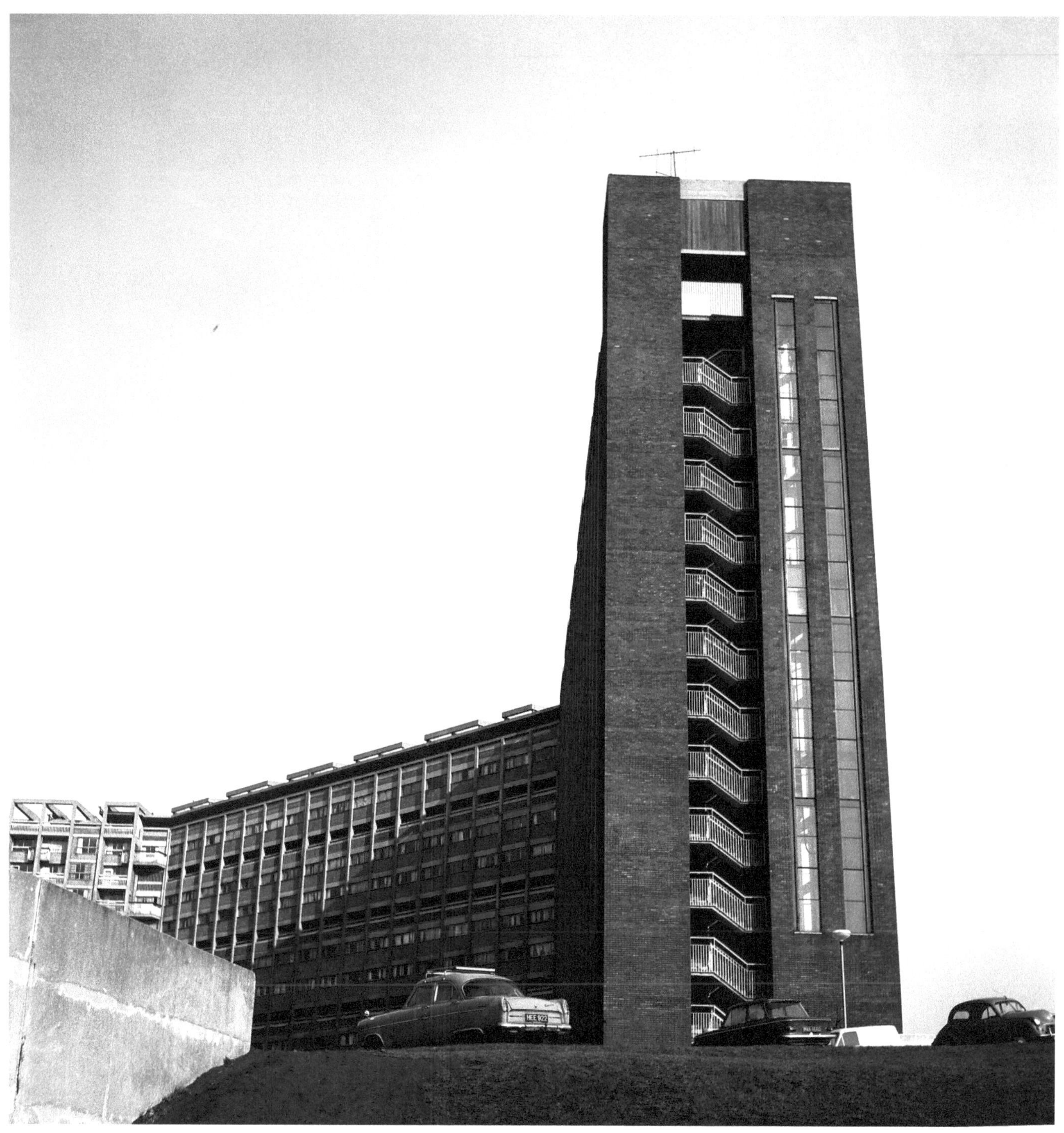

I like the contrast here between the beautiful old classic cars and the brutalism of the architecture of Hyde Park. The glass lifts were unusual at the time.

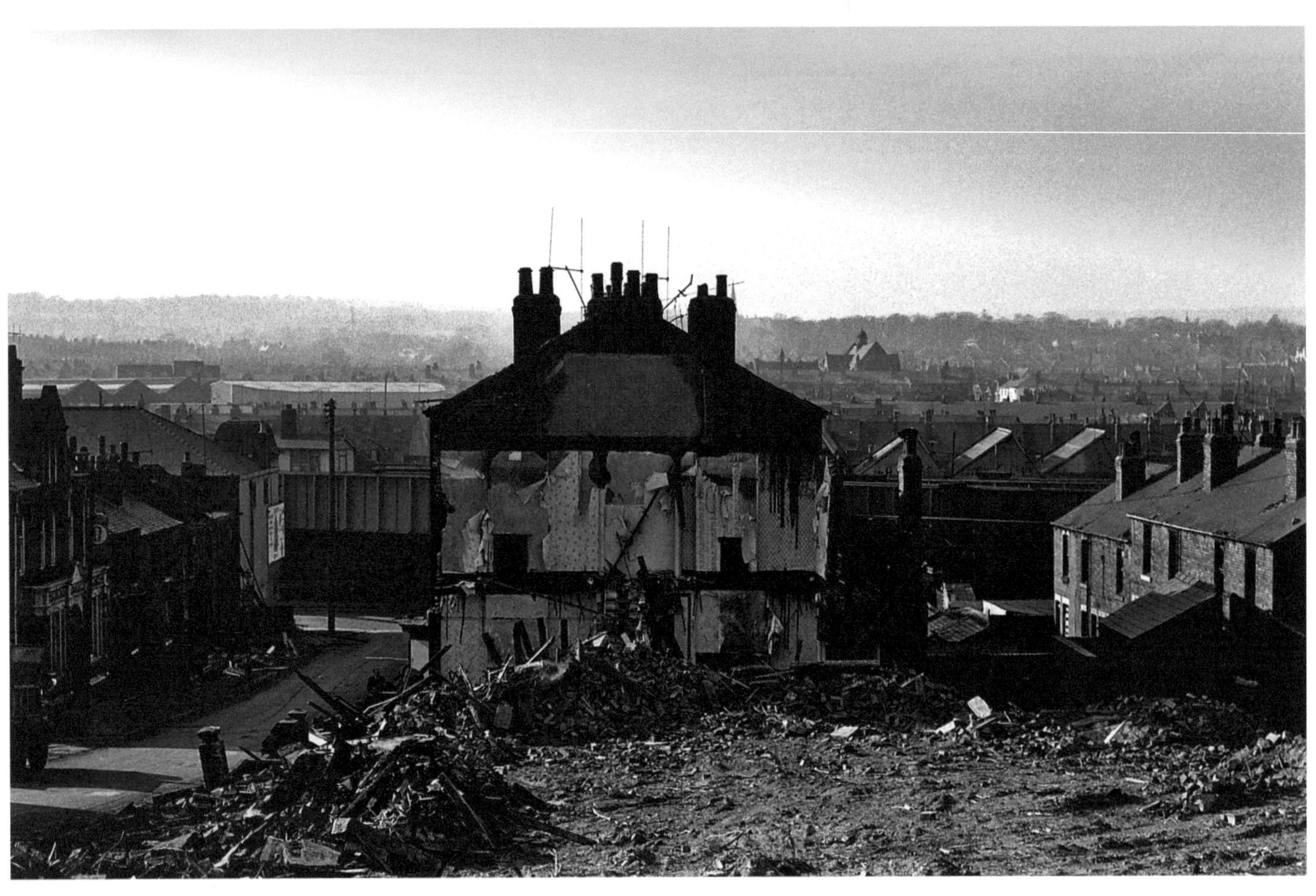

Demolition of Oak Street, Heeley. I suppose in some ways it was sad, but their new house was likely to have all mod cons like an inside toilet and bath.

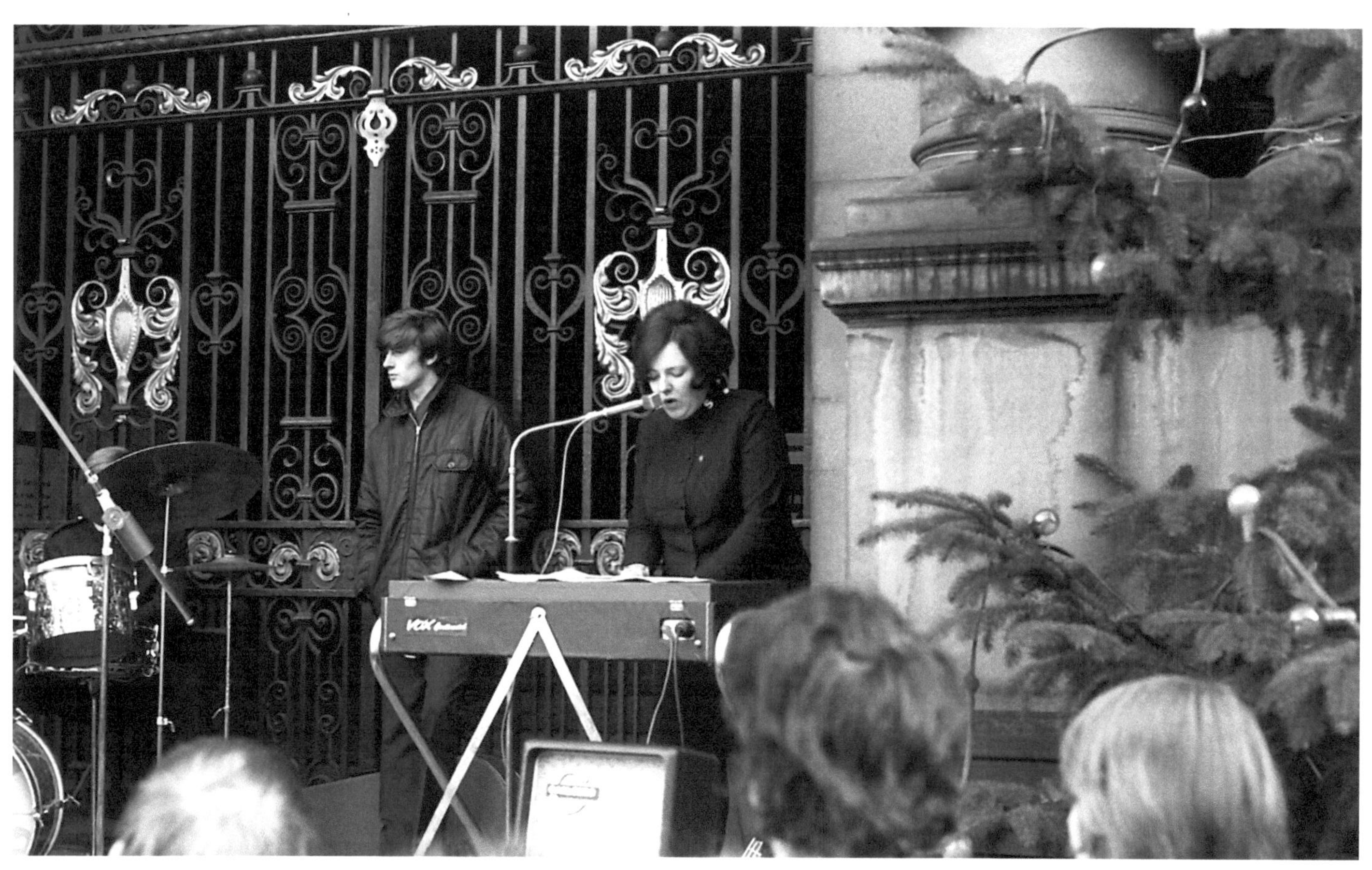

The Salvation Army on the Town Hall steps at Christmas

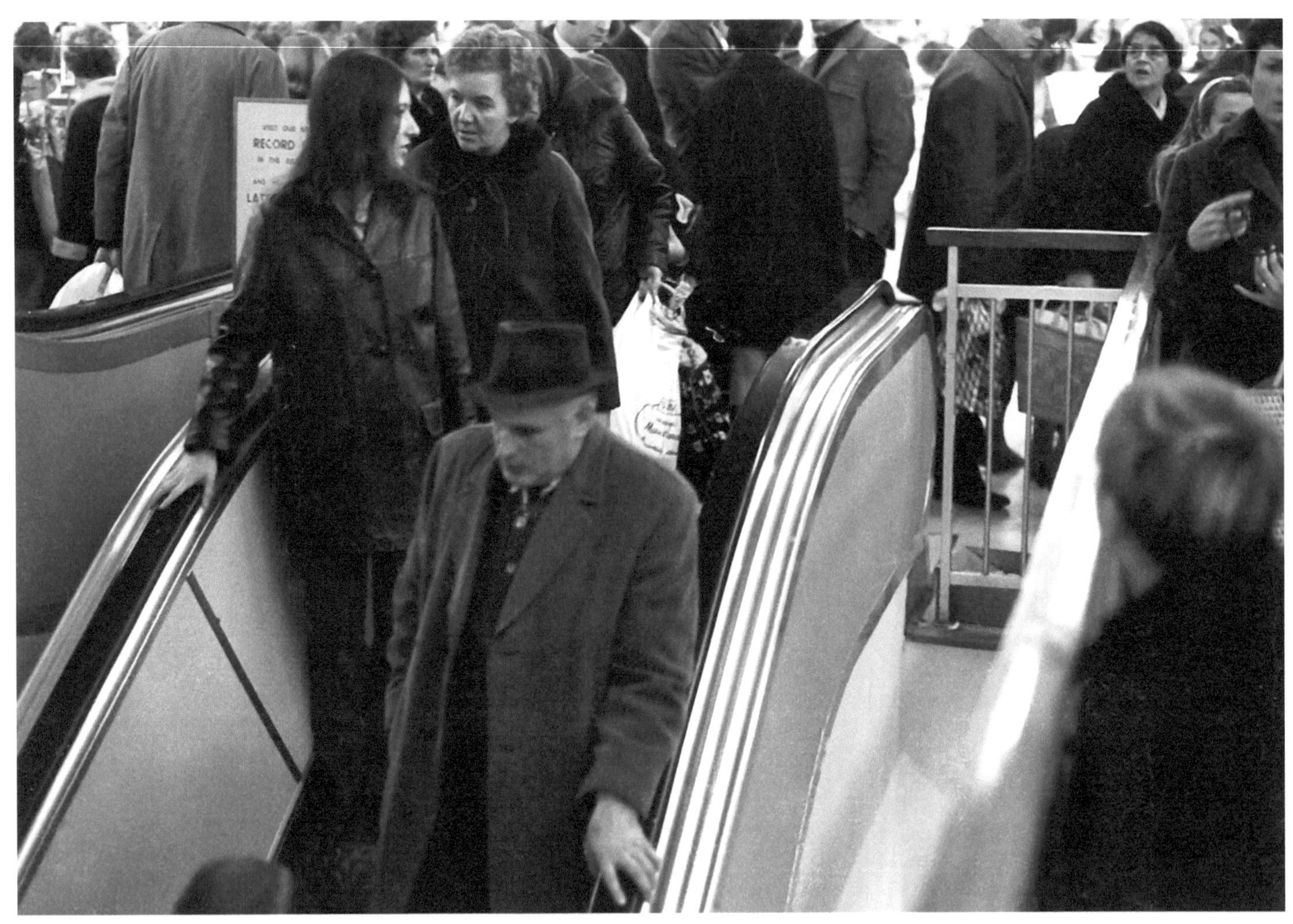

Escalators at Pauldens. Town is packed, so I suspect it was a Saturday.

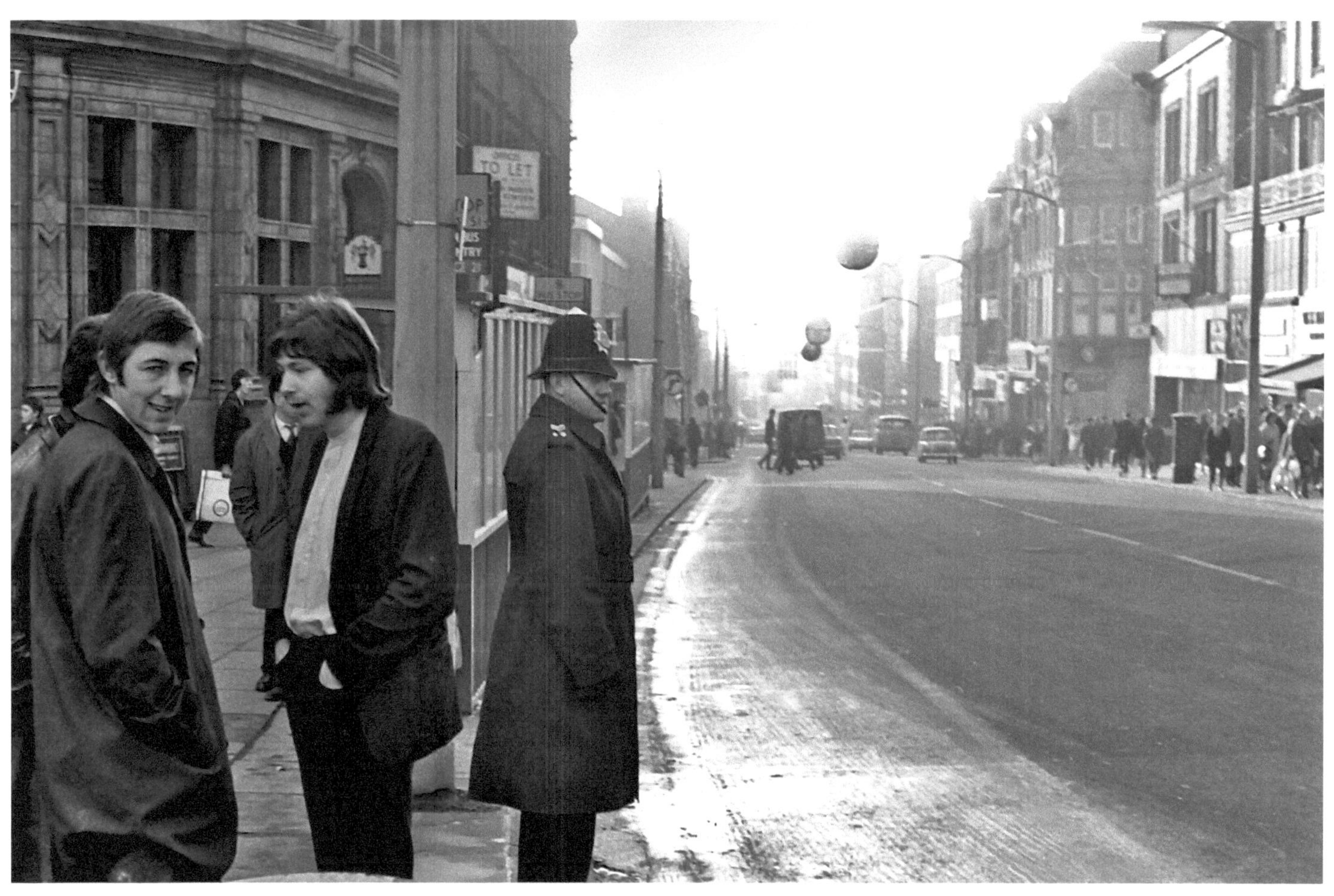

Pinstone Street looking down towards the Moor, Christmas 1969. The police sergeant has been identified. Apparently, he was well known and respected. You don't see "bobbies" on the beat these days.

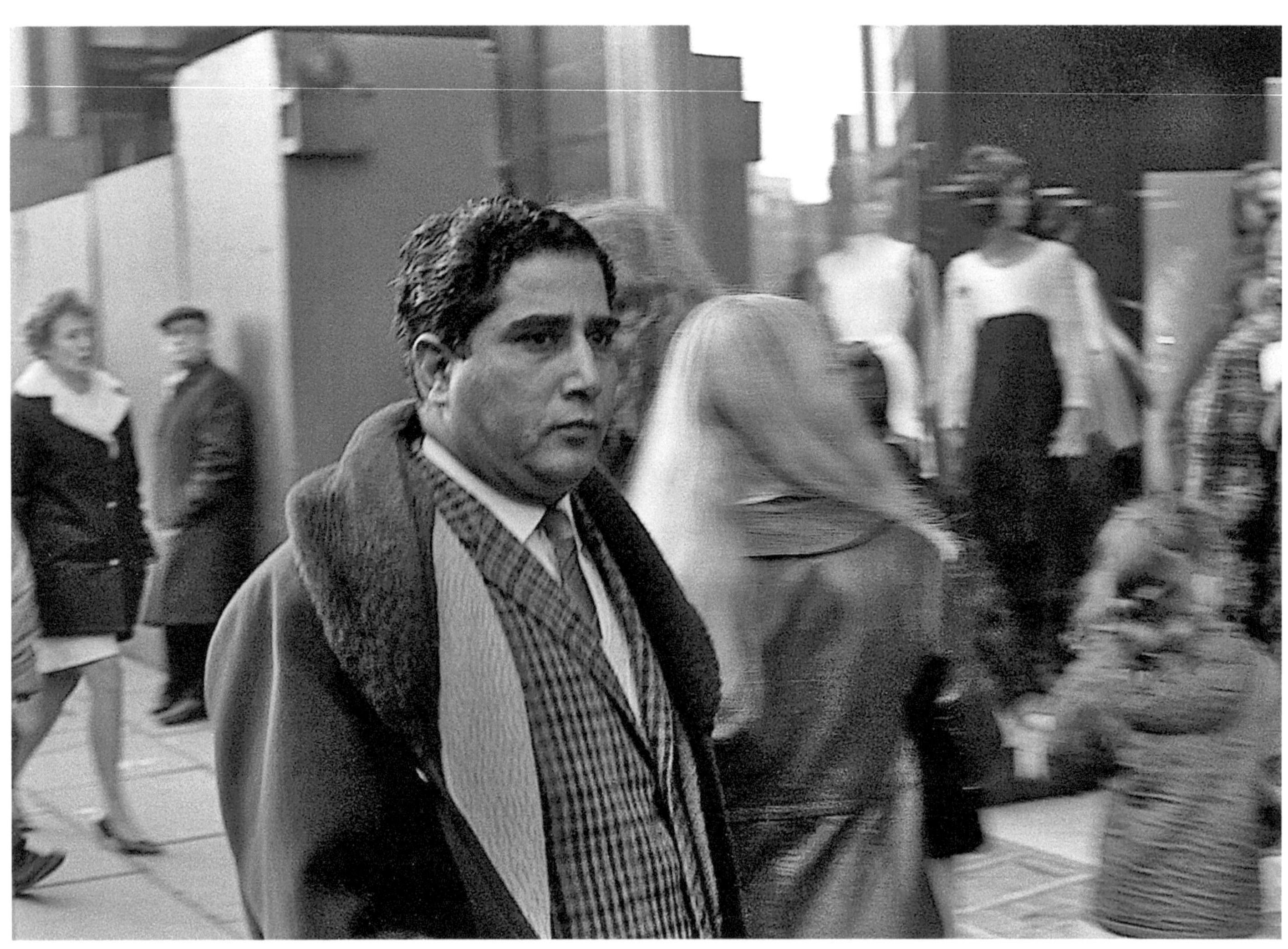

High Street shoppers.

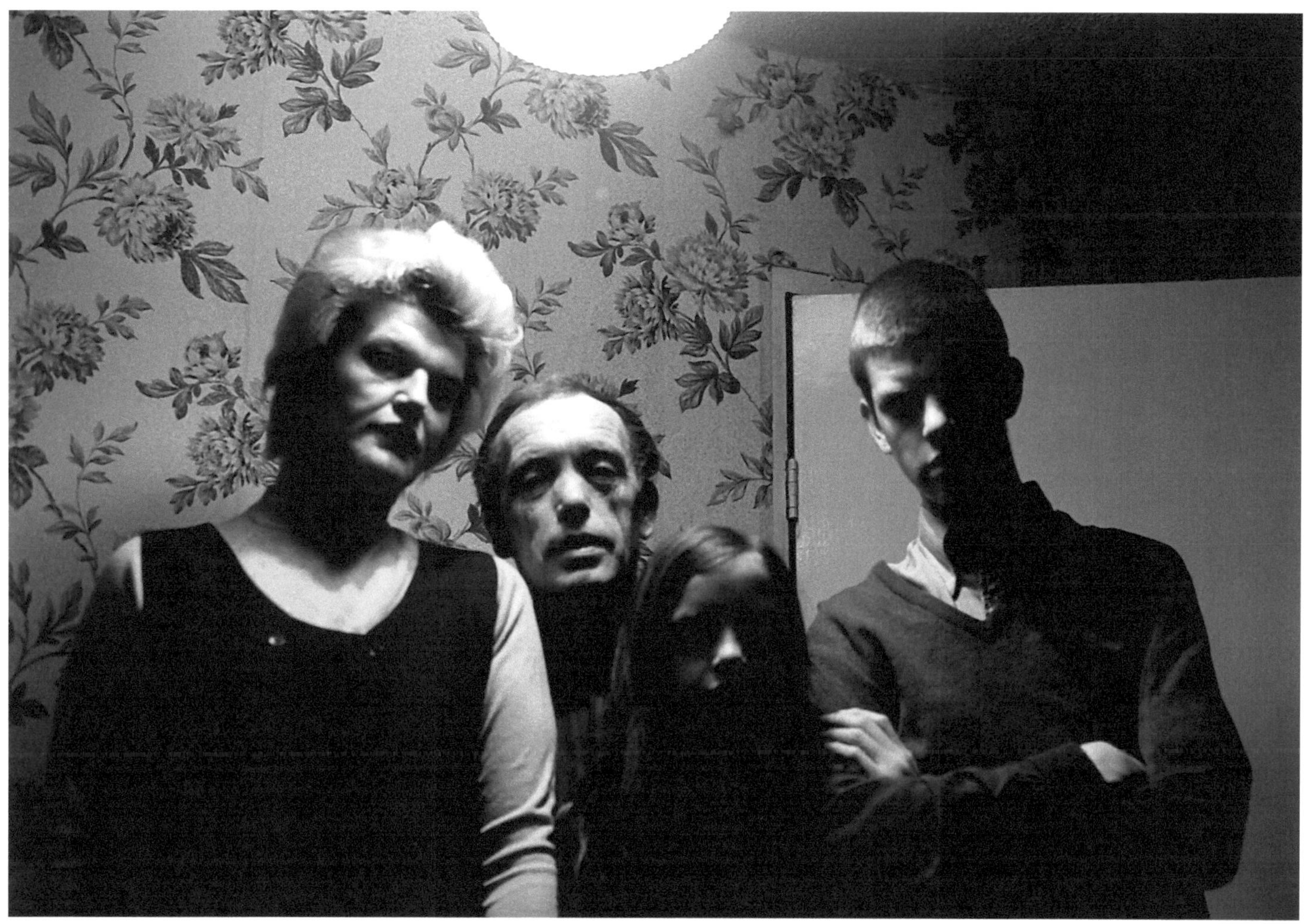

My family: Mum (Mary), Dad (Jack), Anita and Sean. It took ages to get them to pose seriously for this; I wanted to play around with different lighting and mood. Mum worked most of her life — we were latch-key kids but I loved that because it meant I was in charge, being the oldest. Both mum and dad worked hard and played hard. Dad was a hod-carrier — some said the best in Sheffield — running up and down ladders with two hods, if you believe the stories. He'd sometimes take us to work with him and we'd play in the sand and on the ladders. He was "self-employed" so didn't pay any tax, until they eventually caught up with him and he went bankrupt — not that he had much. He liked a bet on the horses and sometimes spent all his money, so then there was an almighty row; the pots and pans went flying at dad, and my mum would have to go and borrow money, usually from friends. When he won, he'd chuck his money around — feast or famine. We loved them to death though, and had a fantastic life.

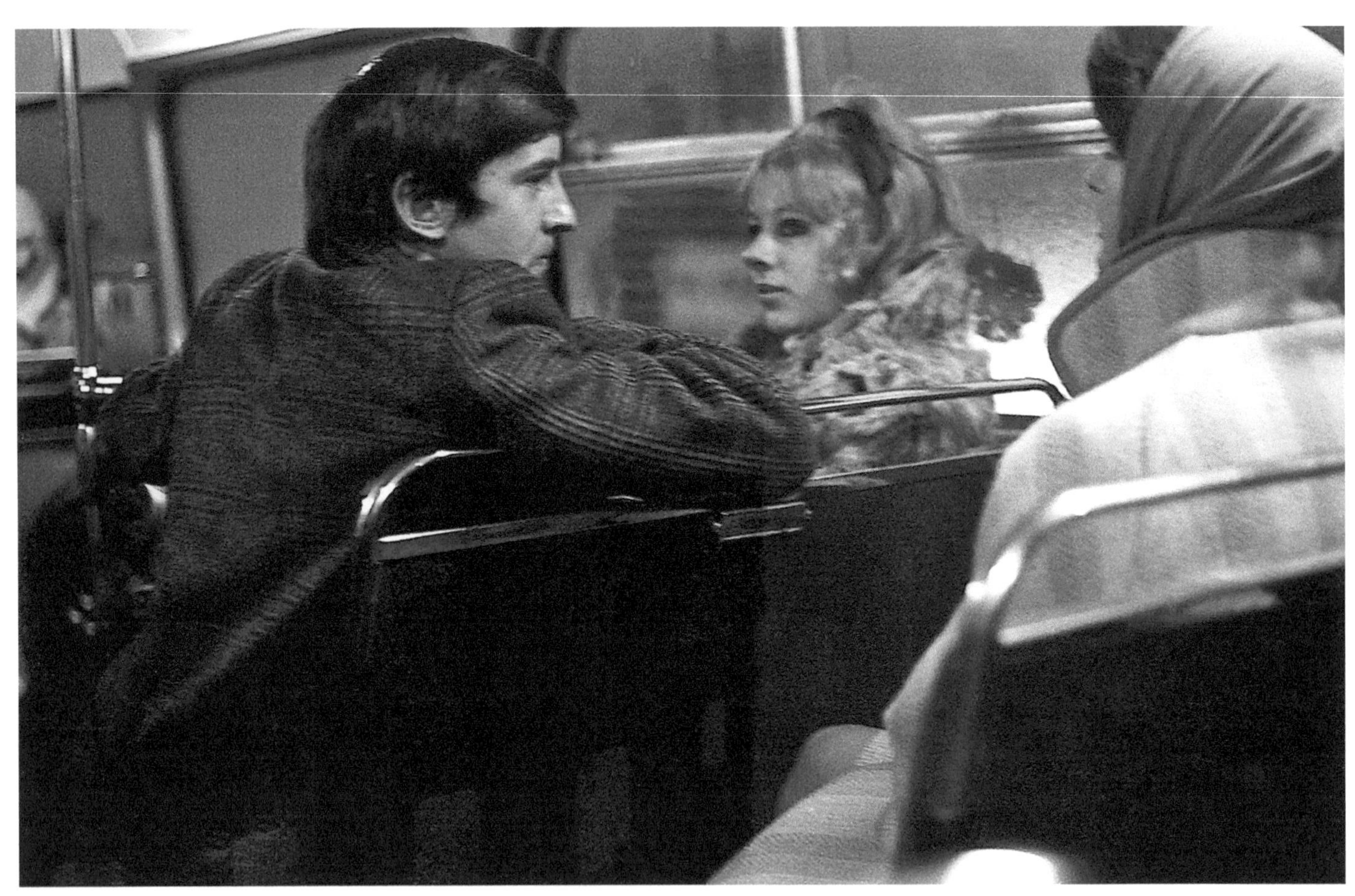

Upstairs on the bus going home.

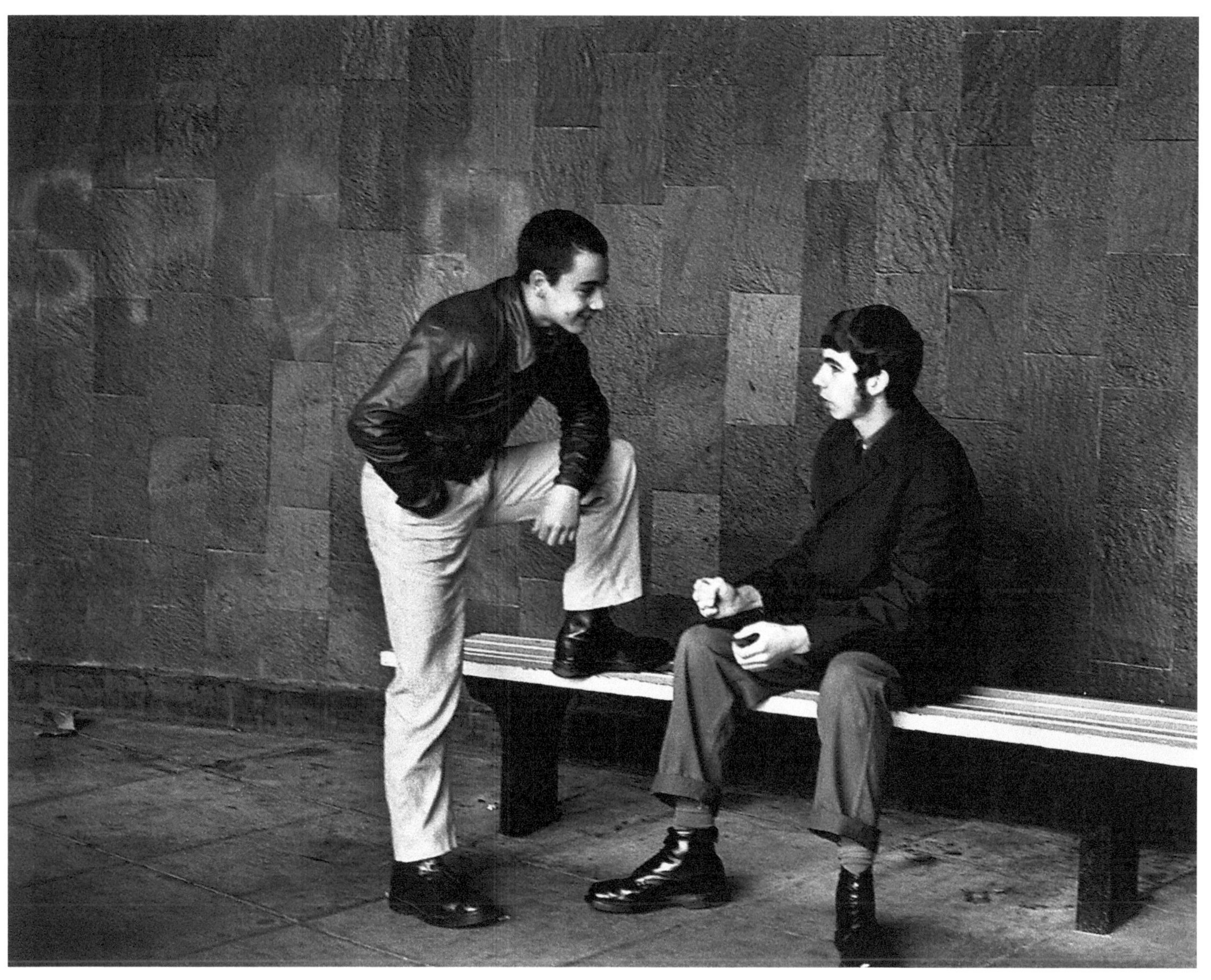

Hole in the Road — Gary Drabble sitting down.
Intellectual graffitti? SPQR — Senatus Populusque Romanus: The Senate and People of Rome (Sheffield is built on seven hills after all). Or is it from Asterix: Sono Pazzi Questi Romani — they're crazy these Romans? There was also an American record label in the 1960s called SPQR records. More sinister was its adoption by Mussolini.

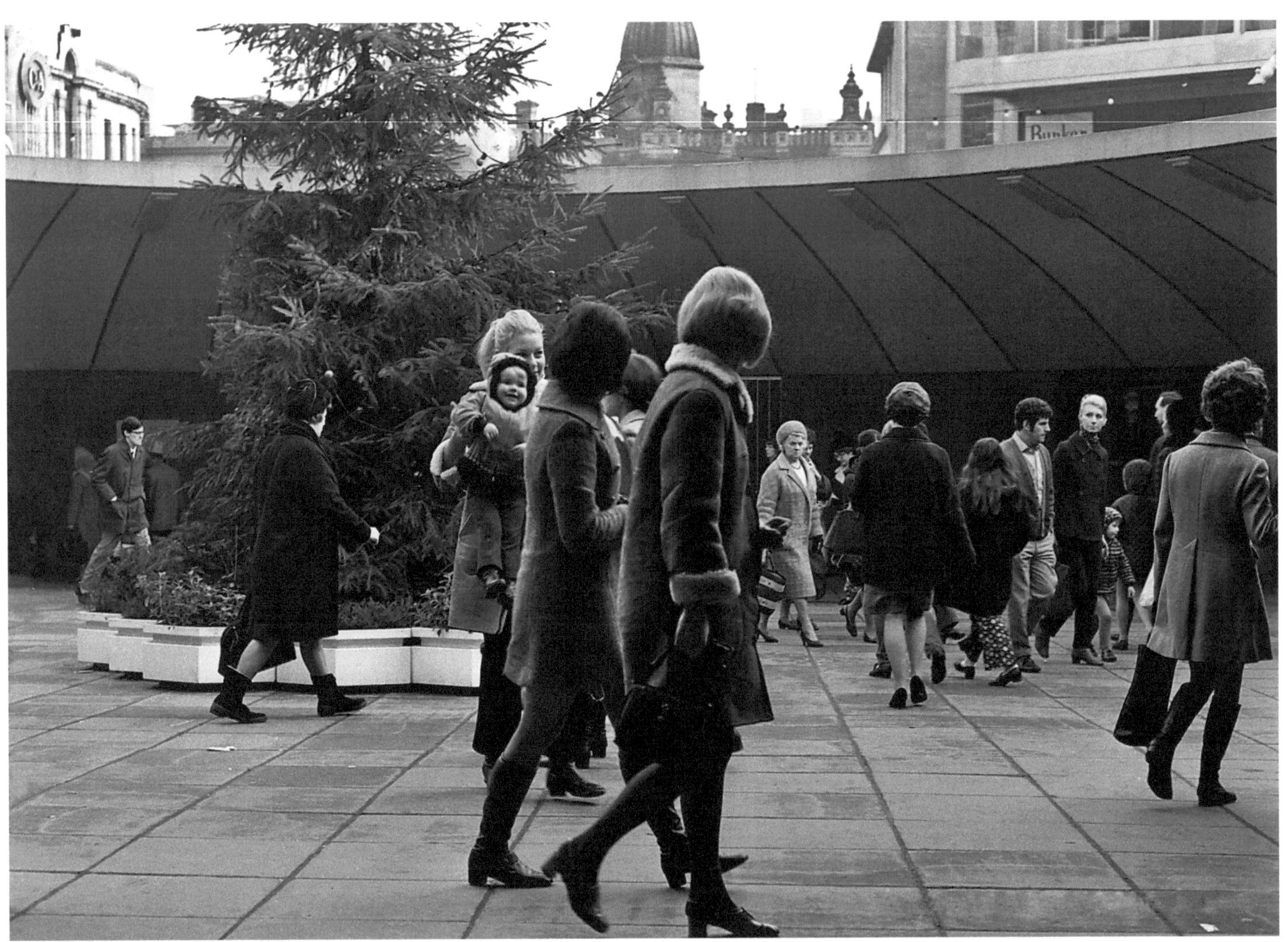

Hole in the Road at Christmas. This is one of my favourite images. Town is busy and everyone is dressed really smartly. I loved Christmas then and still do — it breaks up the winter just nice.

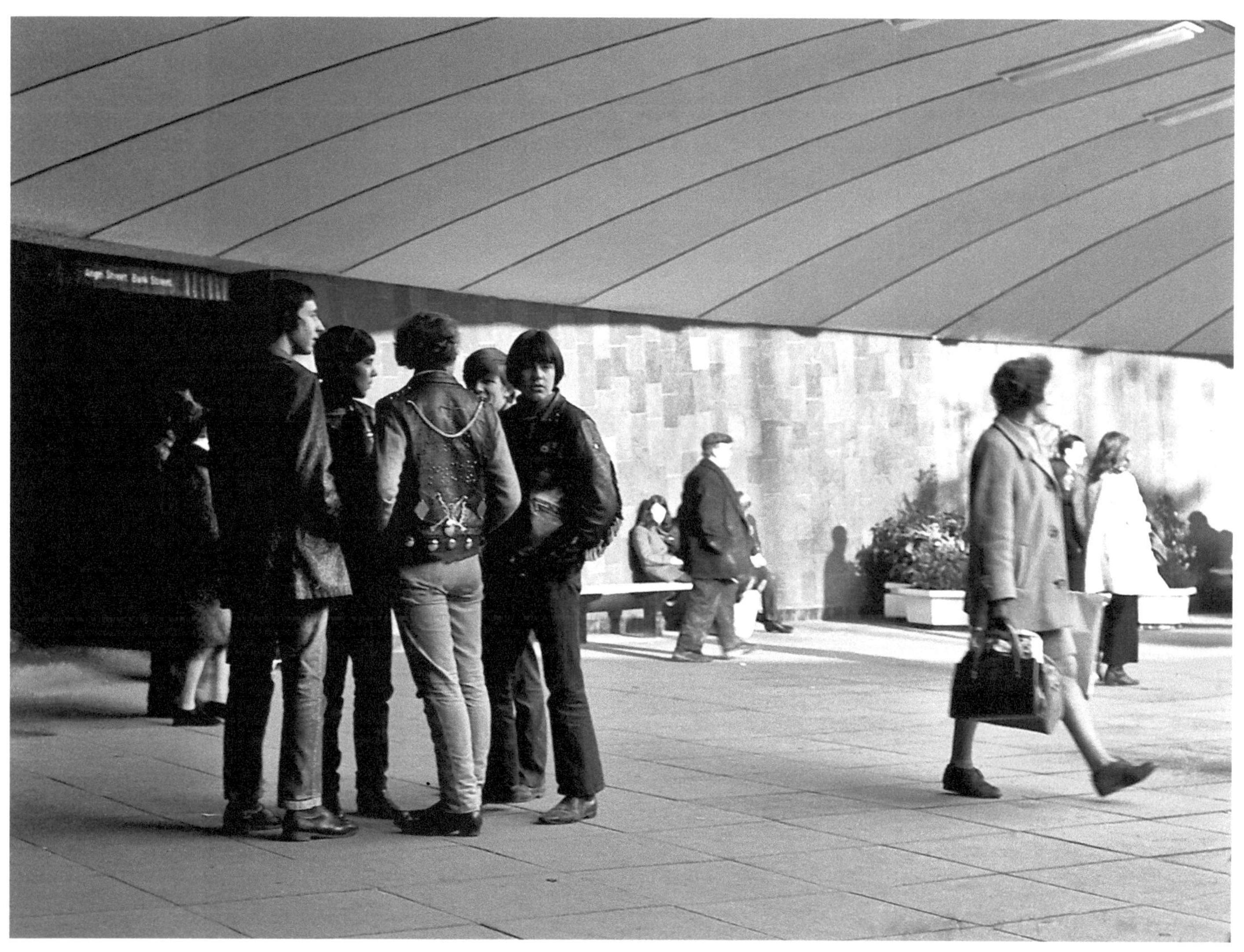

Rockers in the Hole in the Road in late 1969. Although you would get Skinheads and Rockers in the same proximity there was hardly ever any trouble.

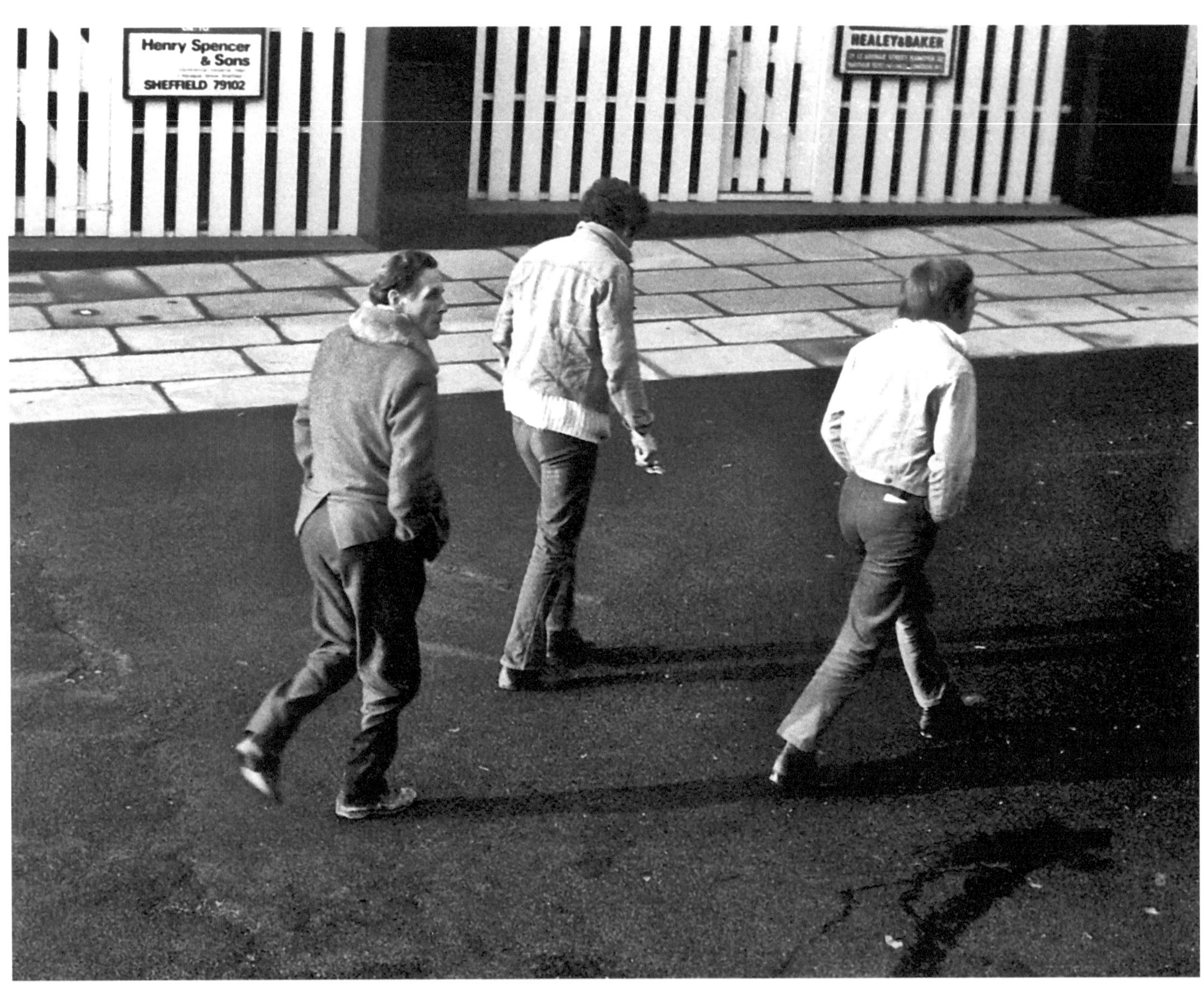

Off to the pub?

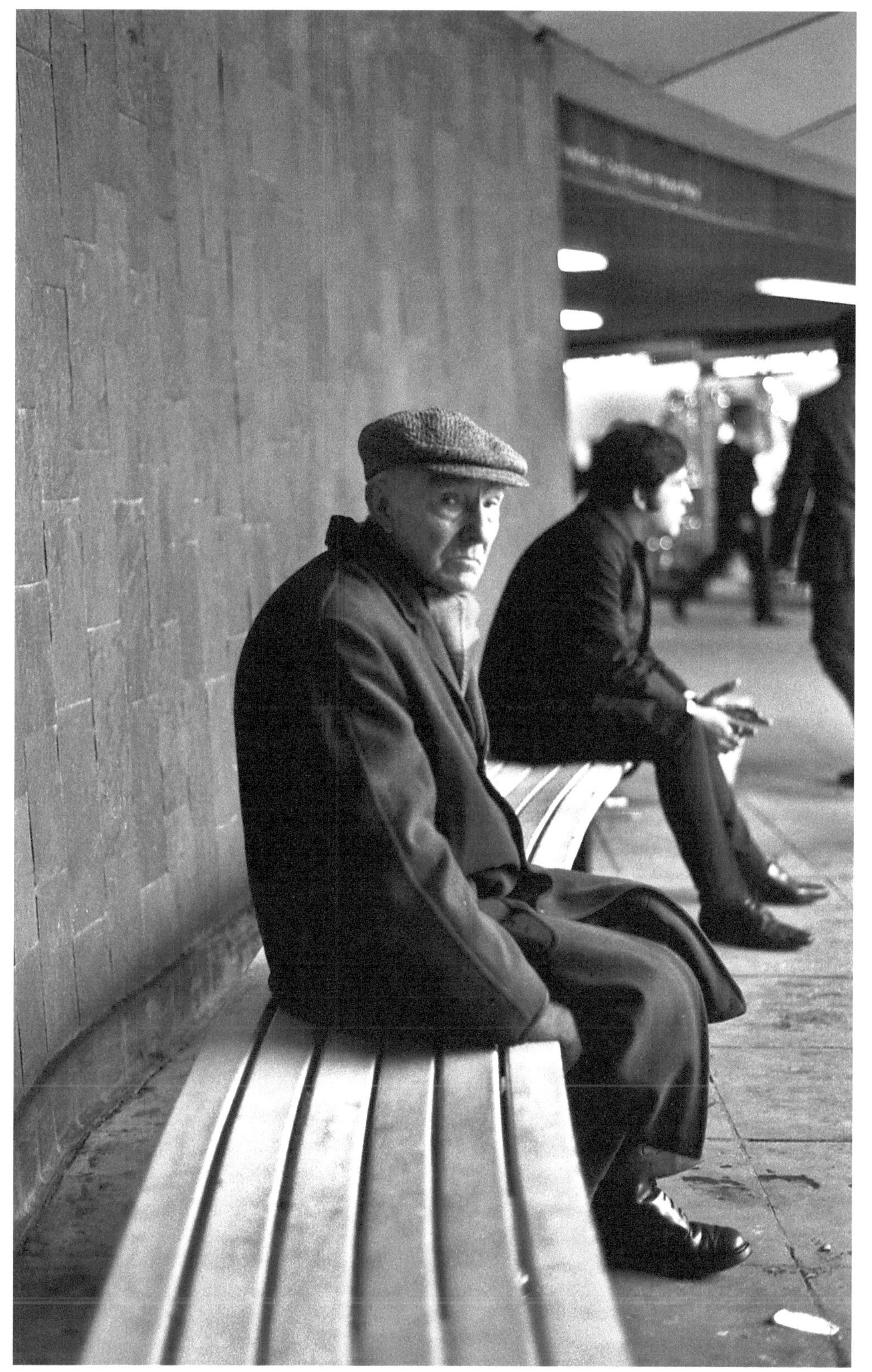

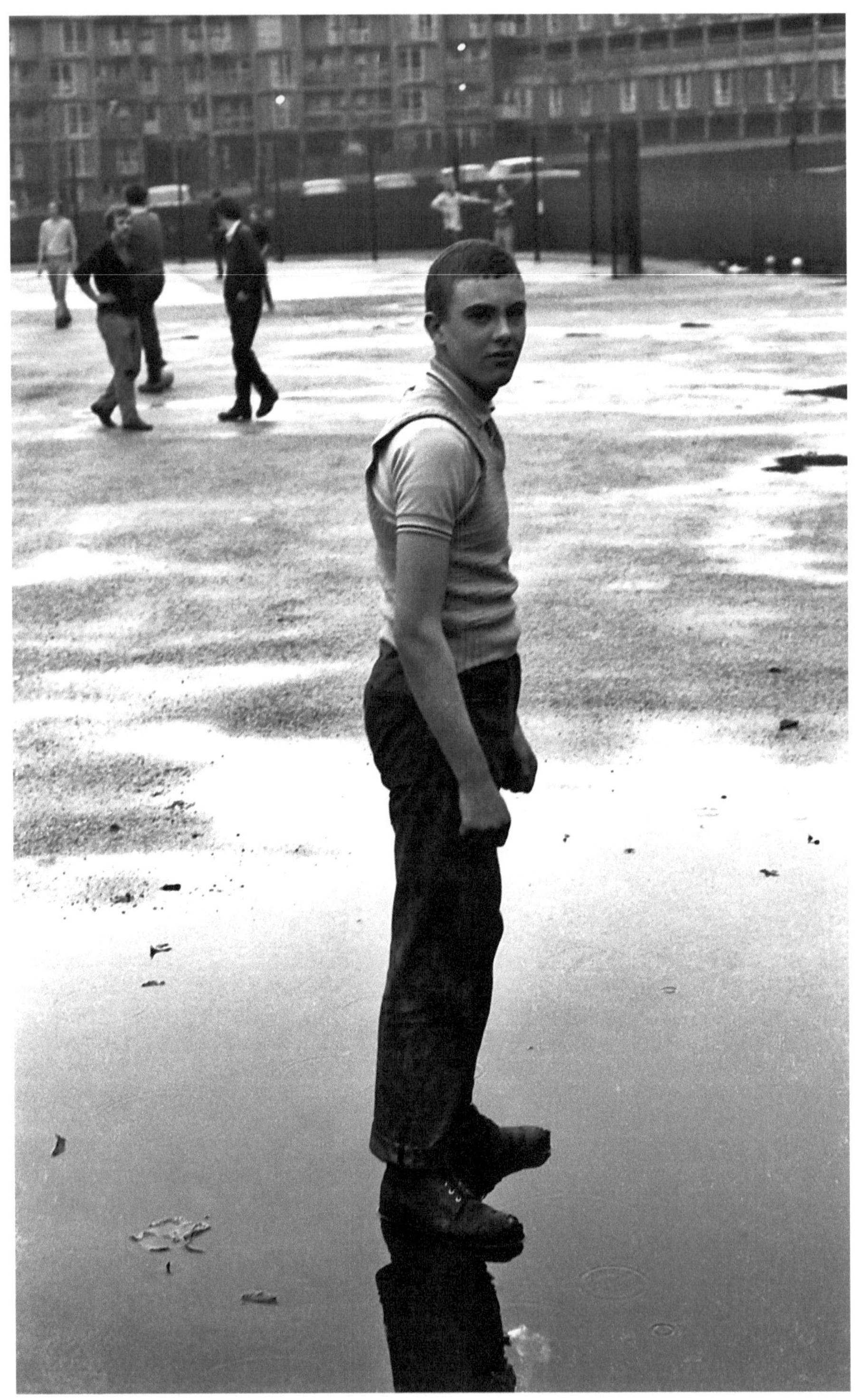

In goal at Park Hill. Steel toe caps: not obligatory but useful.

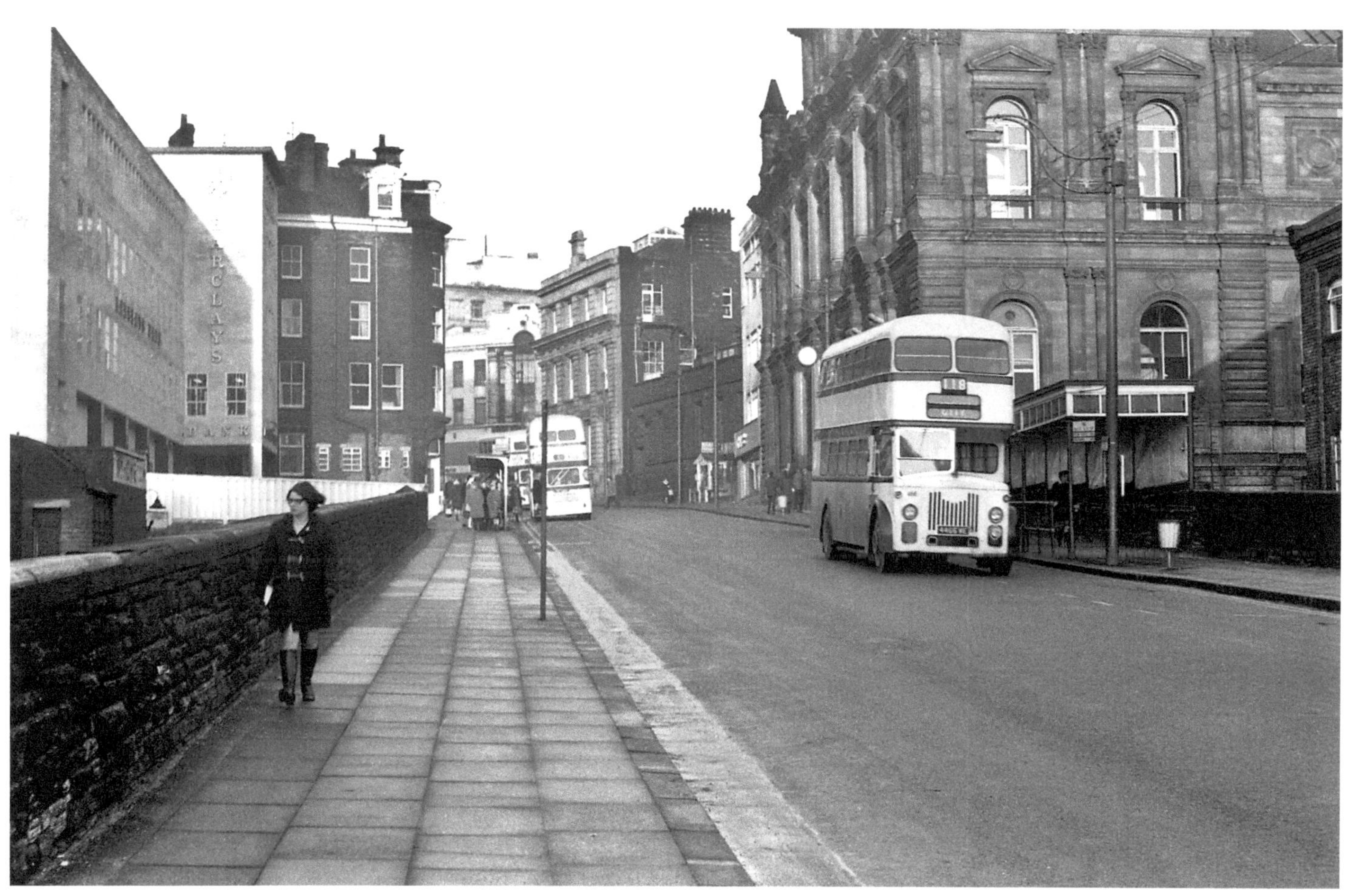

Commercial Street — our main route from Park Hill up into town. Also where I'd catch the bus up to college. As a student I did have a free bus pass, but, living at home, I never got a grant, which I was miffed about as we didn't have much money.

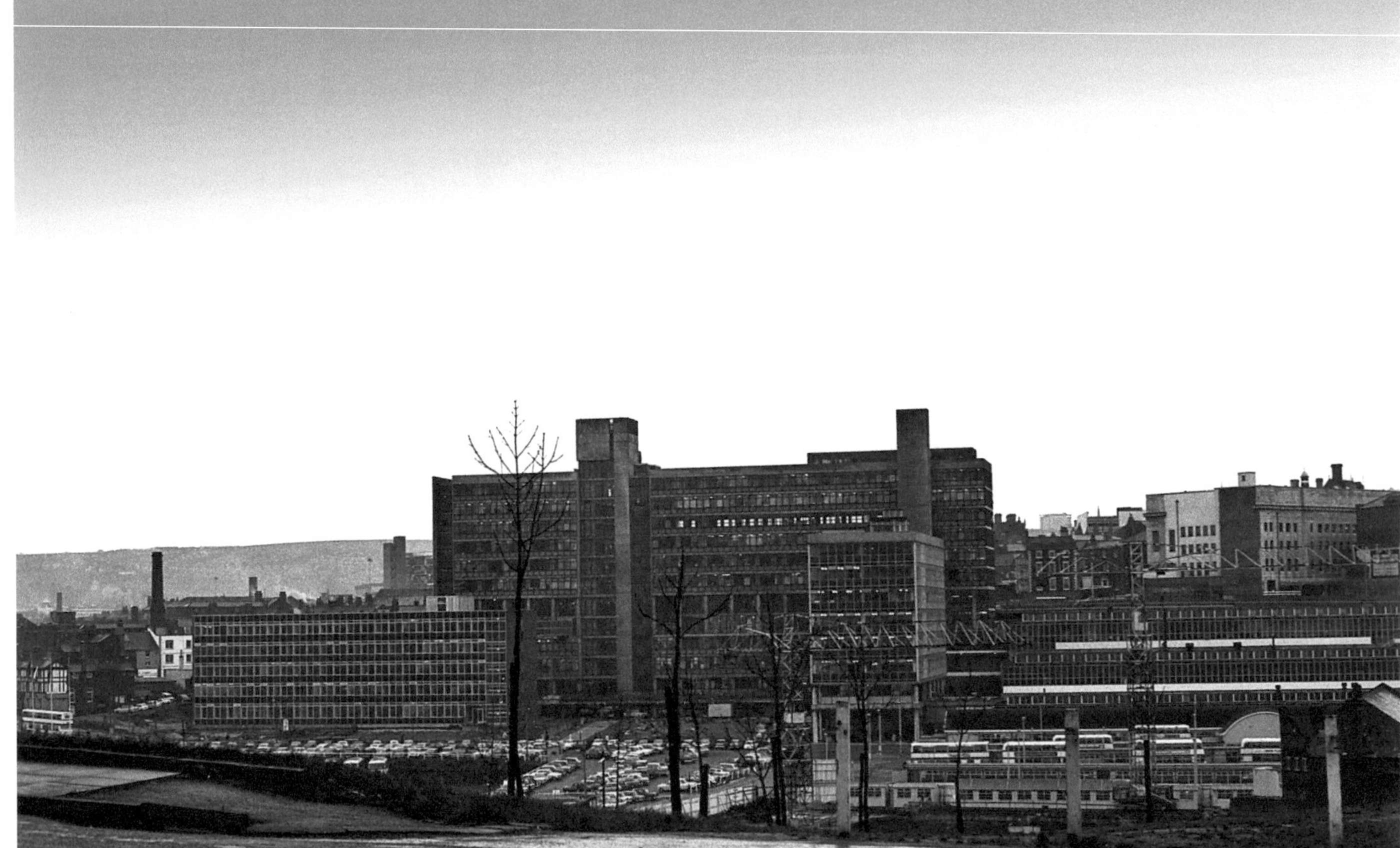

Pond Street bus station and Sheffield Poly from South Street. Graves Art Gallery and central library on the right. The bollards are blocking off what used to be Norwich Street. We often used to sit on this grass in summer and have a great view of Sheffield.

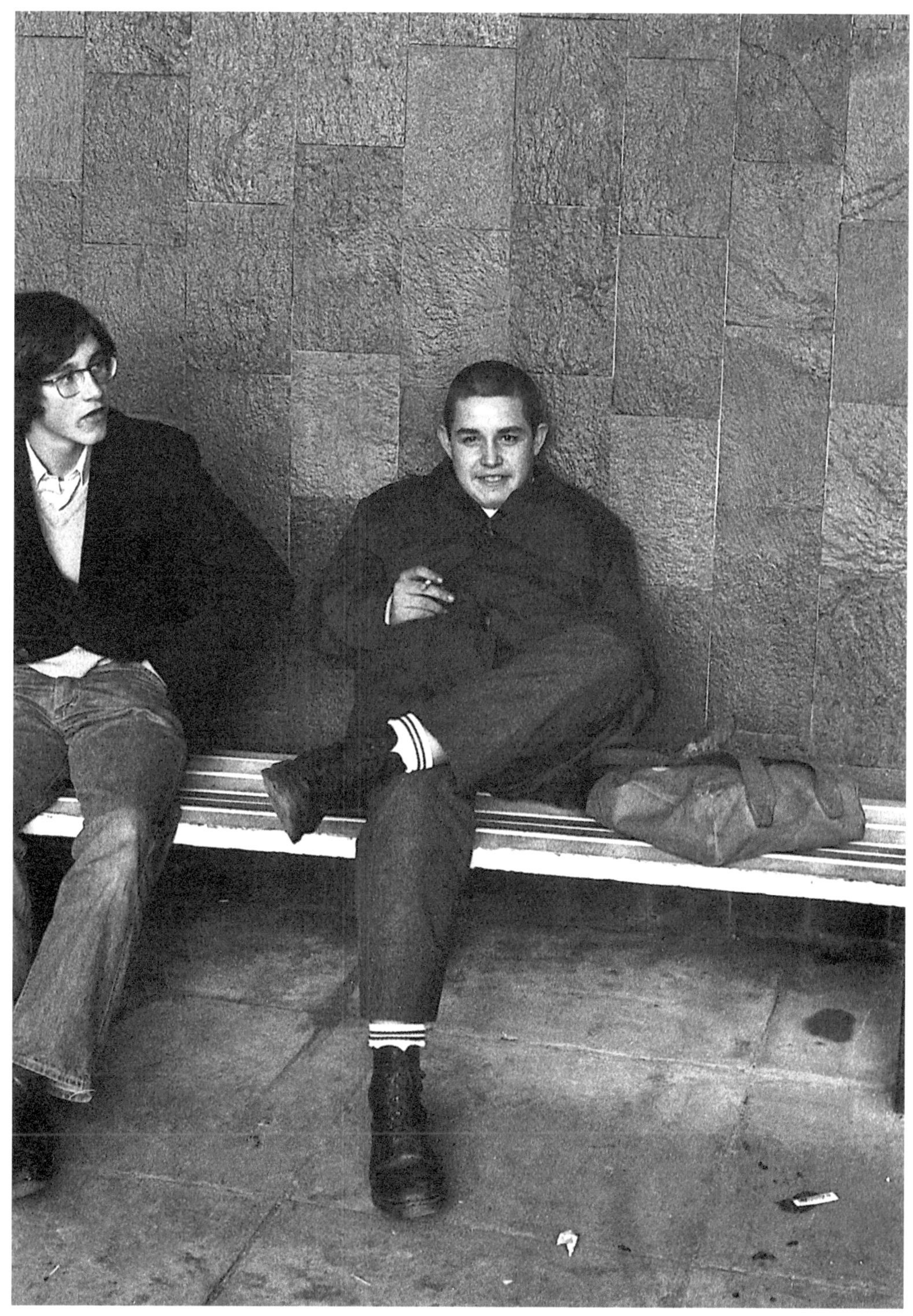

Mick Marshall whose dad had the Scottish Queen. Now fittingly exiled in Scotland. He is a keen fisherman and looks a little bigger. Must be the porridge.

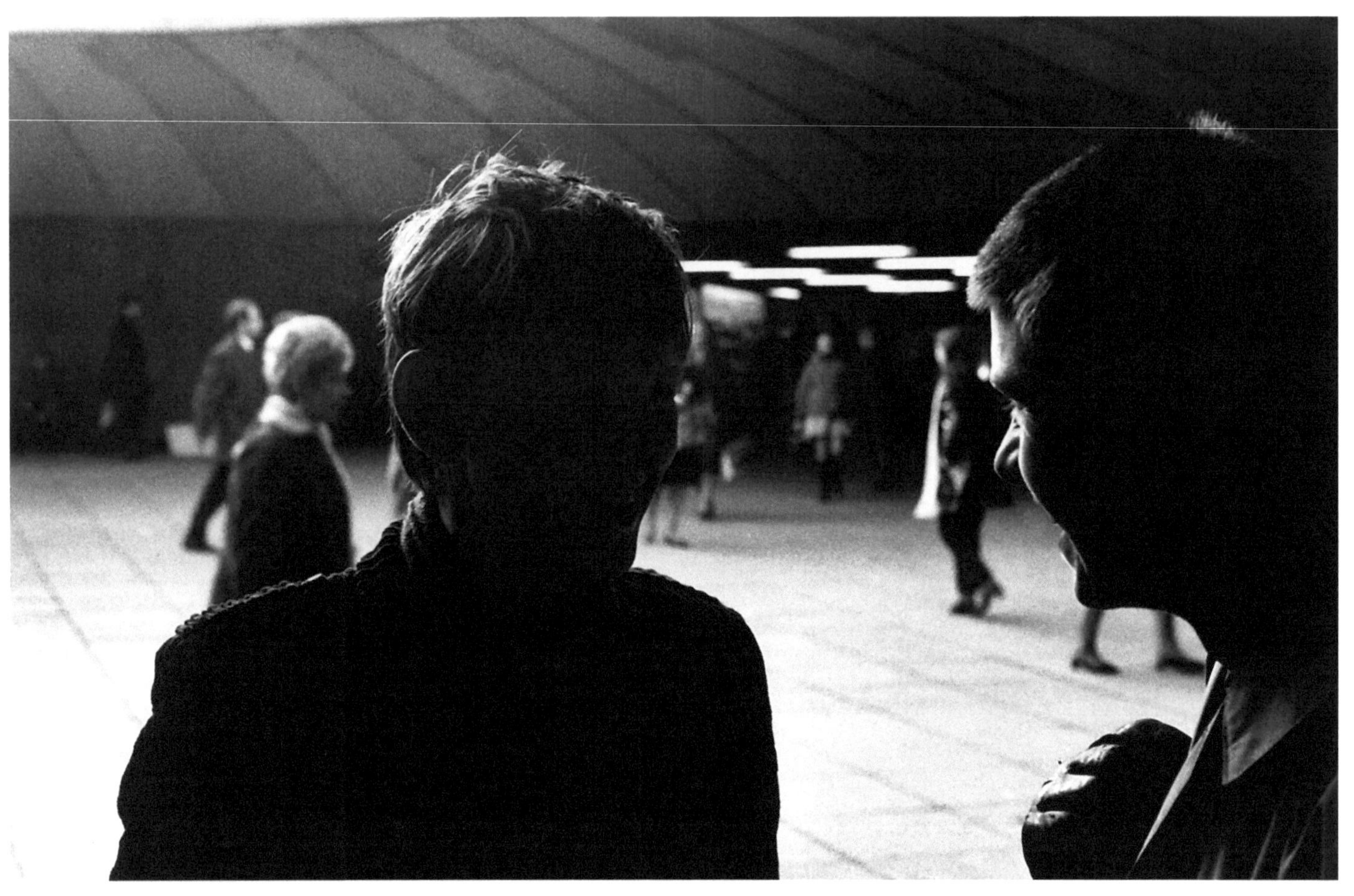

Mick Pierpoint and my brother. Fifty years later both their portraits were in the foyer of The Crucible Theatre for the premier of "Standing at the Sky's Edge." About a dozen past residents' portraits were shown in the foyer.

Pauldens' cafe. I thought this young lady was giving me the eye until she put her tongue out.

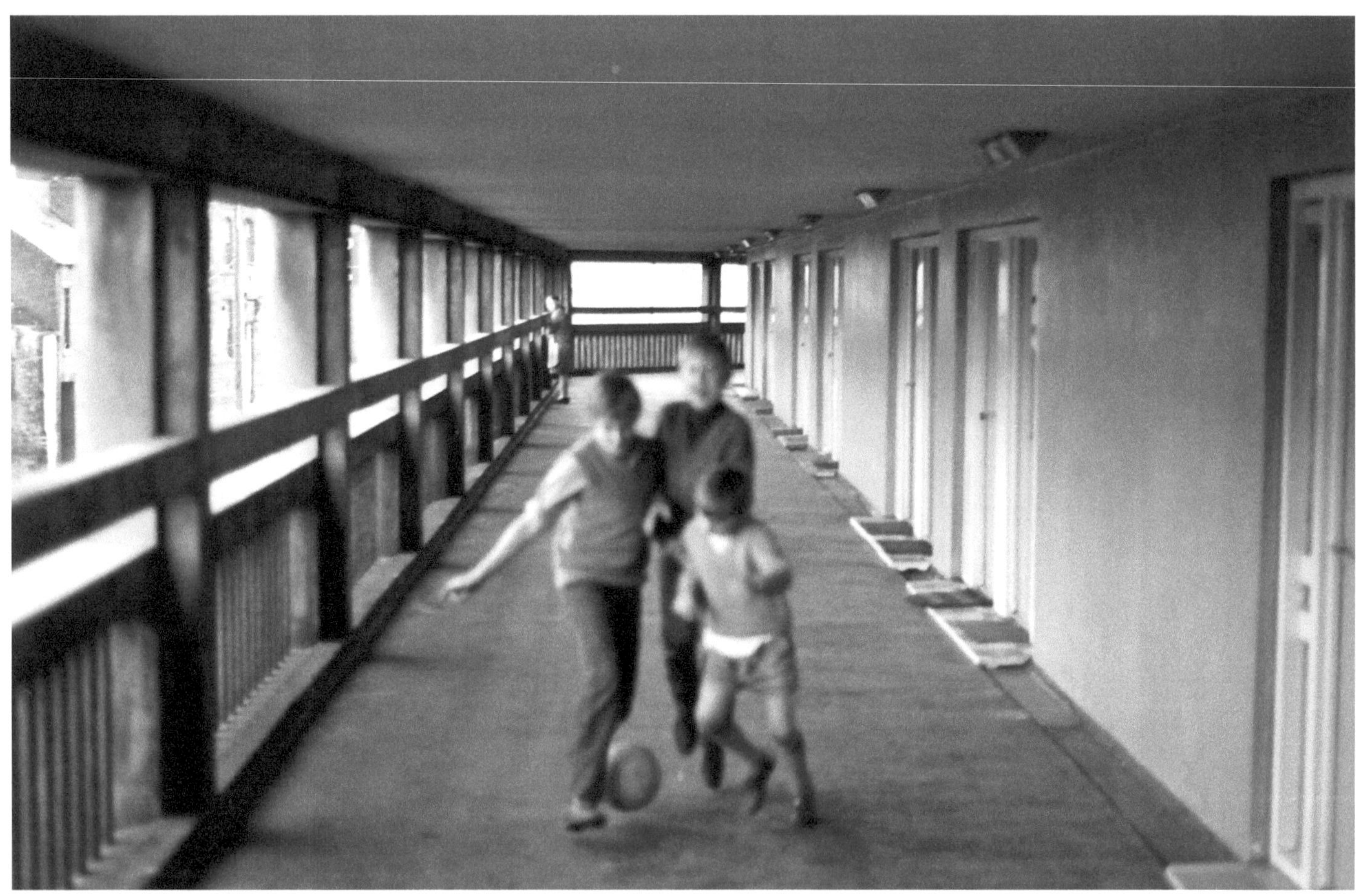

Long Henry Row just outside our house: one of the "streets in the sky." Playing football on the landings at Park Hill was a big "no-no." This was Neil Andrews, Alan Balderson and a friend.

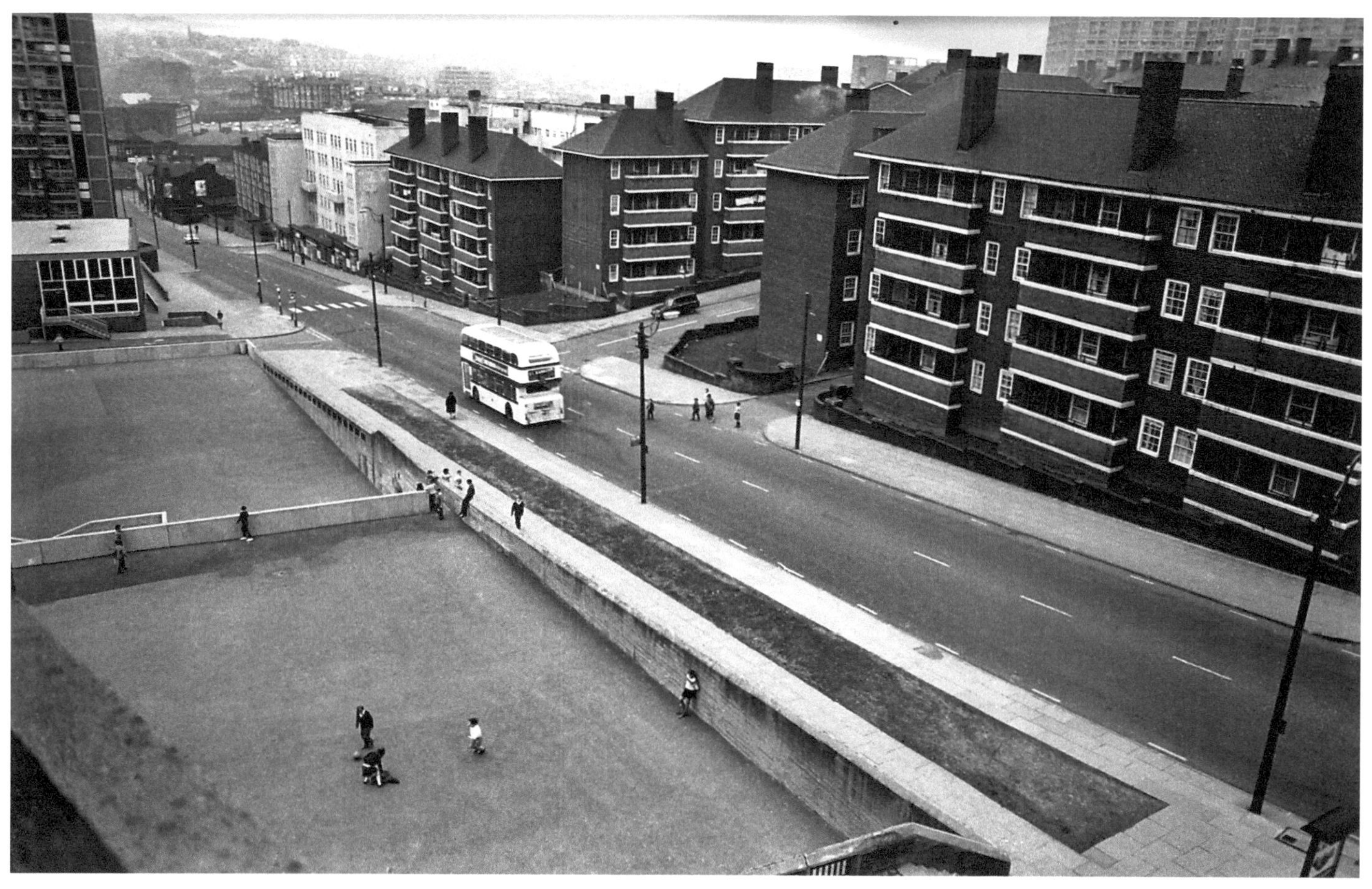

Looking down Duke Street from just outside our front door.
You can see Park Junior School playground, Bard Street and Stepney Buildings. The flats lower down on the right were Embassy Court. To the left, on this side of the road was the Community Centre. There were weekly dances and bingo, along with other activities. I went to the Scouts there but after an hour of tying knots got fed up and never went back.

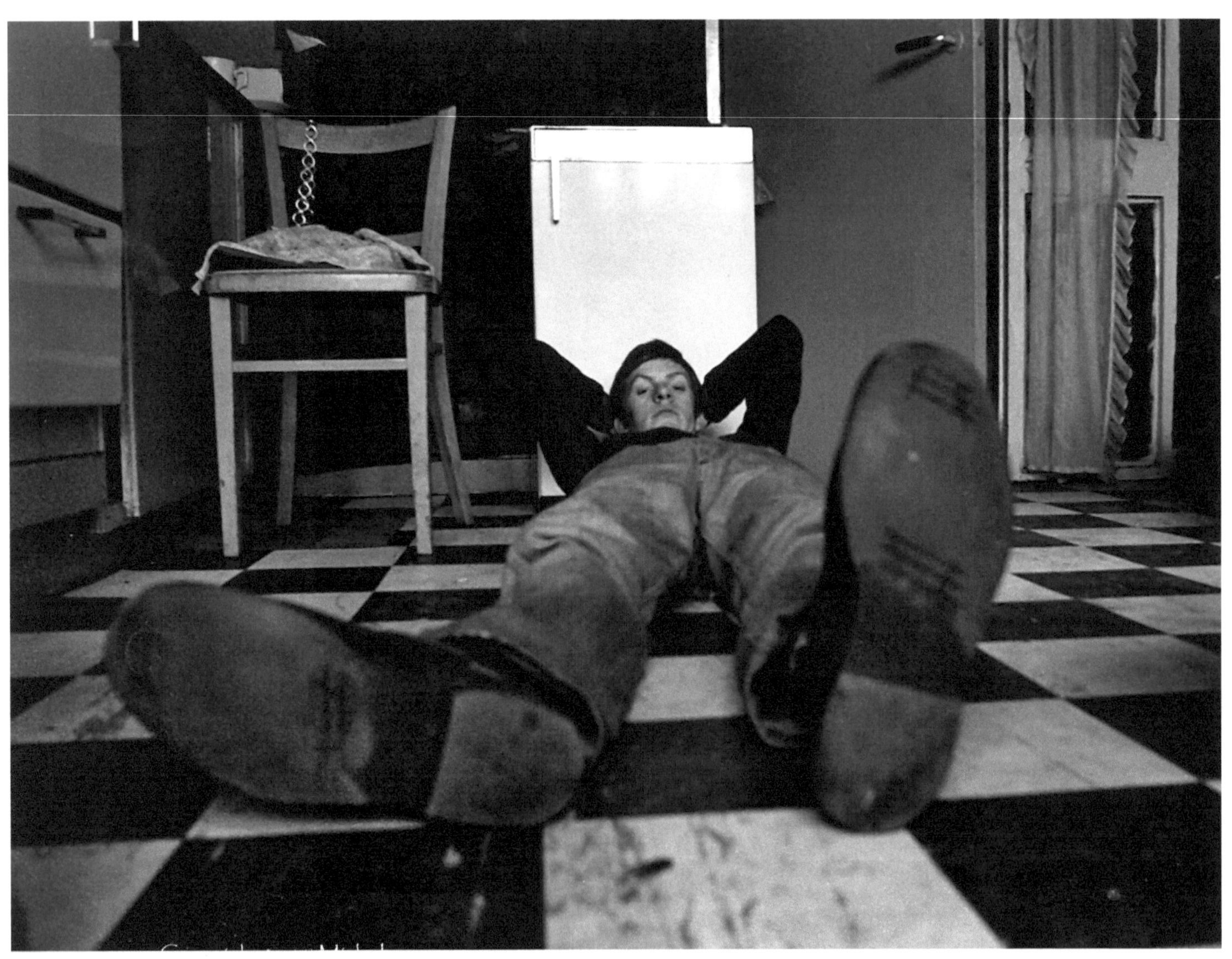

My brother in our kitchen. Note the new fridge: a rarity at that time. Also one of those chain belts belonging to my sister, hanging over the chair. Also of course, in those days, the obligatory net curtains.

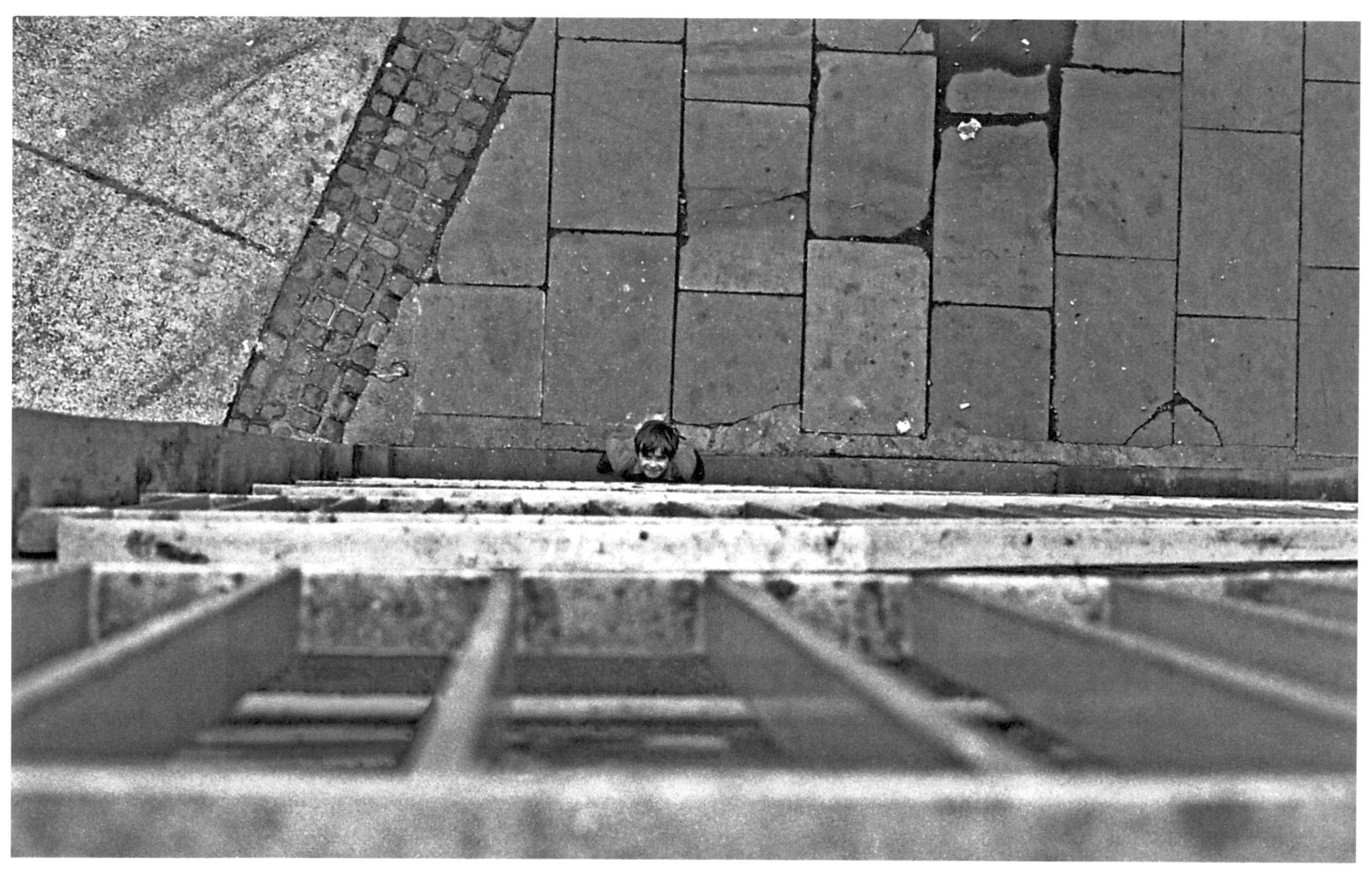

Robert King looks like he's being naughty, but I'm pretty sure the shot was posed. After all there was a public toilet just yards away.

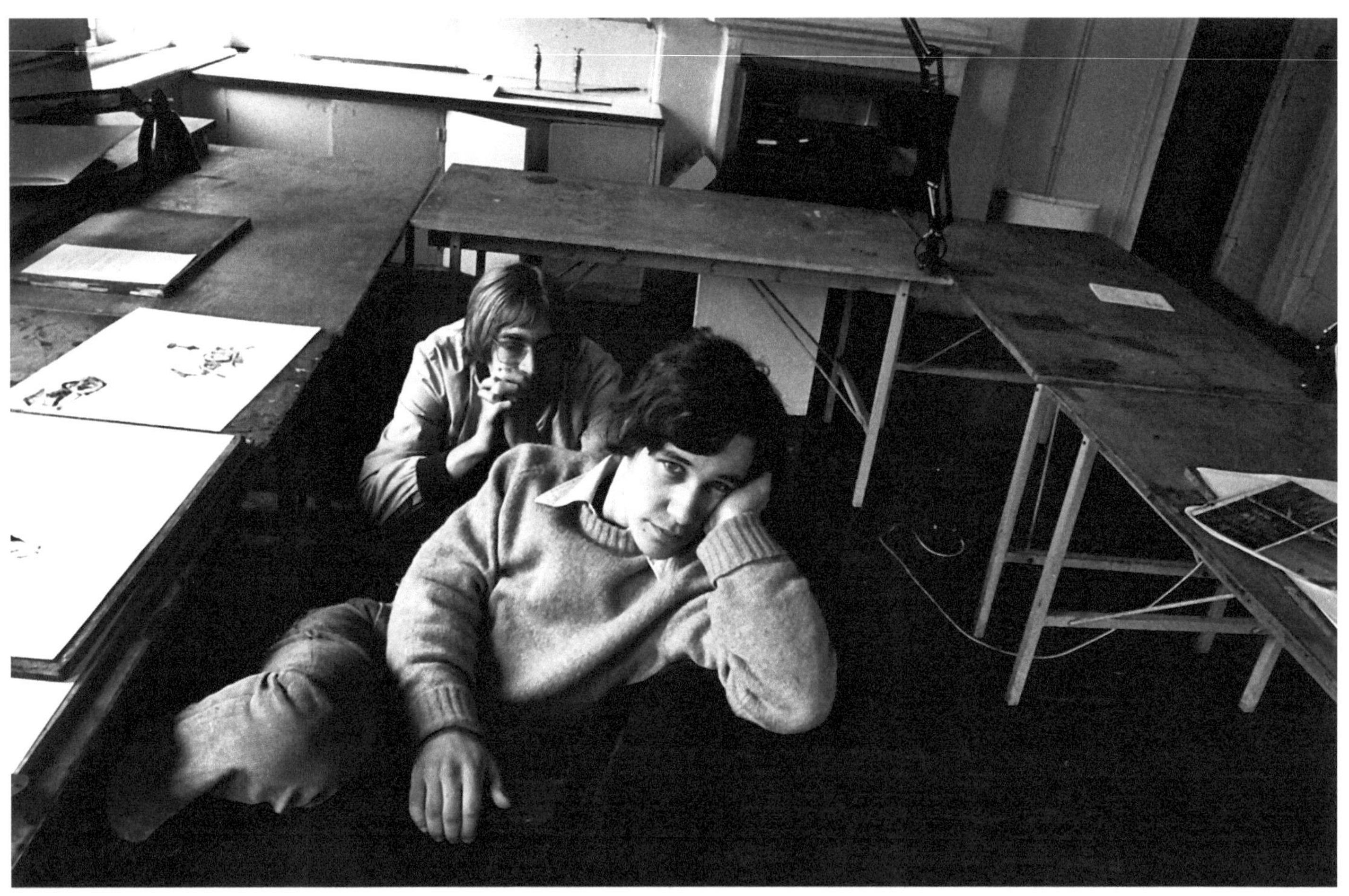

In the second year at Art College. Peter Knowles and Stuart Pinder. As you can see we were always busy.

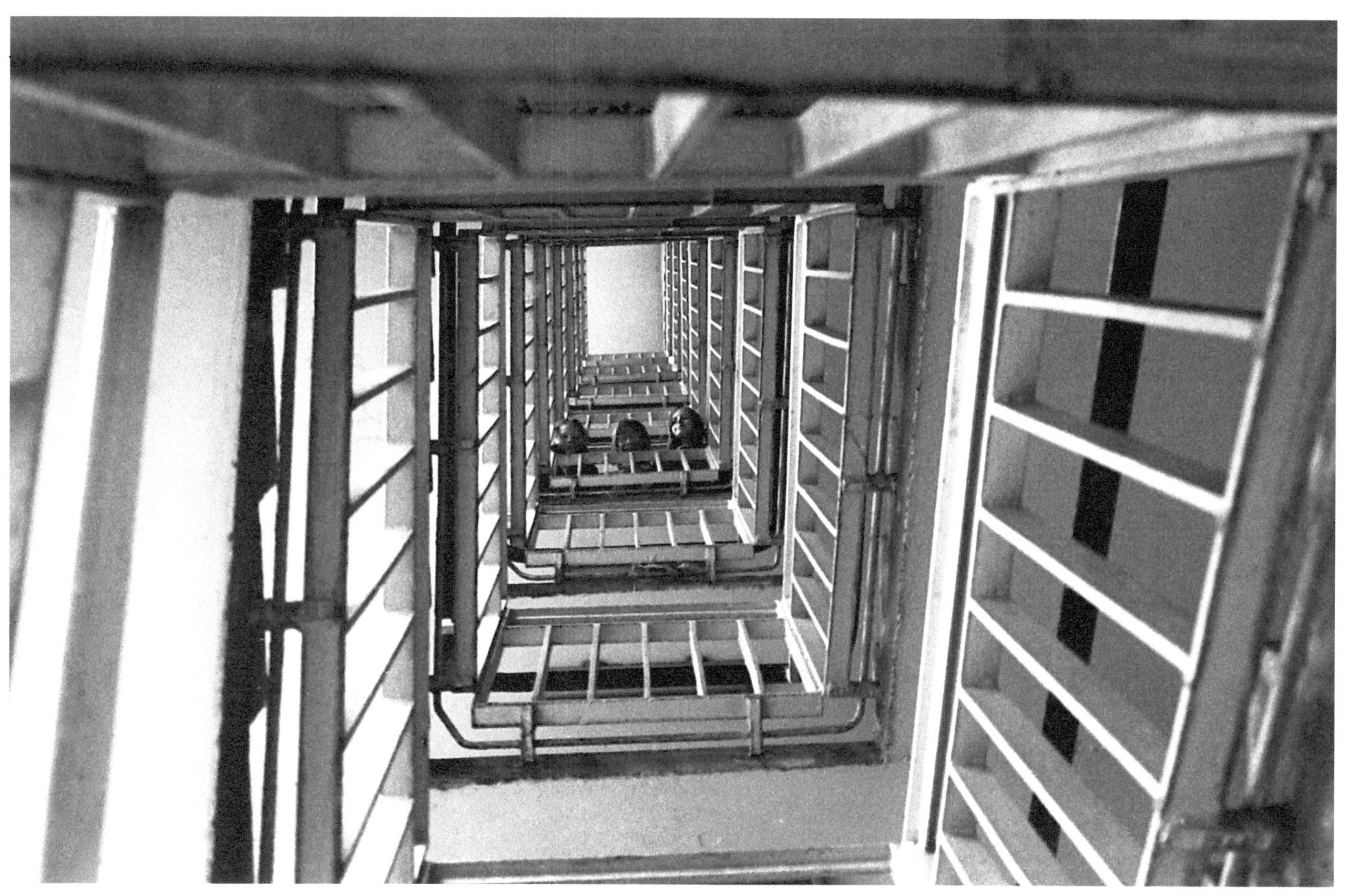

Possibly inspired by the Beatles album cover? Tina, Julie and my sister Anita looking down the stairwell at Park Hill in early 1970.

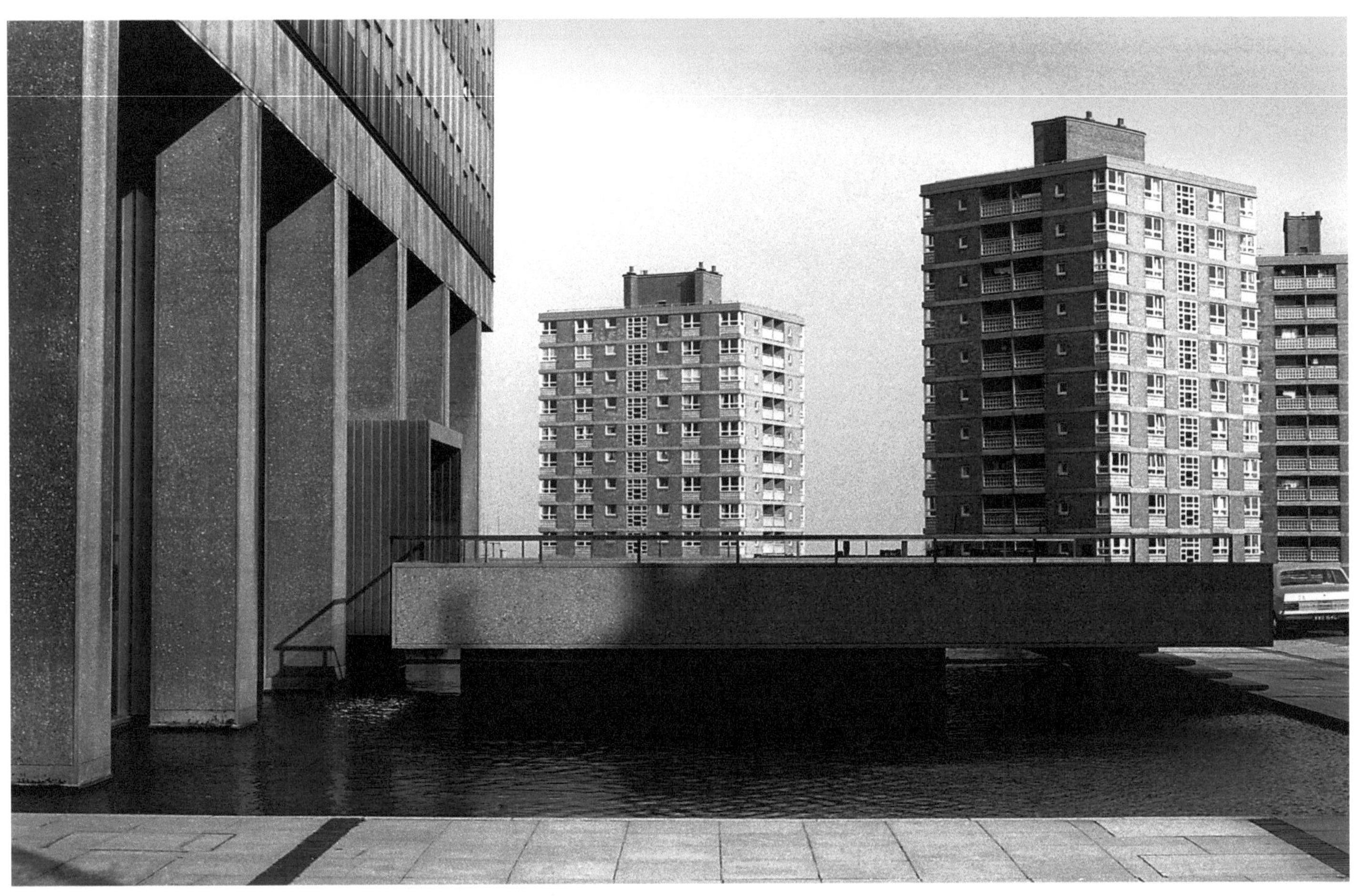

The Arts Tower steps and Netherthorpe flats. The architect's original concept of mixing water, open edges and students failed for some reason and was filled in.

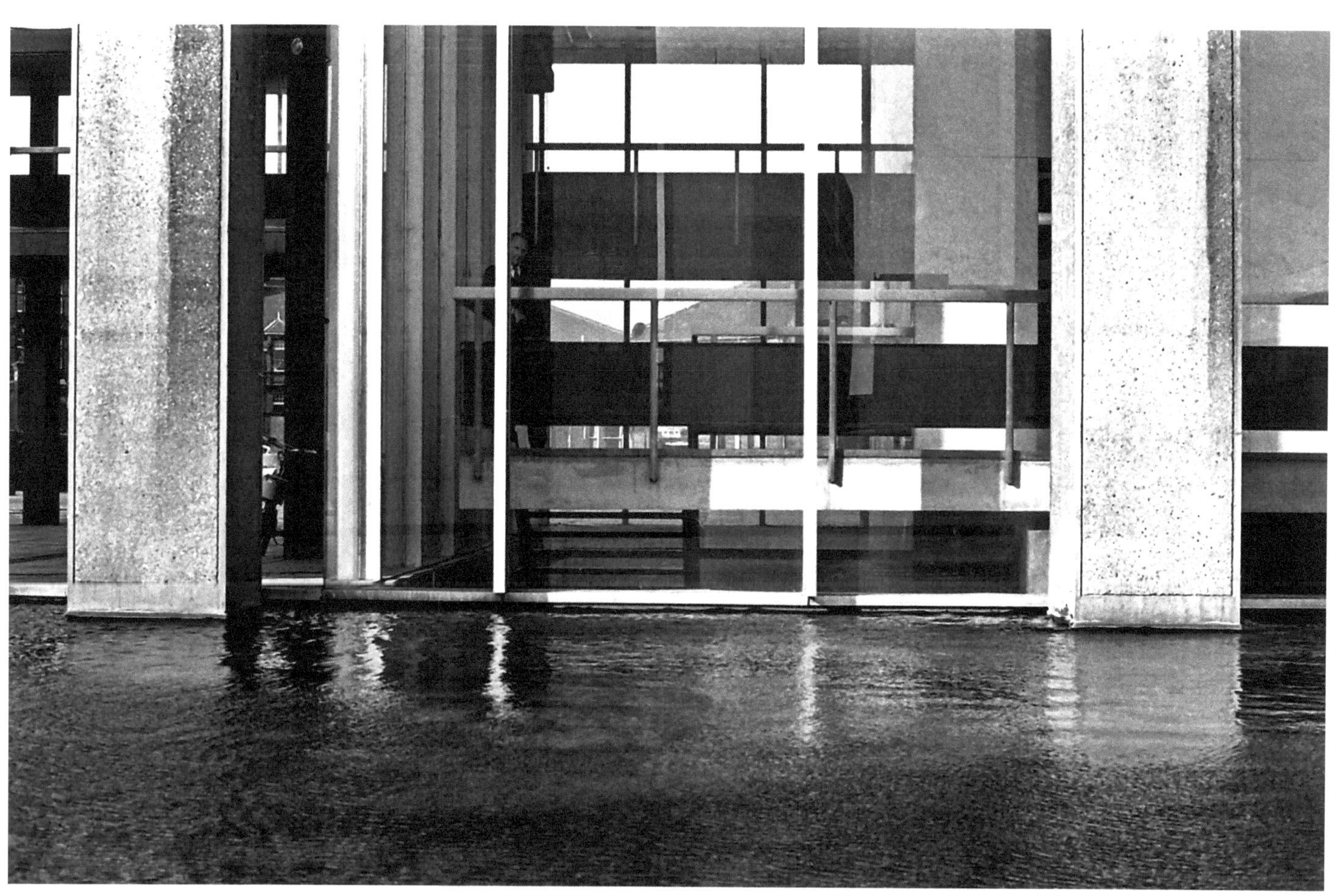

Still got that feeling of being watched.

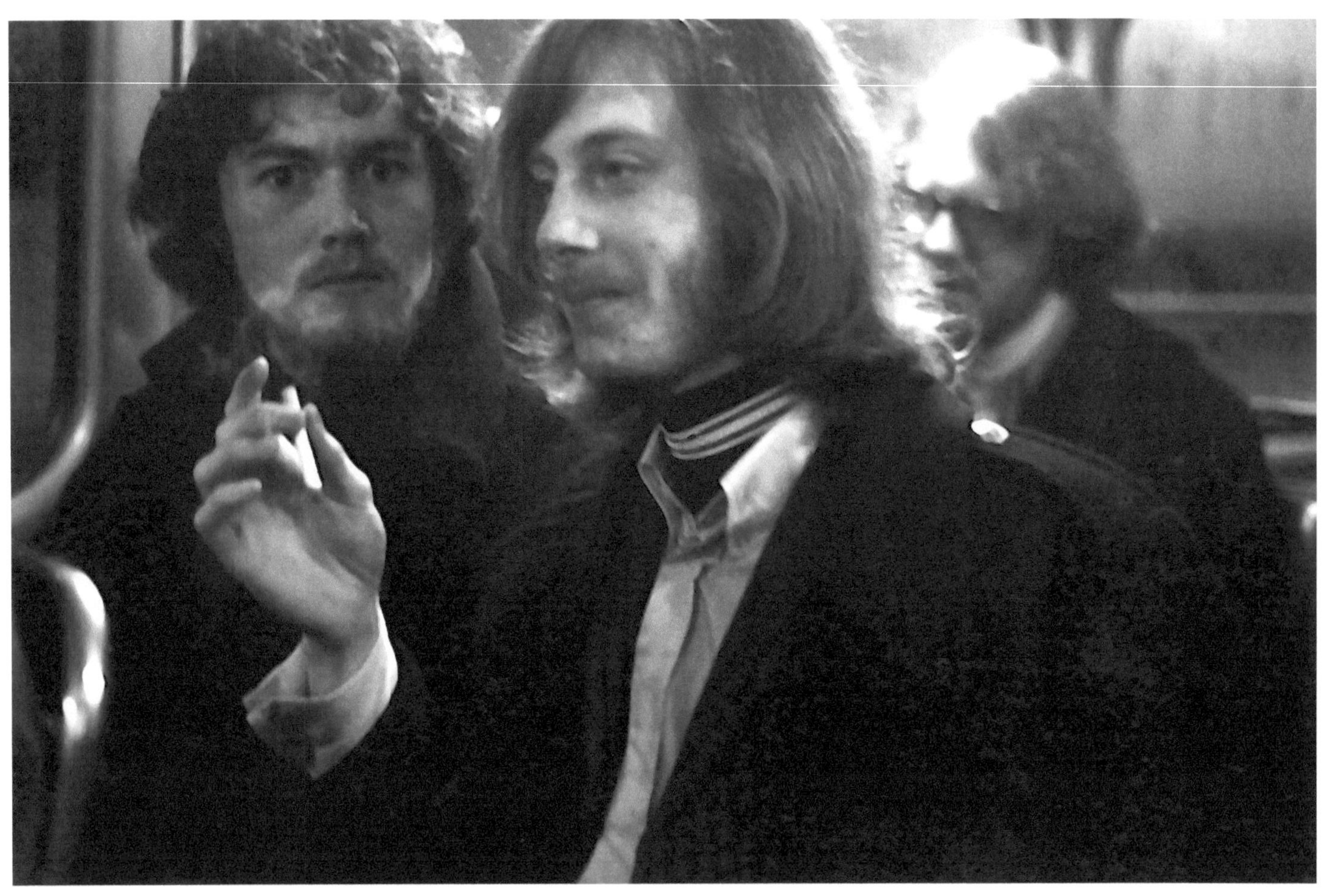

First year students on the bus. I hated going upstairs because I couldn't stand smoking, but that was where all the girls sat, and where the students hung out, so I had to go up.

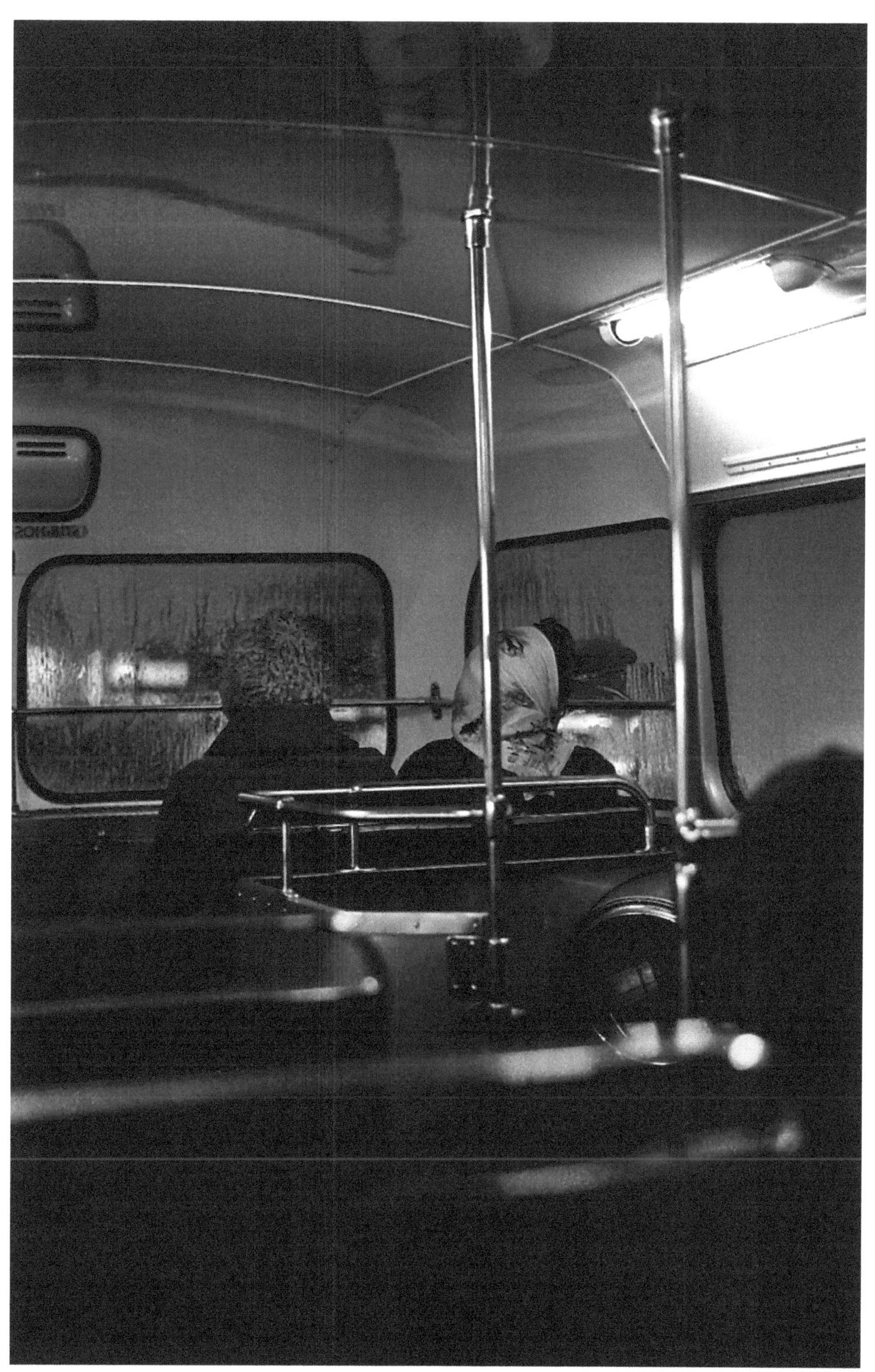

Steamed up windows on the top deck.

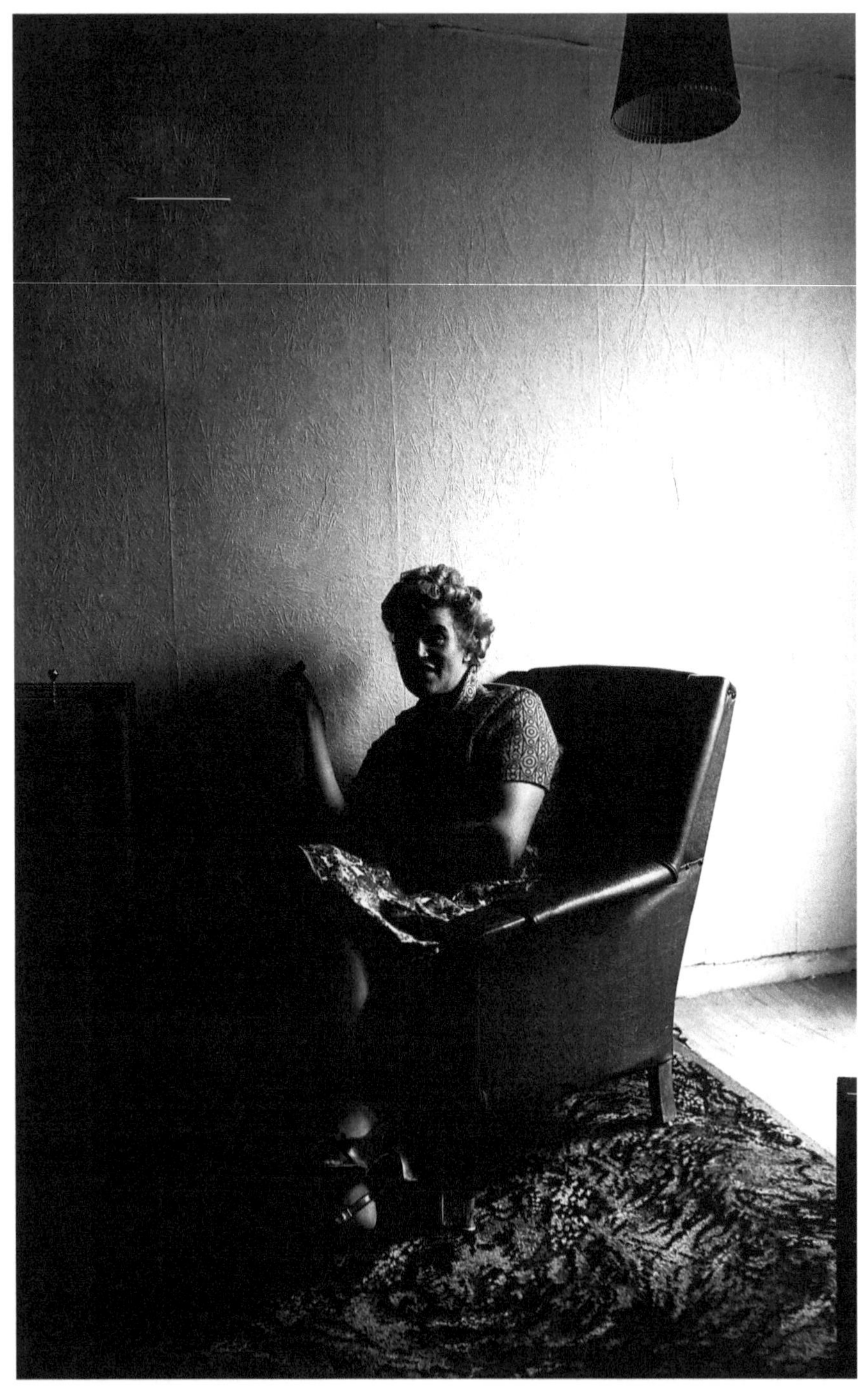

My mum: probably in her 40s here. Note the woodchip on the walls — mum did all the decorating because my dad was useless, but see how it doesn't quite reach the bottom in the corner: "Ah, it'll be all right," she'd say.

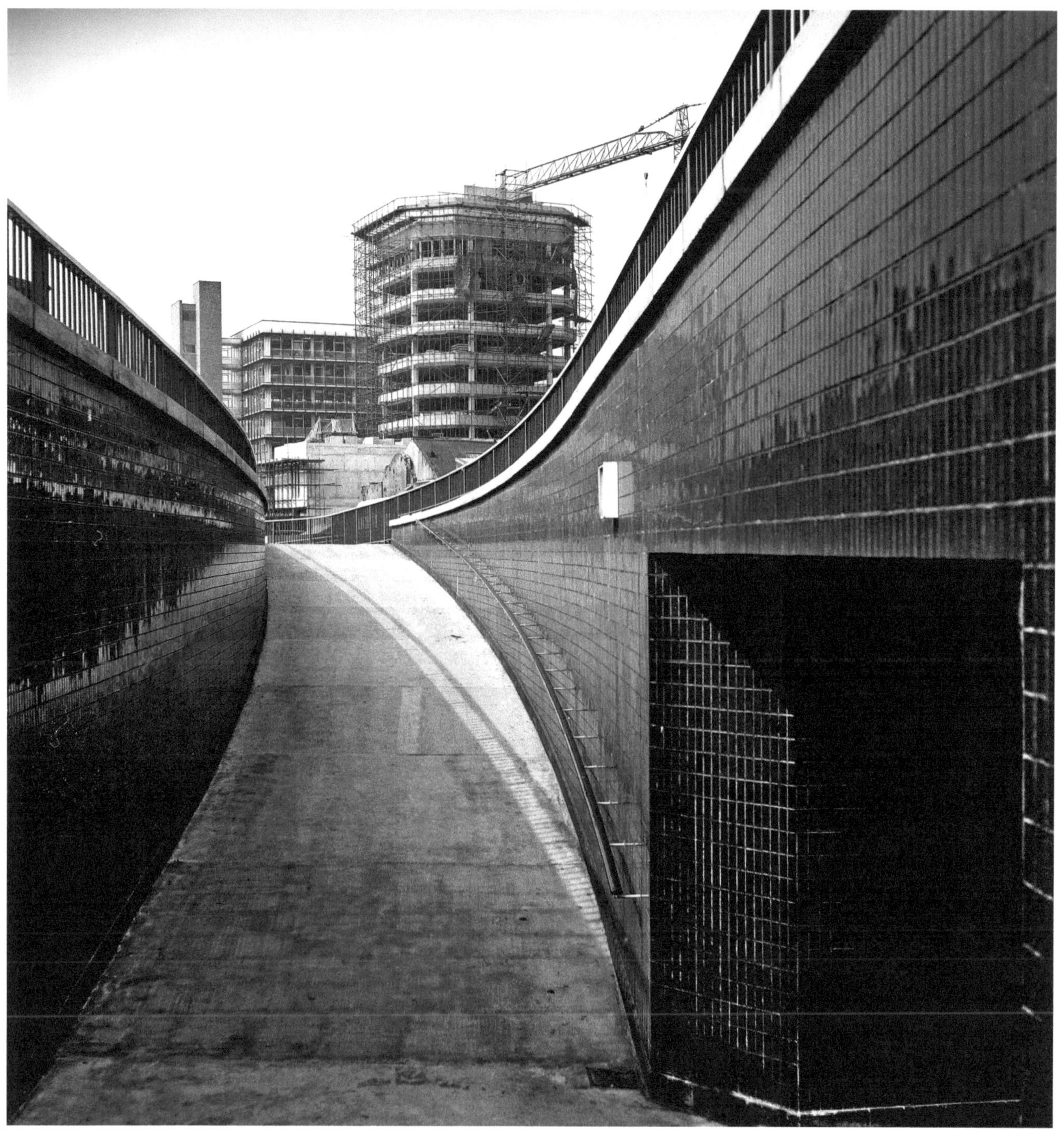

Underpass on Arundel Gate with the AEUW building under construction. I like the contrasts and the shininess of the tiles. Not many years later you wouldn't want to go down there, but at the time it was all new and futuristic.

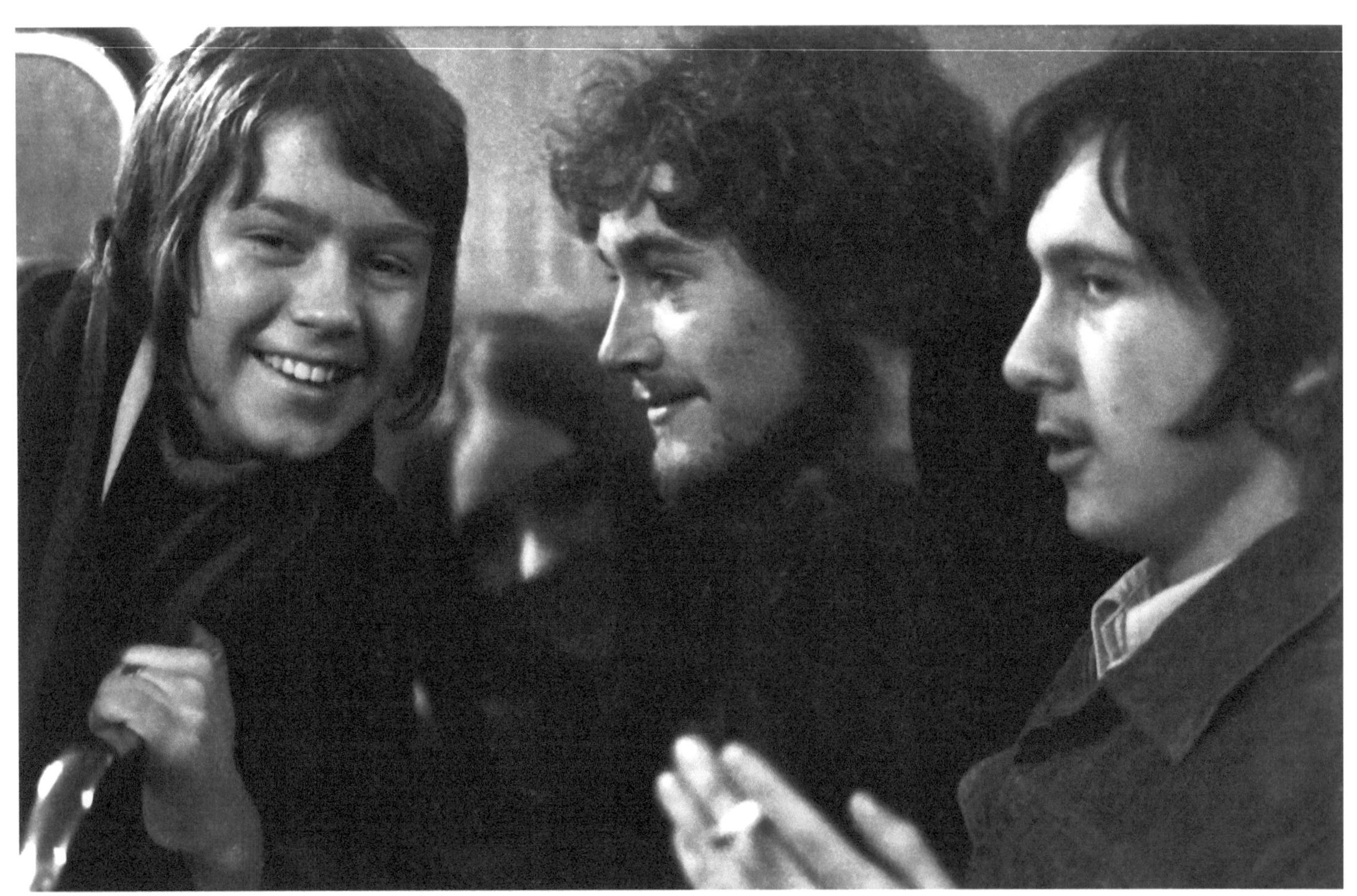

Students on the bus: Joan Parsons on the left in a college scarf was an amazing artist. Goodness knows what happened to my scarf, it was blue, white and black. I thought I looked intelligent when I wore it. But my friends knew different.

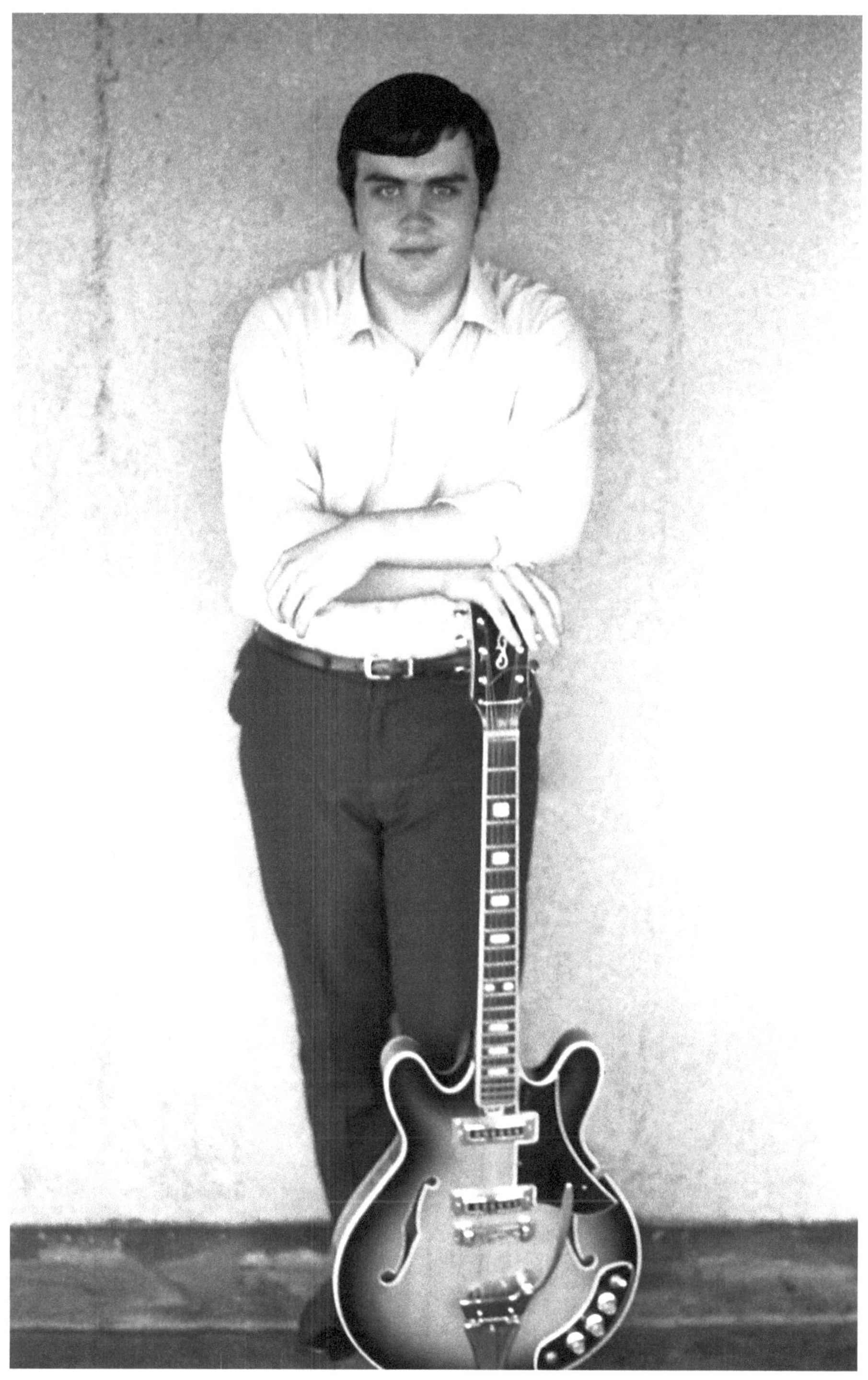

Kevin Cosgrove, Whitsuntide. He asked me to take a picture of him and his guitar — he is sadly no longer with us.

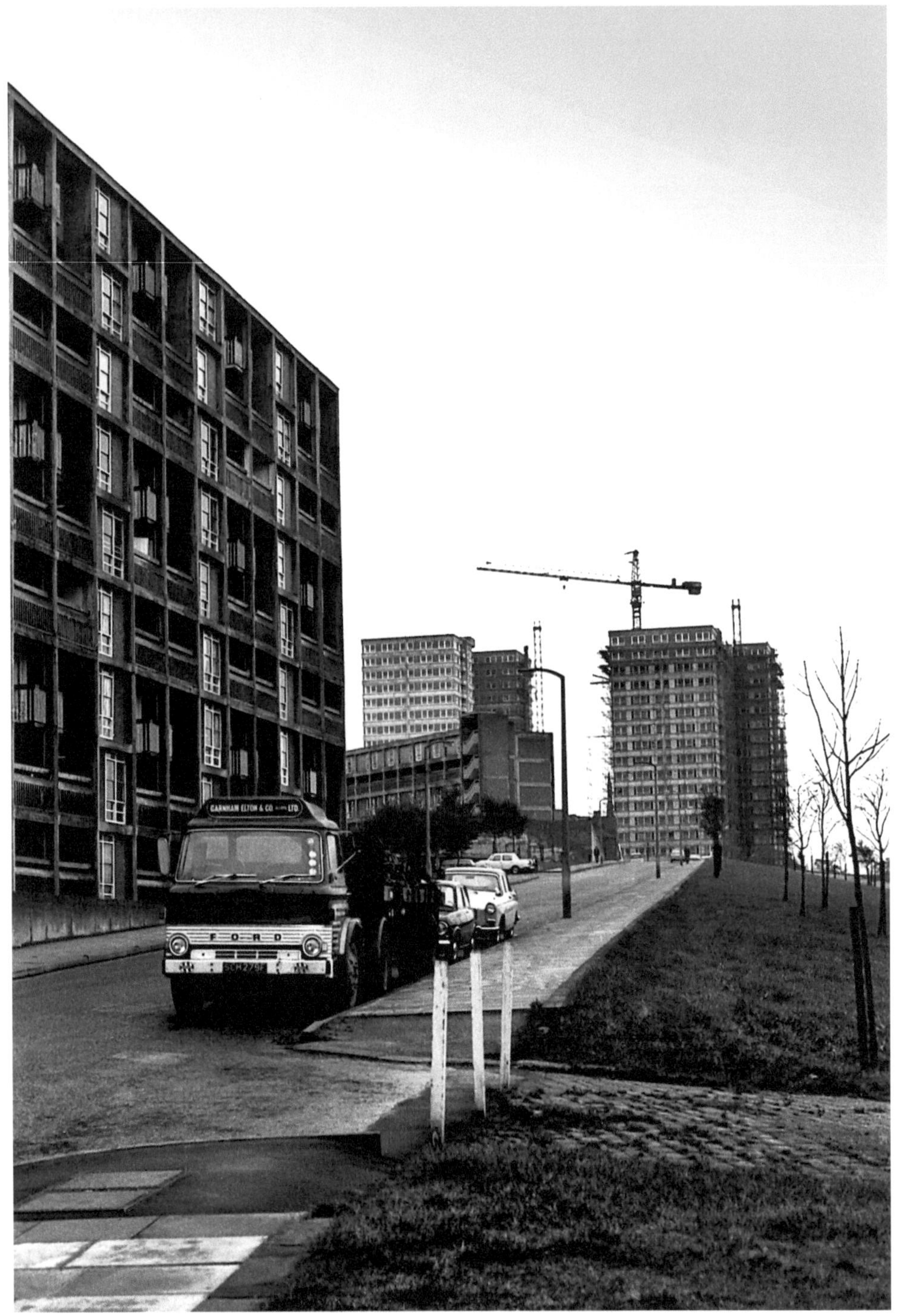

Looking up South Street. Claywood flats under construction. The little bit of cobbled road you can see was what was left of Norwich Street: part of the old Park District once referred to as "little Chicago."

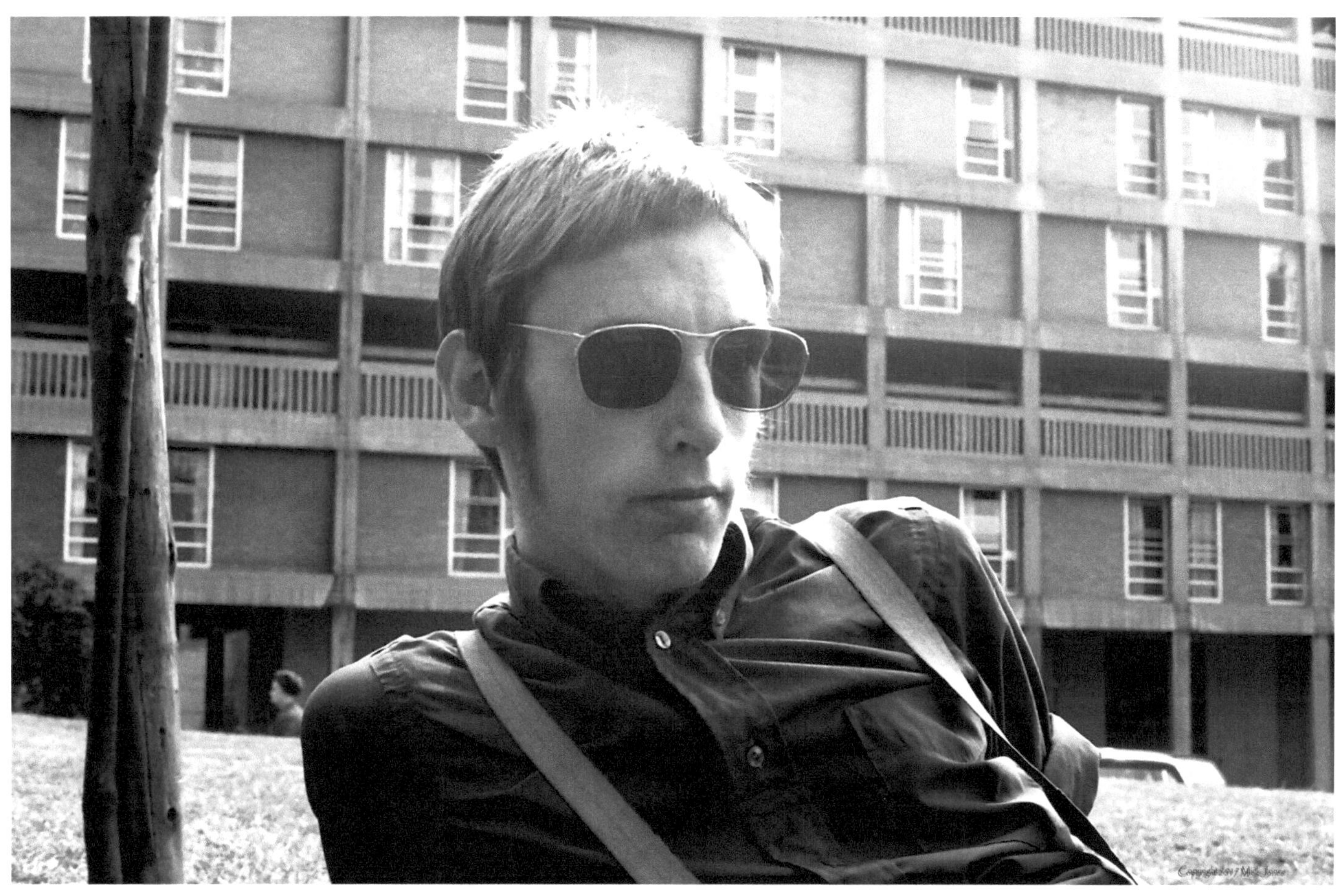

Lounging on the grass outside the flats.

Gary Drabble took this one of me: well, he pressed the button after I set it all up. Park Hill wasn't a concrete jungle: there were loads of grassy areas to sit around on, sunbathe, or listen to music — then if we saw some girls we'd shout them over. They usually took one look at me and bailed out.

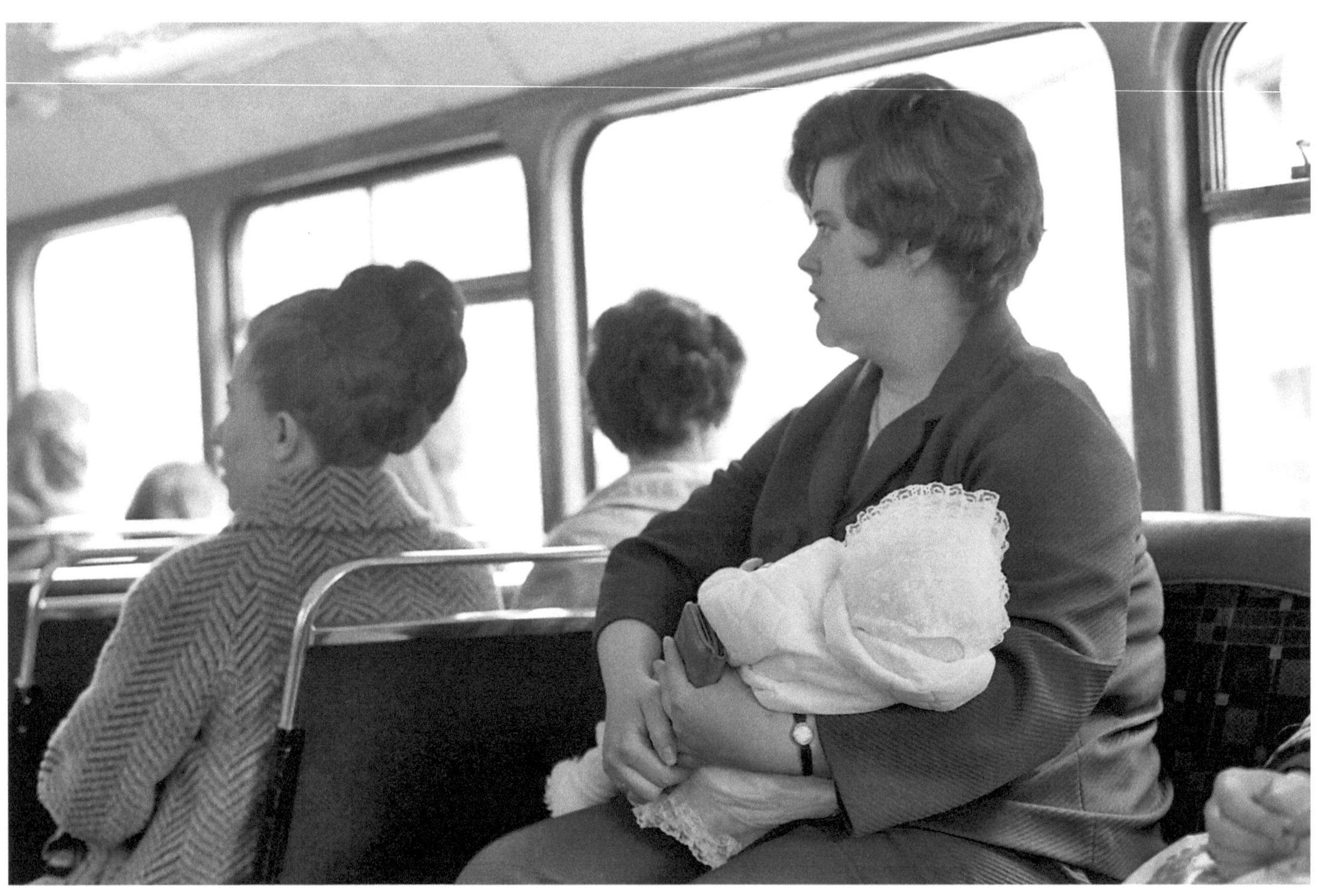

Someone called Lisa Hill came forward having seen this on a social media post. She'd recognised the woman as her mum — so that was her in her mum's arms!

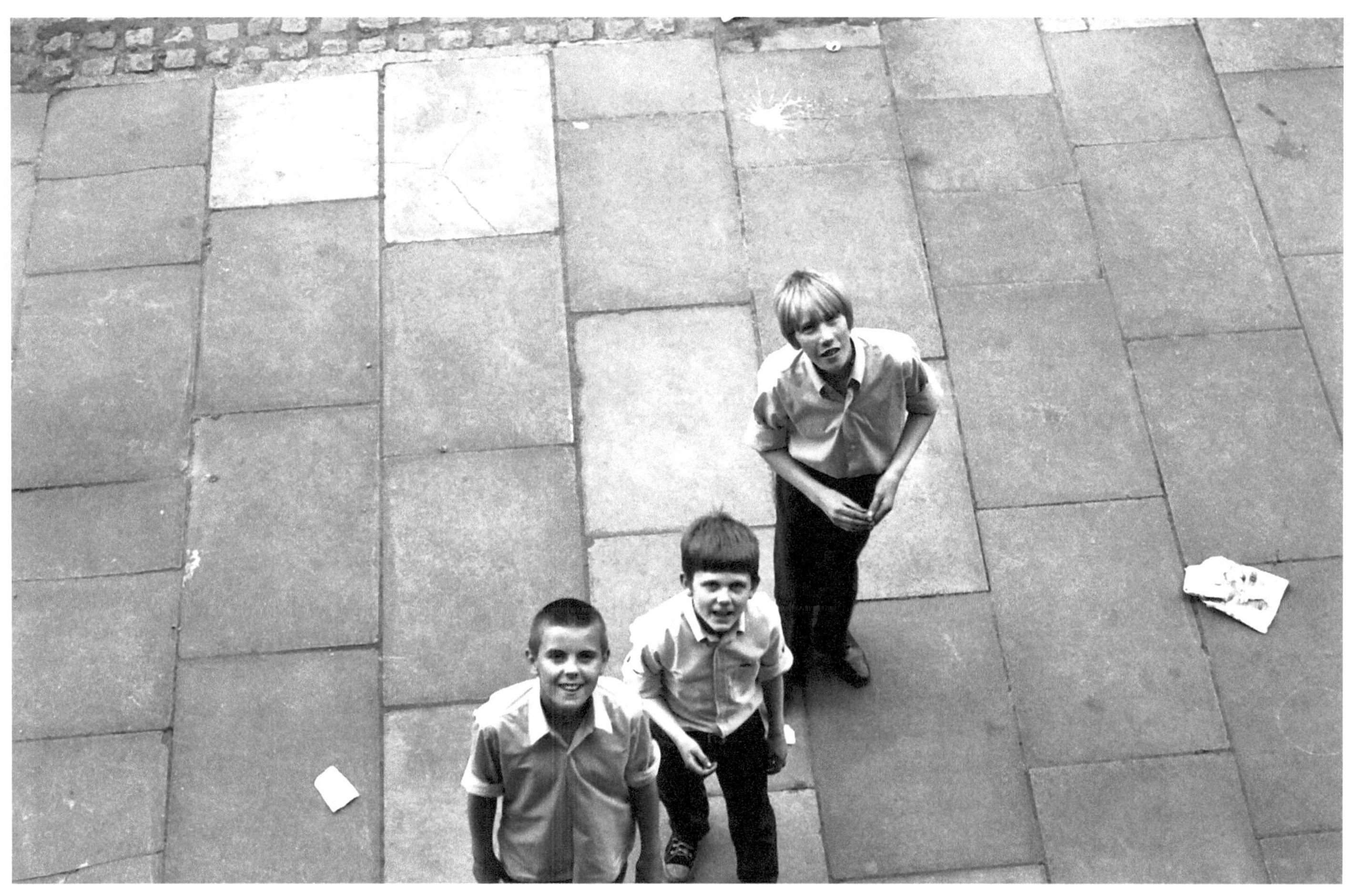

Neil Mappin, Alan Donohoe and Kenny Haywood — friends of our Sean, looking up towards the link. I was stood on Hague Row when I took this photograph.

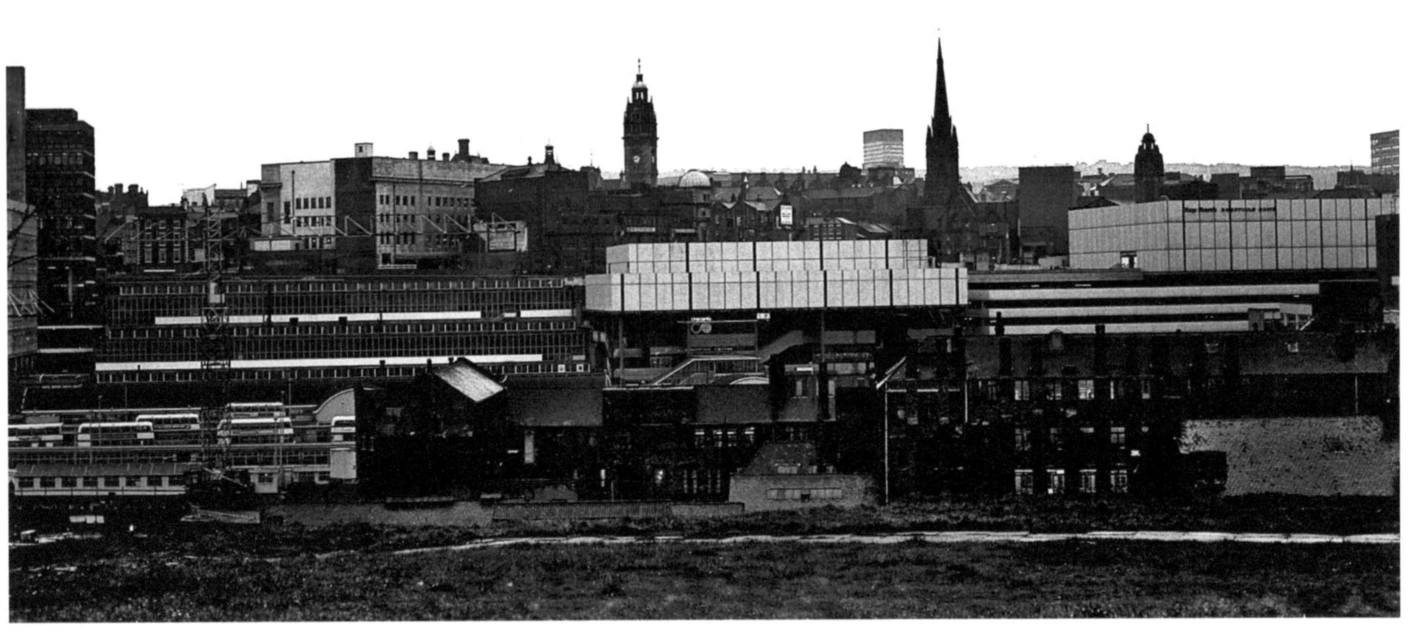

Town from the Hill with the Fiesta and Top Rank night clubs in the mid distance. We were only seventeen but used to get away with going into pubs and clubs — well most of the time. Once, all my mates were outside at the Blue Bell. I had gone to the bar and was returnin with six pints to find them lined up against the wall by some coppers for under-aged drinking. I returned to the bar sharpish — I only briefly considered drinking the six pints before deciding it was wiser to just scarper.

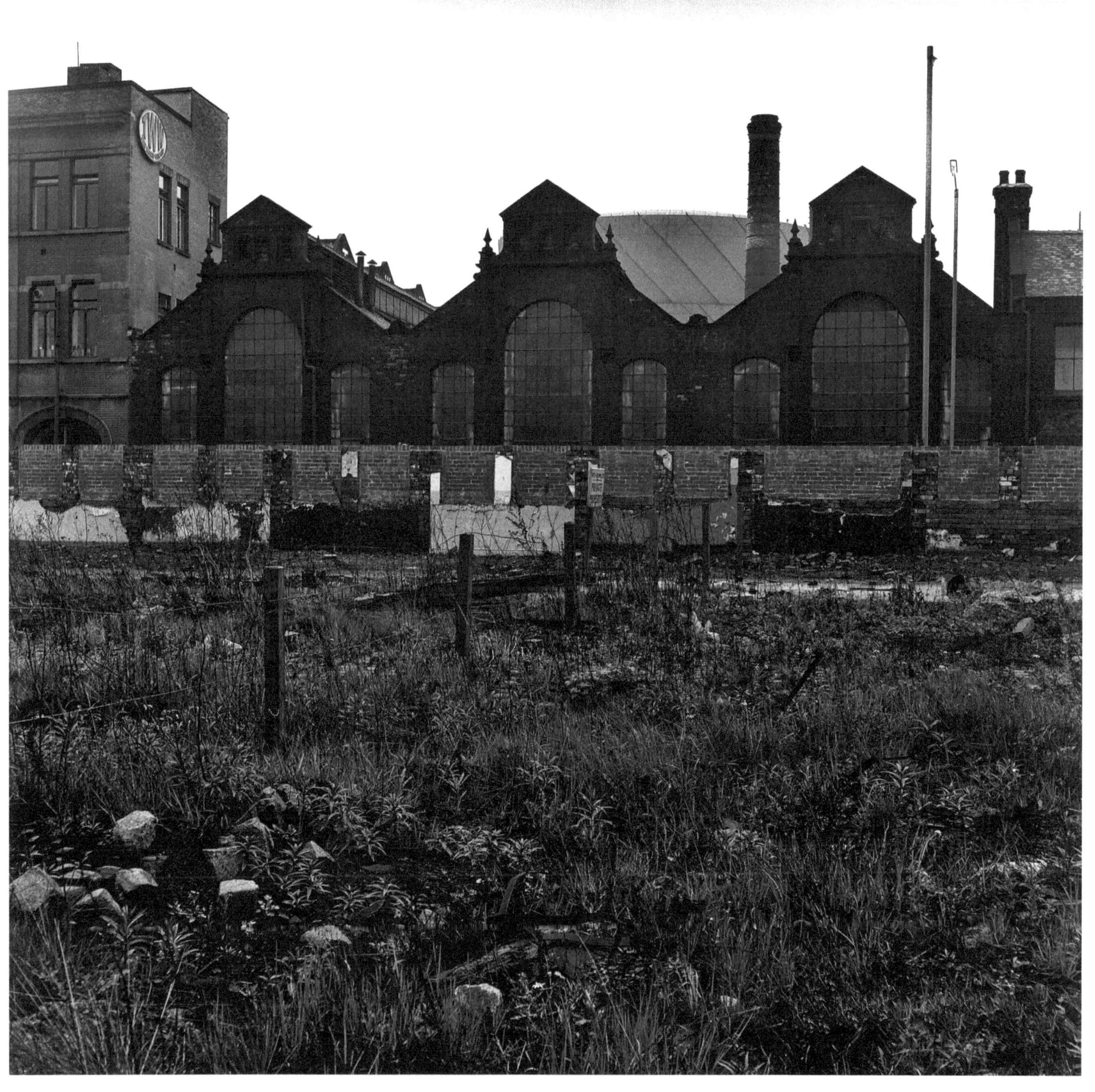

Savile Street from the old Wicker goods yard : Thomas Ward's factory; now Vauxhall
Pentagon.

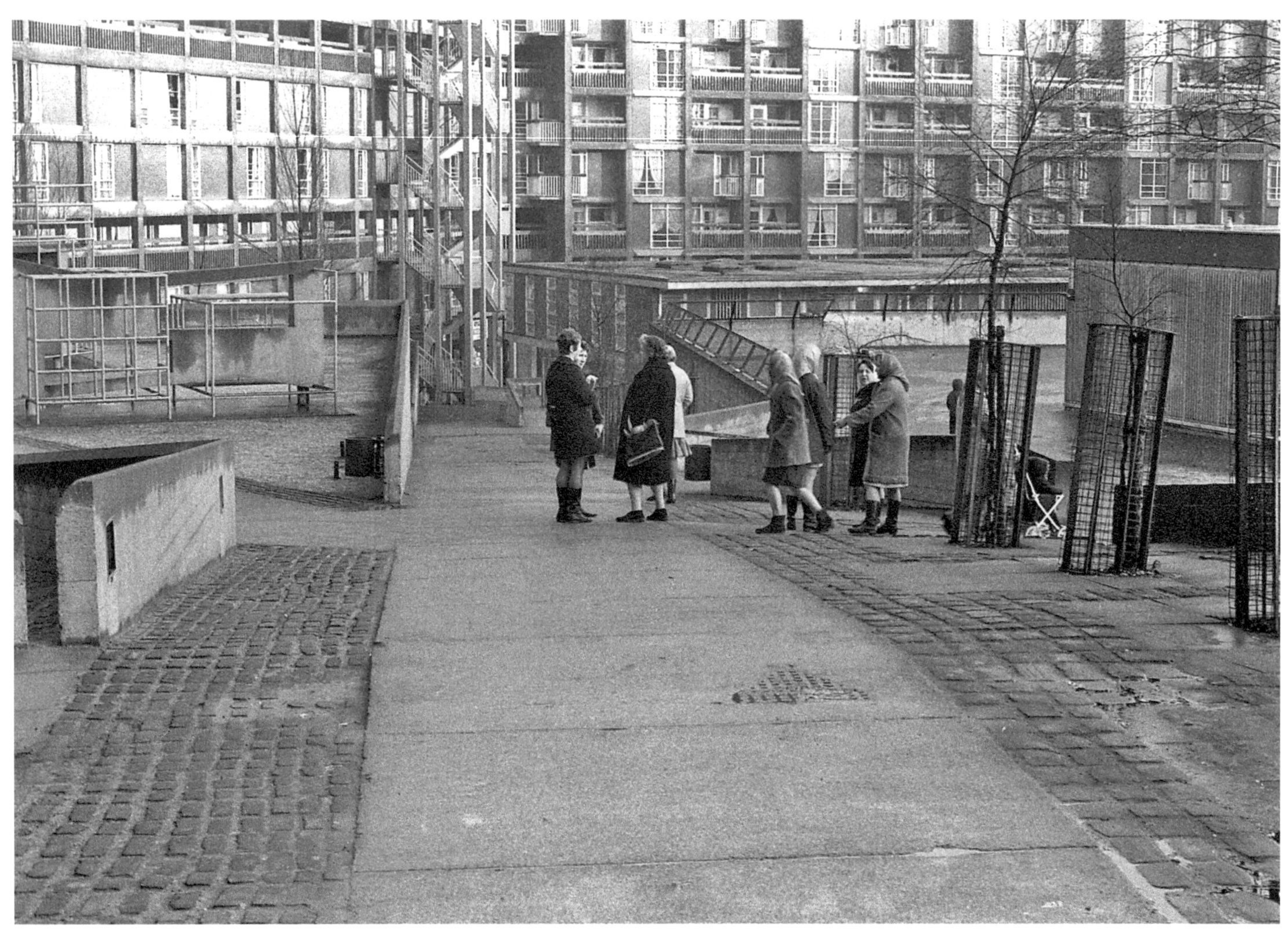

The school run, 1969. Taken outside the Scottish Queen, with the washhouse to the left and the bars that kids used to play on — and fall off. Most families had an old pram to carry the washing to and from the washhouse.

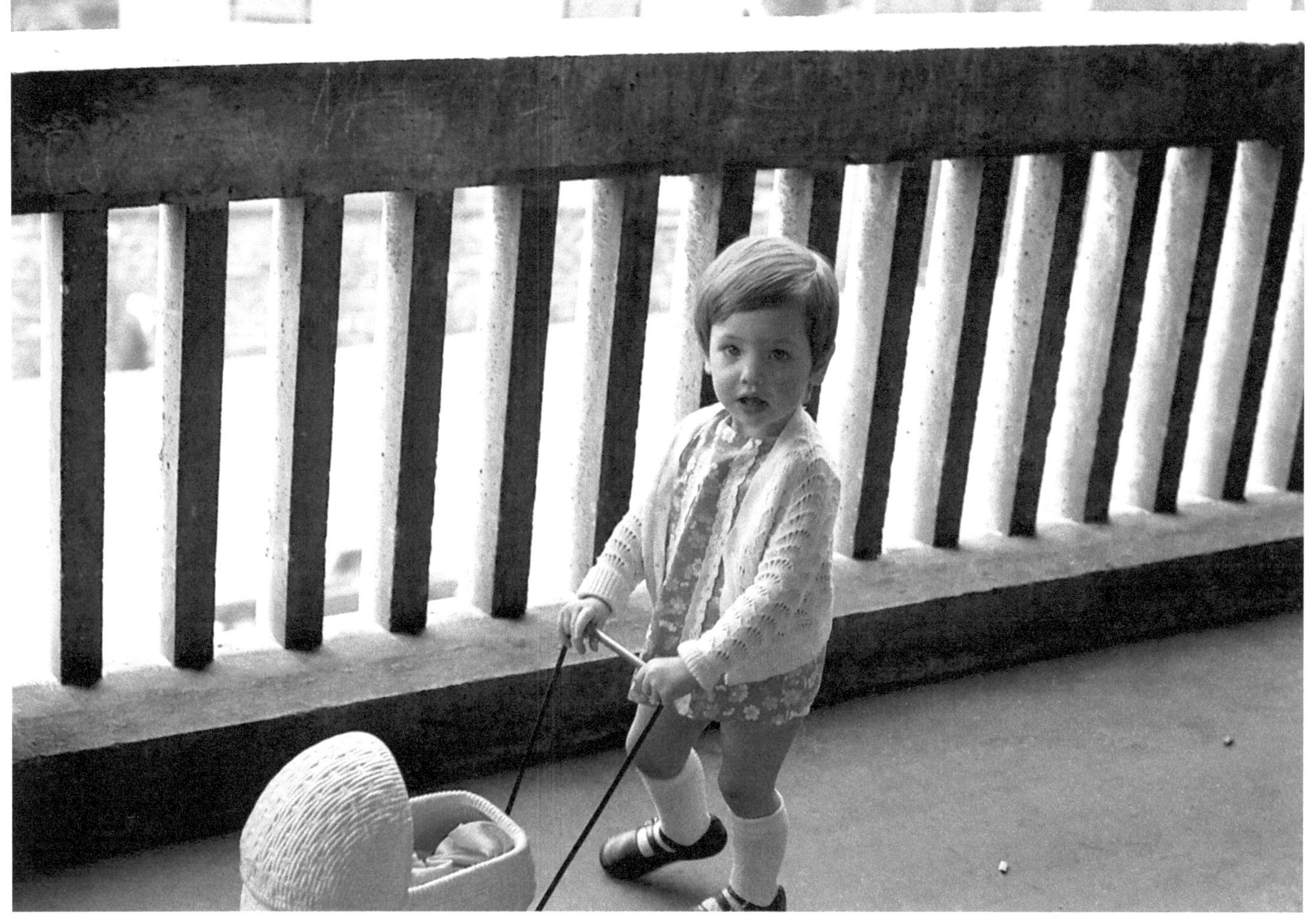

Lisa Calcott in her Sunday best. The Calcotts lived near us; they had a famous fishing tackle shop off the Wicker — it was badly hit in the 2007 floods and never recovered.

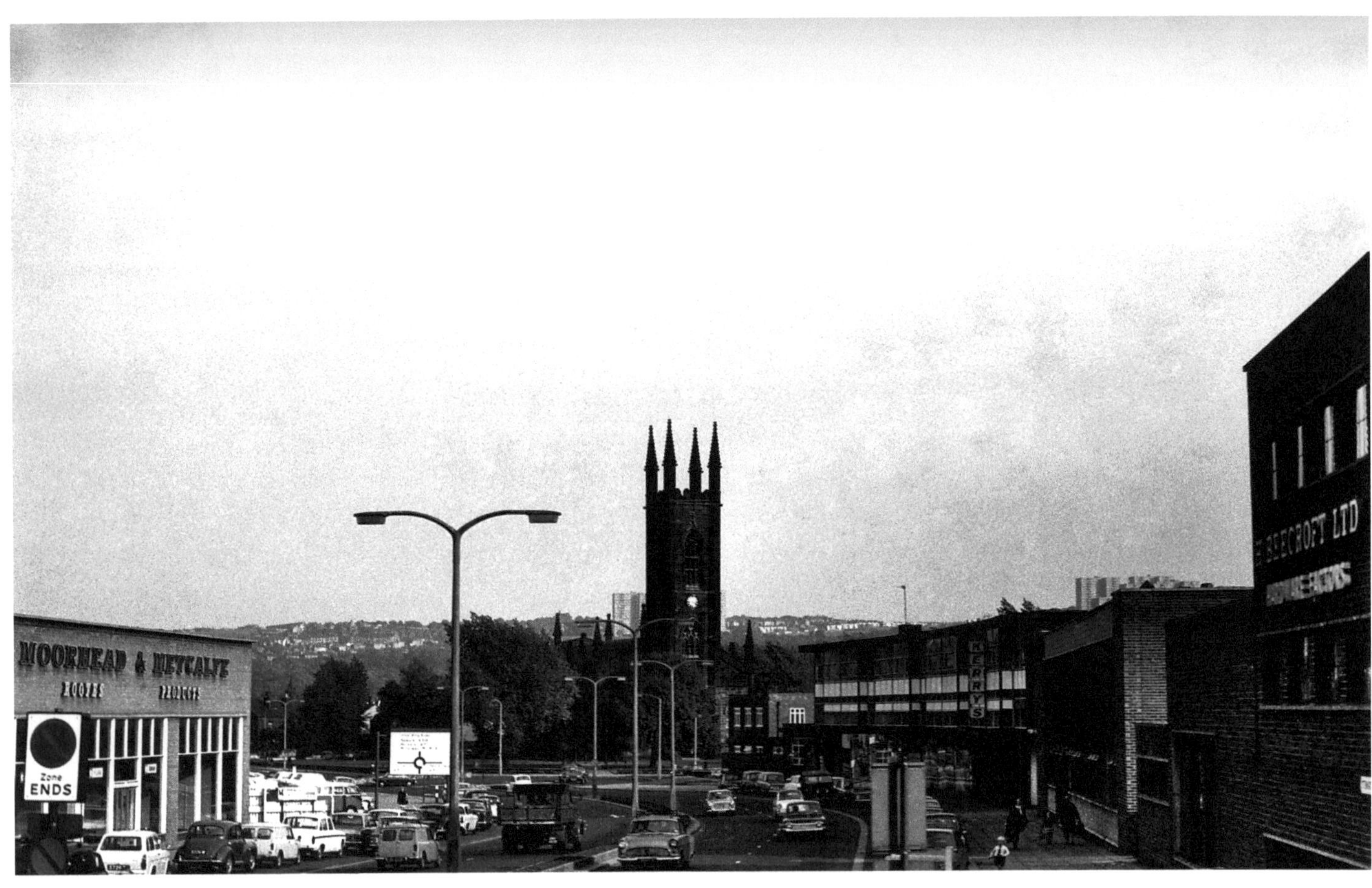

St Mary's Road — people forgot what colour some of these old buildings were supposed to be: the stone was black from soot. There used to be a disco at the church hall that skinheads used to go to — I remember the floor moving as everyone was jumping up and down.

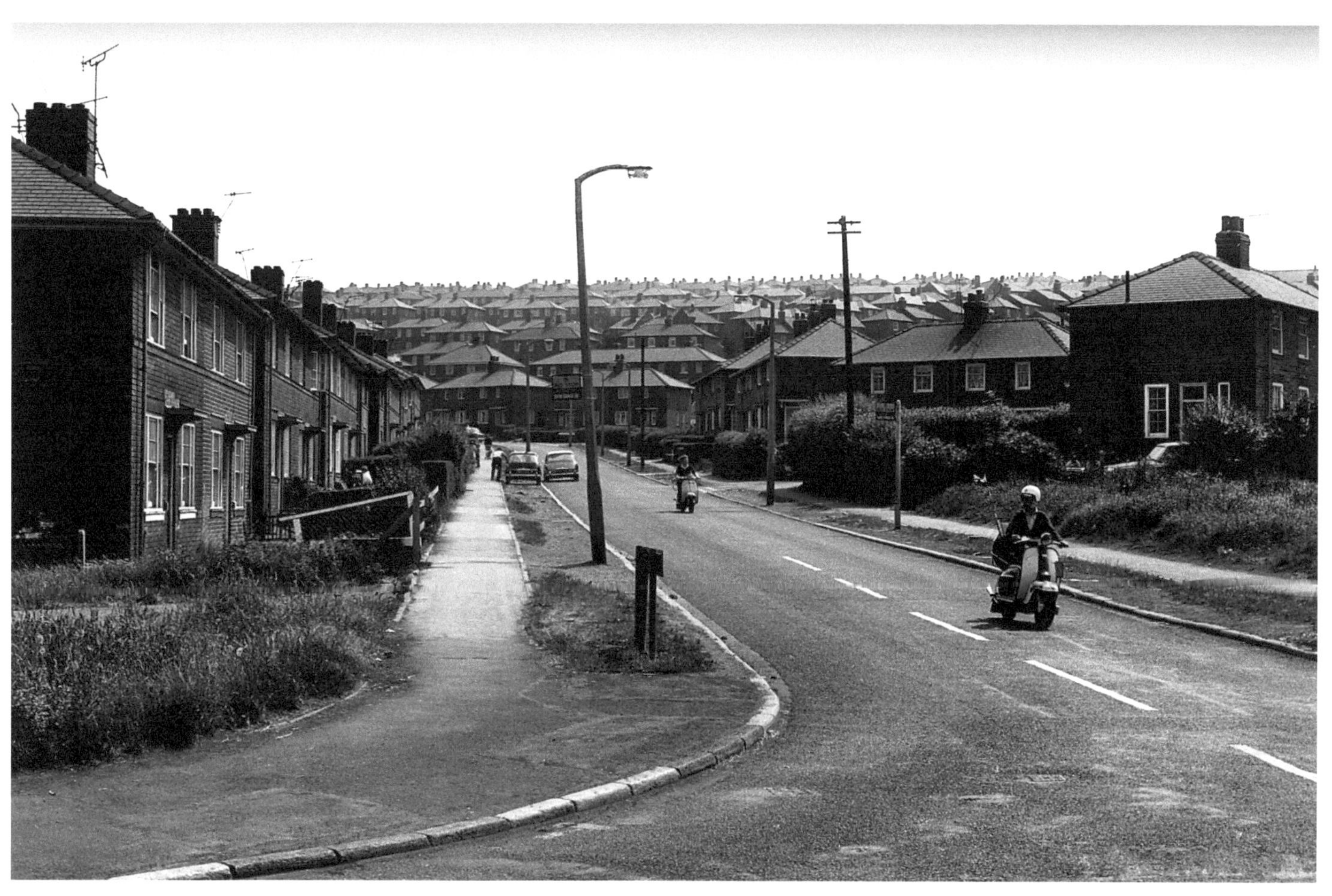

Cricket Inn Crescent and the Wybourn Estate. I used to wish I had a Lambretta, but it was out of my league. Closest I got to a scooter was a Tri-Ang when I was about six.

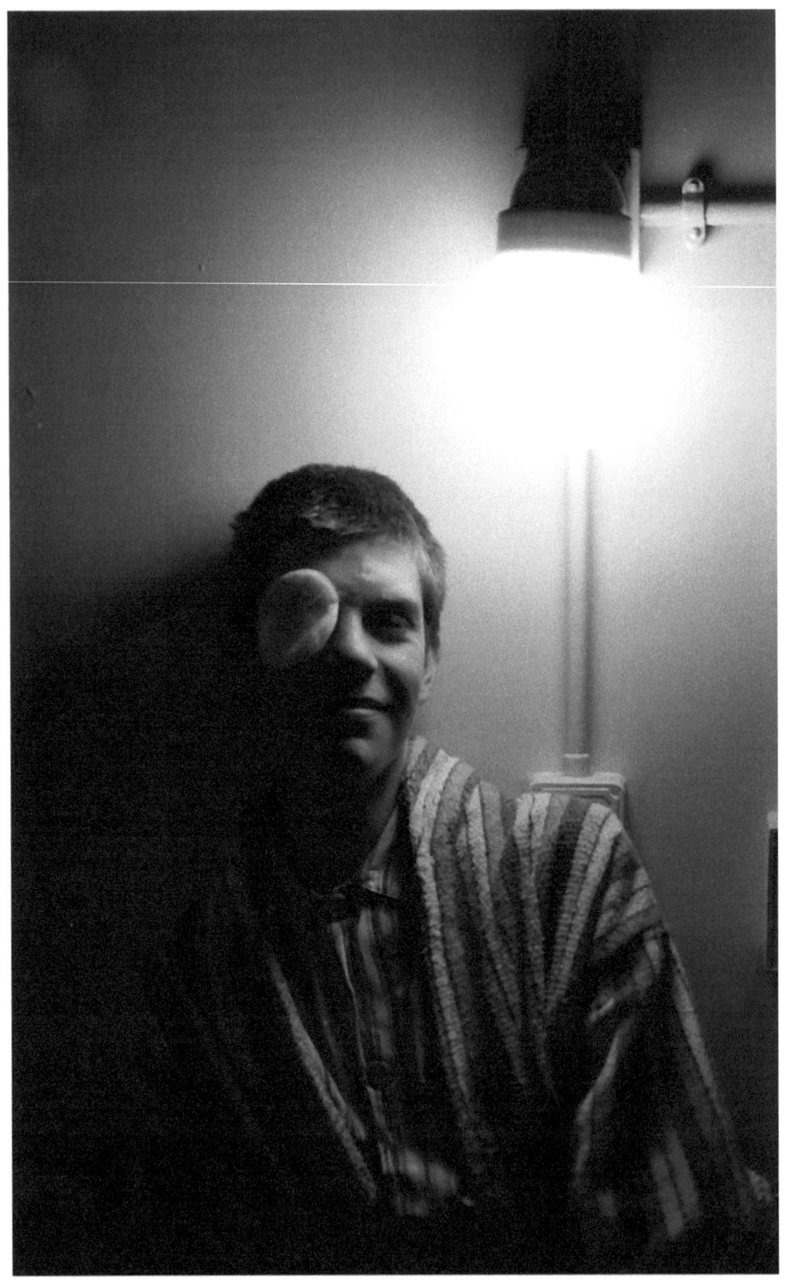

My brother after he injured his eye at Osborn Mushet tools. I was fortunate in getting to go to college: I was probably the more academic one and they couldn't afford to send him to college too so he started working at 15. I was a bit jealous of his £4 a week. The apprentices had a gang: "the nail gang" — they wore a bent nail on their lapels. It was when bending a nail that it went in his eye. He still got £500 compensation for lack of eye protection.

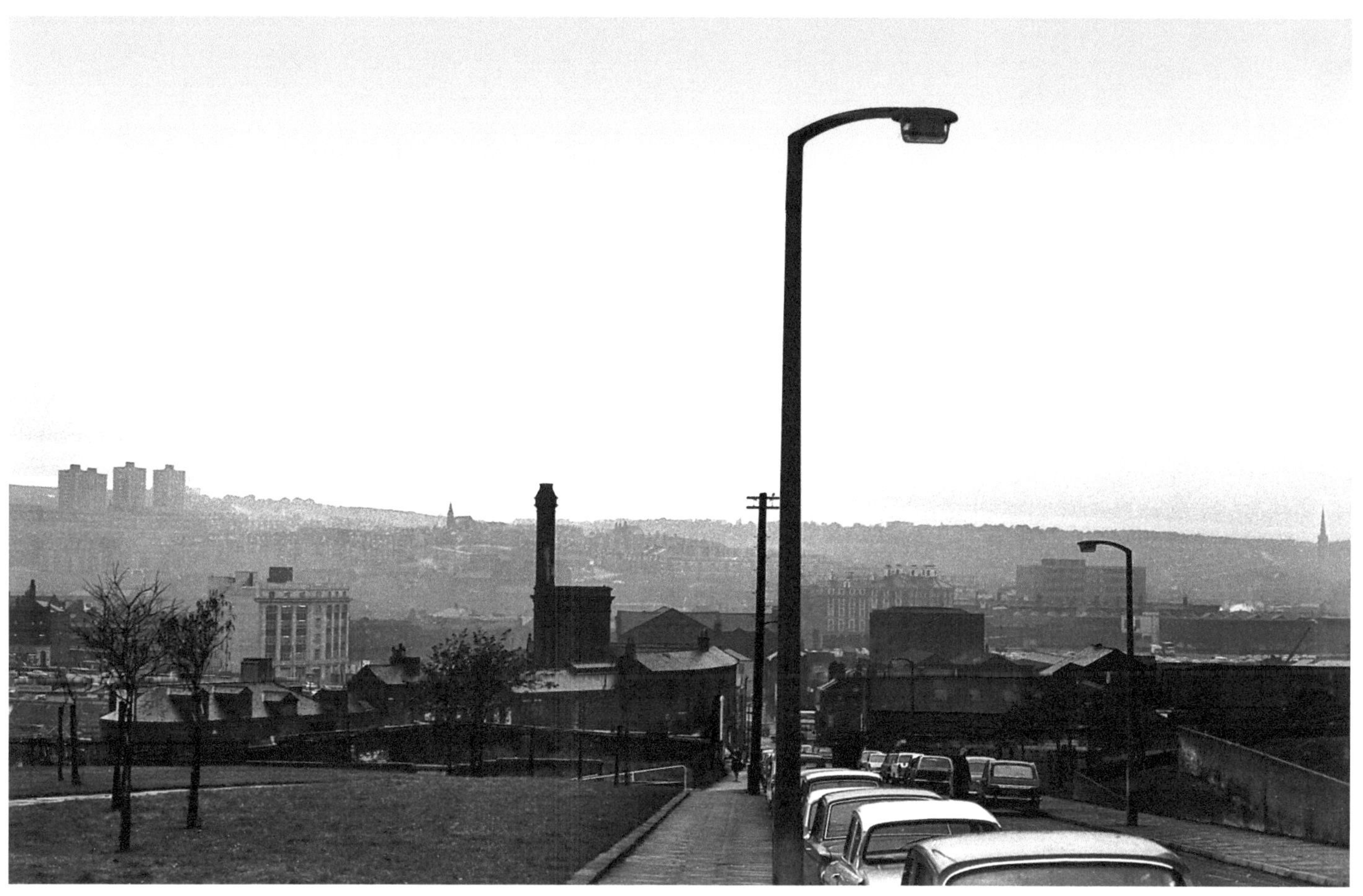

Looking down South Street towards town. At the bottom of the hill was the canal basin; there was a rowing boat place there where we'd sometimes hire boats and row up the canal. When out of sight we used to have fights, splashing with the oars and getting each other soaked. Inevitably an oar would get broken and the bloke would go mad. Guaranteed we'd have some sort of rash the next day from the polluted water — it was always a funny colour.

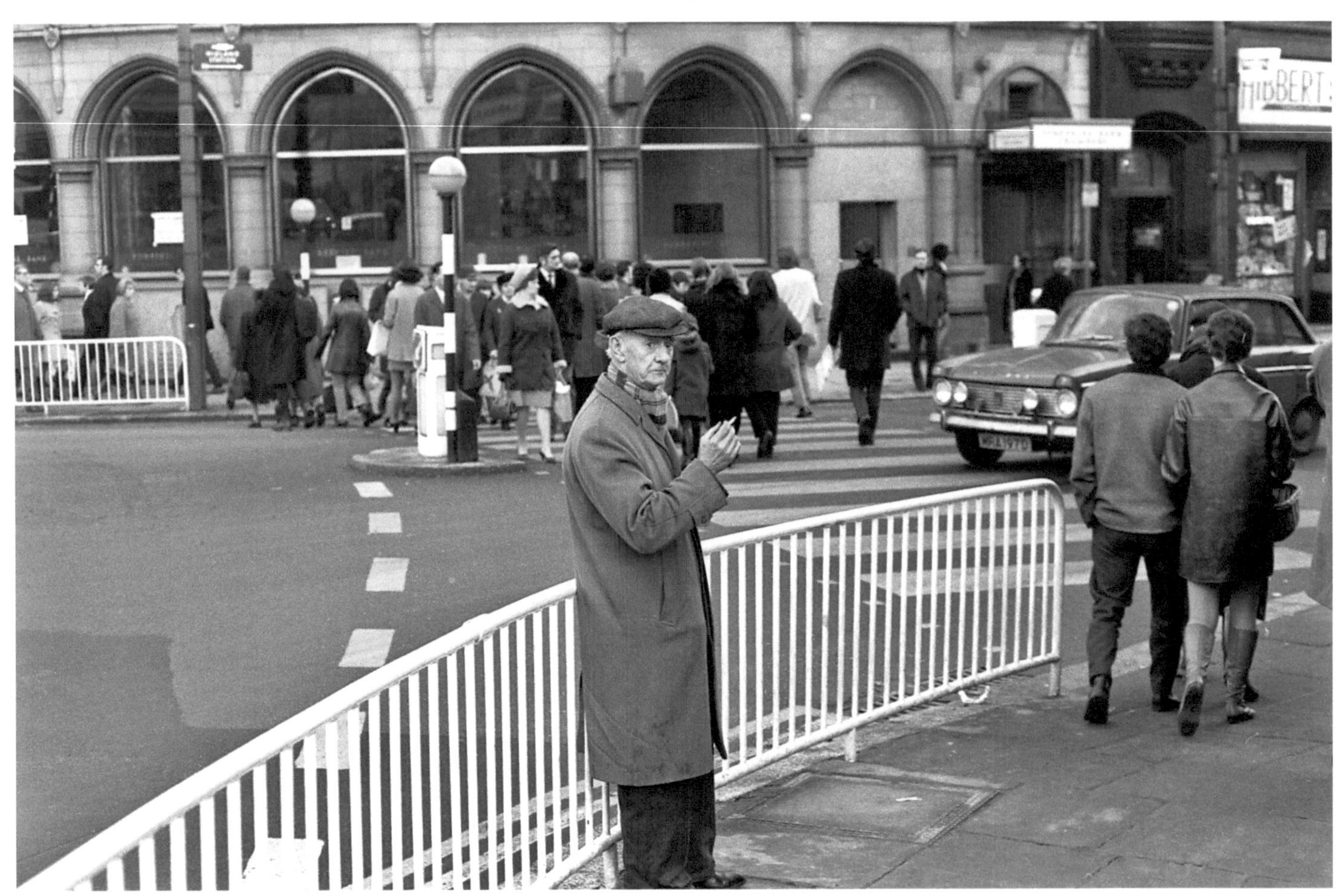

End of Surrey Street

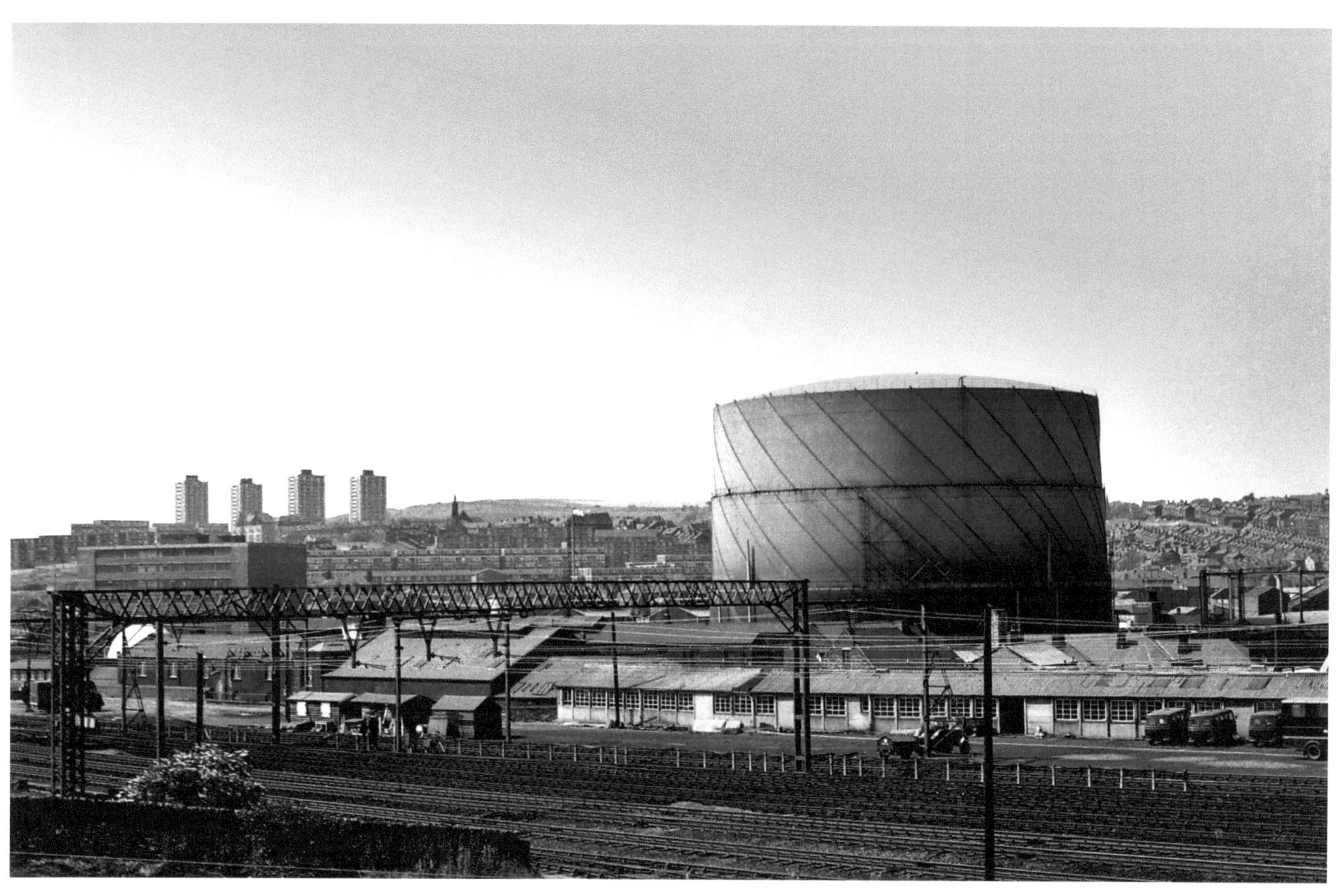

Overlooking Nunnery sidings and Effingham Street Gas holder. Four and a half years later there was an explosion at the gas works in which six people died.

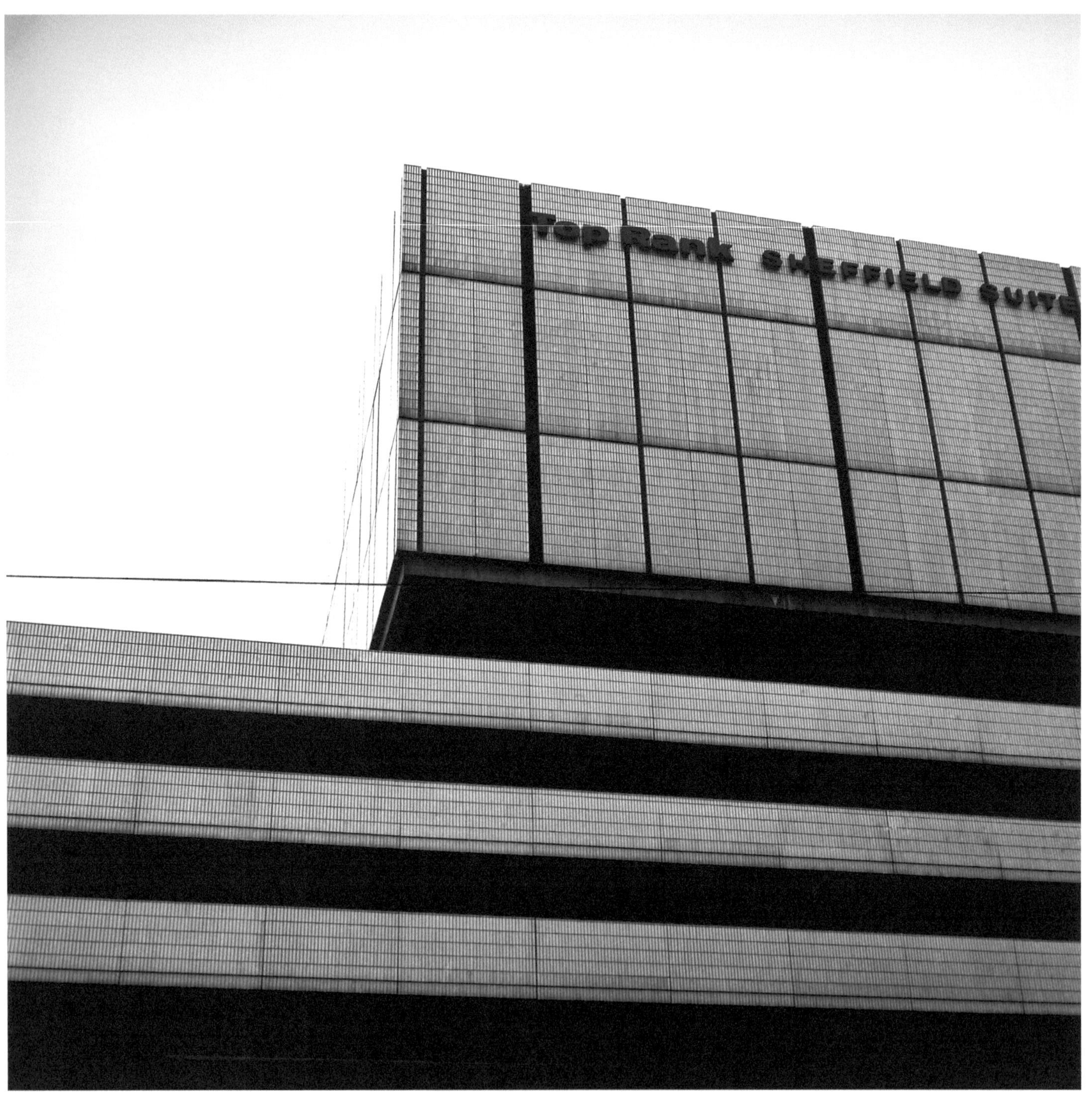

I saw some of the greats at the Top Rank: The Four Tops, Jimmy Ruffin, and The Temptations. Living on Park Hill meant we could walk to all the night clubs in just a few minutes. Staggering home at 2:00am took rather longer.

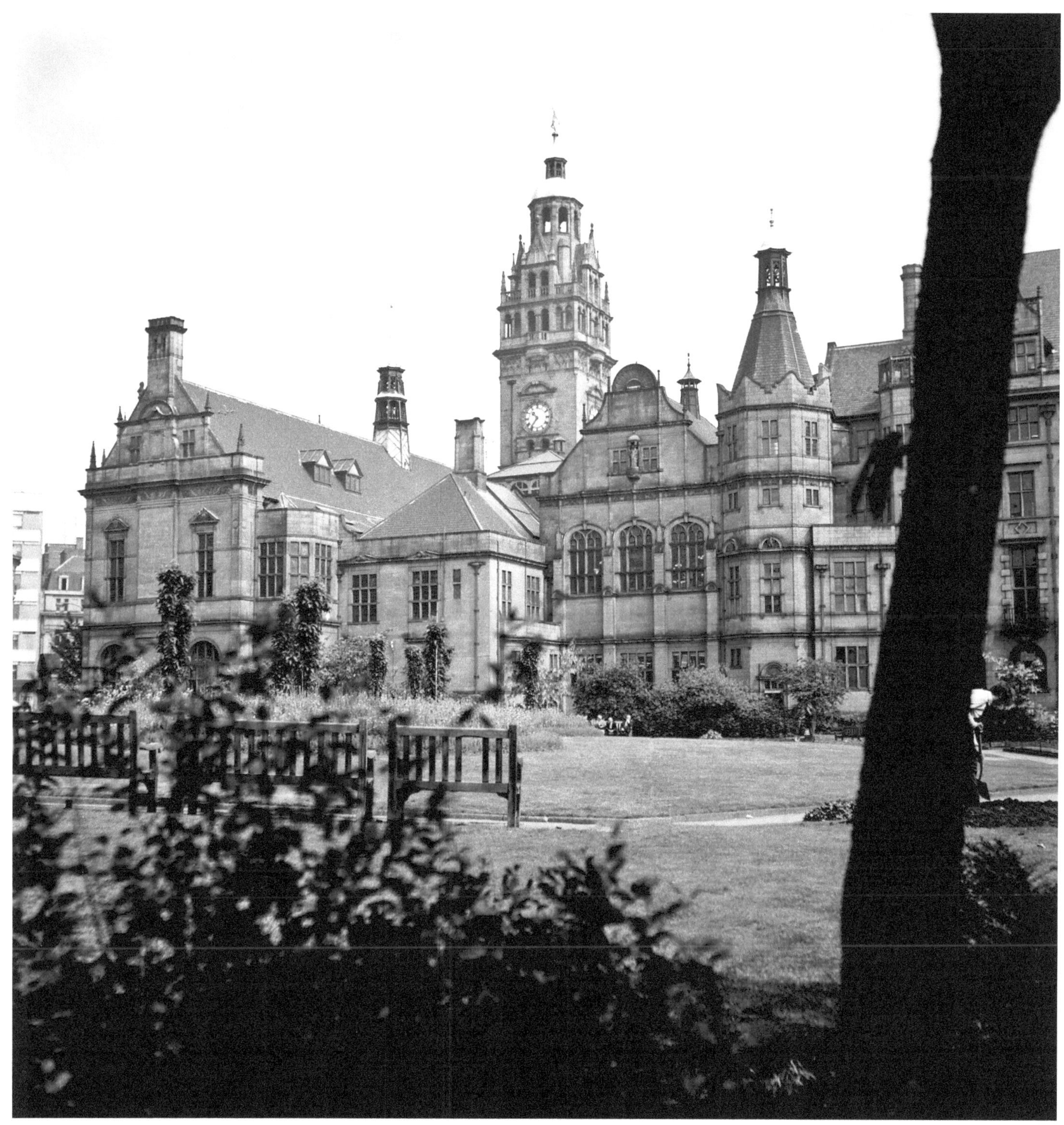

The Peace Gardens as they used to be, early summer 1970.

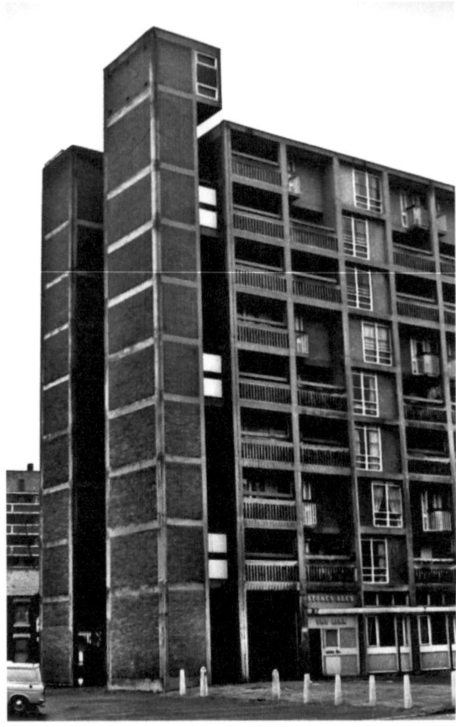

This was where I lived between 1961 and 1974. It was the family home and inspired the title of this book. It's Park Hill Flats of course, and our house was on the second landing, which was called Long Henry Row. The landings can be recognised by the white facia attached to the lift shaft. Our kitchen was the first one to the right with mum and dad's bedroom above, and to the right of the bedroom was the living room. It was on "the Hill" that I took some of my photographs and got much of my inspiration whilst at Sheffield College of Art between 1968 and 1970.

A few people have helped and influenced me over the years. Apart from my family and my dear wife of 46 years, Sue, I can probably count them on one hand. One such person who taught me all about photography was Emeritus Professor Roger Taylor. He was my tutor between 1968 and 1969 and put a lot of effort and time into helping me through the course. I would also like to thank Steve Kay who has helped me publish this book and nagged me into making sure that the people of Sheffield were able to view my work. I would also like to thank Neil Kitson for his kind words and encouragement towards this project.

Without the good people of Sheffield there would be no photographs, so I would like to thank anyone who is a subject, and, more often than not, never knew they were being photographed.

Finally, there are a number of people in the book that are sadly no longer with us. I hope my images bring comfort to the families that have lost loved ones.